CONTRACT LAW AND THE UNEXPECTED

The question explored in this book is how contracts can manage uncertainties.

Commercial parties face uncertainties on a regular basis. Market fluctuations, new laws and regulations, pandemics, rapid technology advancements and geopolitical tensions are all examples of events whose nature cannot be easily foreseen or captured by the contractual parties' expectations.

One possible way of addressing the uncertainty generated by such risks and events is through reliance on established contractual doctrines, such as variation or frustration. Under English law, these doctrines are traditionally limited. Another, and typically preferable, method is for contract drafters to include clauses that modify, suspend or terminate the obligations or liabilities of one (or both) of the parties, or clauses that at least open up the options for renegotiation. Examples include material adverse change (or effect) clauses, hardship clauses, performance clauses, termination or suspension clauses, remedies clauses, and variation clauses.

Such clauses raise a range of issues concerning their interpretation, effect and enforceability; the consequences that follow when the clauses do not work as planned; the consequences of allocating contractual discretion to a party to determine the existence of the relevant risk or event; and the extent to which the existence of specific clauses changes the options available to the parties beyond what general contract law principles offer.

This book advances the understanding of how the law deals with the unexpected and is an essential read for academics, students and practitioners, including contract drafters, legal advisors and litigation lawyers.

Contract Law and the Unexpected

Edited by
Paul S Davies
and
Magda Raczynska

•HART•
OXFORD • LONDON • NEW YORK • NEW DELHI • SYDNEY

HART PUBLISHING

Bloomsbury Publishing Plc

Kemp House, Chawley Park, Cumnor Hill, Oxford, OX2 9PH, UK

1385 Broadway, New York, NY 10018, USA

Bloomsbury Publishing Ireland Limited, 29 Earlsfort Terrace, Dublin 2, D02 AY28, Ireland

HART PUBLISHING, the Hart/Stag logo, BLOOMSBURY and the Diana logo are trademarks of Bloomsbury Publishing Plc

First published in Great Britain 2026

A catalogue record for this book is available from the British Library.

A catalogue record for this book is available from the Library of Congress.

Library of Congress Control Number: 2026936548

ISBN: HB: 978-1-50998-900-3
ePDF: 978-1-50998-902-7
ePub: 978-1-50998-901-0

Typeset by Compuscript Ltd, Shannon

For product safety related questions contact productsafety@bloomsbury.com

To find out more about our authors and books visit www.hartpublishing.co.uk. Here you will find extracts, author information, details of forthcoming events and the option to sign up for our newsletters.

PREFACE

When we organised the first commercial contracts conference at UCL in May 2019, on 'Contents of Commercial Contracts: Terms Affecting Freedoms',[1] we already had plans for two further conferences, one in May 2020 and another the year after. But then the unexpected happened – the COVID-19 pandemic hit – and our plans for the conferences, like many plans back then, were scuppered. We eventually returned with a commercial contracts conference in 2023, and on 16 May 2025 we were able to hold a conference at UCL focused on a theme. As for that theme … we were totally uncreative. The idea of 'Contract Law and the Unexpected' arose organically.

The papers, which were discussed at the conference and which now feature in this book, explore how different actors deal with unexpected events – contracting parties through contract design, courts through contract doctrines, lawmakers through new rules, and market participants through market standards. We understand 'unexpected events' broadly, and there is no shortage of examples: natural disasters, pandemics, and economic, political and technological shifts.

This topic matters both in theory and in practice.[2] Just as in life – which can only be understood backwards but must be lived forwards (to borrow from Søren Kirkegaard[3]) – we must continue to draft, interpret and enforce contracts without knowing the next economic, political, social, natural or technological upheaval. It is easier to tackle uncertainties with a better understanding of the law. The events that can have an impact upon contracts are varied, and the responses of laws, parties and markets have become similarly varied, nuanced and sophisticated. This book is not intended to provide a comprehensive overview of the possible ways of responding to unexpected events, but it shows that the range of possible responses to unexpected events is wider than often thought. The book begins by considering difficulties with the doctrine of frustration, and then discusses other contract law doctrines, including interpretation, implication, and mistake, as well as market interventions which can be deployed when managing the unexpected. Further chapters analyse the importance of various contract clauses, and the way they interact with the general contract law.

[1] See P Davies and M Raczynska, *Contents of Commercial Contracts: Terms Affecting Freedoms* (Oxford, Hart Publishing, 2020).

[2] For an excellent overview by a sitting judge, see D Foxton, 'When Everything Changes: Adapting Contracts to Fundamental Changes in Circumstance' [2025] *Journal of Business Law* 161.

[3] *Søren Kierkegaards Skrifter* (Søren Kierkegaard Research Center, Copenhagen, 1997) vol 18, 306.

The first two chapters outline the key features, incidence and rationales for the doctrine of frustration, and the ways in which changes of circumstances are dealt with by the courts. In 'Contract Law and the Unexpected: A Comparative Perspective' (chapter one) John Cartwright's comparison of English law with civil law jurisdictions, focusing on French law, throws into relief the narrowness of the English law doctrine and the general reluctance under English law to relieve a party from its obligations if circumstances have changed since the contract was formed. Cartwright also highlights the importance of interpretation and implication as tools at the courts' disposal which deal with changes of circumstances that do not constitute frustration of contract. Paul MacMahon tackles the basis of frustration in 'Constructing Frustration' (chapter two). He argues that frustration is best viewed as a matter of contractual construction and suggests that valuable insights might be gained from economic analysis of the law, which is often neglected in discussions of English law.

The book then takes a broader look at strategies of dealing with unexpected events. Jo Braithwaite, in 'Managing Unexpected Events in Global Markets: Lessons from LIBOR' (chapter three), shows the limitations of focusing on law, and that parties can be resourceful in drafting to prevent or mitigate disruption to contracts from supervening events. This is easiest when parties deal on standard terms. Braithwaite highlights the significance of public-private partnership in devising amendments to standard terms, and the residuary role of legislation.

Sarah Green, 'Smart Contracts and the Unexpected' (chapter four), considers new challenges of dealing with unexpected, but foreseeable, events when a contract is concluded through the automatic operation of a code, rather than parties' 'meeting on the trading floor'. Green argues that unilateral mistake should potentially be available where contracts have been formed in an automated fashion, and that it should suffice if the non-mistaken party has constructive knowledge of the other's mistake. This would open the possibility of claims in unilateral mistake succeeding in circumstances where the coder failed to anticipate commercial and technological events that an objectively reasonable programmer would expect or provide for.

The remainder of the book is dedicated to contract interpretation and particular contract clauses, designed to deal with changing circumstances, and the challenges as well as the opportunities they bring about. In 'Interpreting the Contract in the Light of Unexpected Events' (chapter five), Catherine Mitchell analyses whether problems posed by unexpected events can be resolved through the process of contract interpretation. This is especially important if other doctrines are often ill-equipped to deal with such issues. Mitchell highlights that a shift away from a more contextual interpretative enquiry towards one which is more focused upon the precise contractual language used may make it harder for contract law to respond to unexpected events flexibly.

Miriam Goldby also considers questions of interpretation in 'Purposive Interpretation of Longer-term Charters' (chapter six). She argues that a purposive approach to interpretation should be adopted, drawing on insights from relational contract theory. Goldby contends that focusing too much on certainty can lead to opportunism, which is contrary to a contract's purpose, and this can be illustrated by examining longer-term charter arrangements.

In 'Hardship' (chapter seven), Ewan McKendrick considers the options open to contracting parties in situations where an unforeseen change of circumstances has caused significant hardship to one or other of the parties. He argues that while it is relatively easy to draft a term which gives a party the right to walk away from a contract on the occurrence of an event of hardship, it is harder to draft a contract to ensure that there is effective renegotiation of the terms of the contract, especially since it is difficult to determine what remedial consequences might follow from a failure to reach agreement.

Jordan English's chapter, "Hell Or High Water' Clauses' (chapter eight), examines clauses under which a party promises to perform come what may. Such absolute obligations are often found in finance leases. English argues that there is no scope for frustration to operate where the parties have agreed to a hell or high water clause. However, some statutory protections against unfair terms may provide some relief to parties bound by hell or high water clauses.

Charles Mitchell and Magda Raczynska, in 'The Idea of Variation' (chapter nine), consider variation clauses that empower the parties to vary the terms of a contract by acting jointly, which can be deployed to manage unexpected events. They argue that the characterisation of changes to a contract as 'variation' as opposed to 'a new contract' is a matter of law, and not for the parties to determine, although in many cases the parties' decision to vary will comfortably fit within the legal concept of variation. They also show that what it means to vary may be different depending on specific contexts.

In 'Specific Performance Clauses' (chapter ten), Solène Rowan considers clauses which provide that specific performance should be available at the election of the injured party on the occurrence of a breach. Such clauses are not common, but Rowan argues that they could be more widely agreed and enforced, provided that there are safeguards to weed out abusive and unacceptable terms.

At the conference, each chapter was commented upon by a practitioner in a session chaired by a judge. We are very grateful to Sir David Foxton, Dame Nerys Jefford, Lord Sales and Dame Joanna Smith, for acting as chairs, and to Sushma Ananda, Sir William Blair, Charles Clark, Kate Gibbons, Philippa Hopkins KC, Charles Kerrigan, James Leabeater KC, Peter MacDonald-Eggers KC, Georgia Quenby, Adam Sanitt, Adam Temple, and Andrew Twigger KC, for being commentators. We would also like to thank Norton Rose Fulbright LLP, and in particular Tara Pichardo-Angadi and Richard Calnan, for their generous support. The conference was well-attended, and the discussion lively. All the chapters were improved by feedback both at and after the event.

We have benefitted from the excellent research assistance of Adam Zahid, and the team at Hart Publishing have, as ever, been a pleasure to work with: particular thanks to Roberta Bassi, Linda Goss, Sasha Jawad, Sinead Moloney, and Verity Stuart. Paul would also like to thank the Leverhulme Trust for their generous support through a Philip Leverhulme Prize.

Paul S Davies
Magda Raczynska
December 2025

CONTENTS

CONTRIBUTORS

Jo Braithwaite is Professor of Law, London School of Economics and Political Science.

John Cartwright is Emeritus Professor of the Law of Contract, University of Oxford, Emeritus Student (Fellow) of Christ Church, Oxford, and Research Fellow (formerly Director) of the Institute of European and Comparative Law, Oxford.

Jordan English is an Associate Professor in Law at the University of Oxford and a Fellow and Tutor in Law at Magdalen College, and an Associate Member of Three Verulam Buildings.

Miriam Goldby is Professor of Shipping, Insurance and Commercial Law at the Centre for Commercial Law Studies, Queen Mary University of London.

Sarah Green is Professor of Private Law at the University of Bristol and Arbitrator at Newmans Row.

Paul MacMahon is an Associate Professor of Law at the LSE Law School and a Visiting Professor at Católica Global School of Law in Lisbon.

Ewan McKendrick is Professor of Anglo-American Private Law at the University of Leiden, Emeritus Professor of English Private Law, University of Oxford, an Emeritus Fellow of Lady Margaret Hall, a barrister in practice at 3 Verulam Buildings and a Bencher of Gray's Inn.

Catherine Mitchell is Emeritus Professor of Contract Law at Birmingham Law School, University of Birmingham.

Charles Mitchell KC (Hon) FBA is a Professor of Law at UCL.

Magda Raczynska is Associate Professor of Law at UCL.

Solène Rowan is the Law Commissioner for Commercial and Common Law at the Law Commission of England & Wales and Professor of Contract Law at King's College London.

TABLE OF CASES

Australia

Canada

France

Ireland

Israel

Singapore

United Kingdom

United States

TABLE OF LEGISLATION

Germany

Greece

Italy

Netherlands

United Kingdom

United States

US – Louisiana

International and Other Materials

1

Contract Law and the Unexpected: A Comparative Perspective

JOHN CARTWRIGHT

I. Introduction

Commercial parties in all jurisdictions face similar practical problems regarding the allocation of risk of events which they cannot foresee (either fully, or at all) at the time of contracting. However, different jurisdictions provide significantly different legal solutions to these practical problems, solutions which typically reflect broader differences in structure and policy within the jurisdictions' law of contract generally but which also, in turn, give rise to differences in the drafting of contract clauses designed to address potential uncertainties.

This chapter will outline some of the differences between legal systems in the management of unexpected events, comparing English law with the law of some European civil law jurisdictions, in particular French law, but the principal purpose of the discussion is to see what lessons English lawyers might be able to learn from such a comparison. The chapter will touch on topics which are covered in more detail in other chapters, both those which explore the English law[1] and practice[2] relating to change of circumstances after the formation of a contract, and those which reflect on approaches in other jurisdictions.[3]

[1] eg, the doctrine of frustration (MacMahon, below, ch 2) and interpretation of the contract (Mitchell, below, ch 5; Goldby, below, ch 6).

[2] In particular, the attempt to anticipate problems arising from changes of circumstances through contract drafting, such as hardship clauses (McKendrick, below, ch 7), 'hell or high water' clauses (English, below, ch 8), material adverse change clauses, and variation clauses (Mitchell and Raczynska, below, ch 9).

[3] eg, McKendrick, below, ch 7; Rowan, below, ch 10. For the need for a coordinated, global response to a supervening event (cessation of LIBOR) which affected globally interconnected markets, see Braithwaite, below, ch 3.

II. The Challenge of Change of Circumstances and the Significance of Default Rules of the Law of Contract

If there is little or no significant delay between the formation of the contract and completion of performance of the obligations it creates, there may be little or no scope for the contractual relationship to be disturbed by a change of circumstances.[4] But where – as in the case of very many commercial contracts – the contract by its nature or by its particular terms involves a delay between formation and performance, or provides for continuous performance over a (more or less extended) period, the risk of some such disturbance is within the foresight of the parties at the time the contract is formed, and – whether or not in fact they foresaw it or attempted to make provision for it – the change may have an impact on one or other party to the contract for which that party seeks a remedy, such as the release (temporary or permanent) from the contract or the adjustment of some of the terms to take into account the new circumstances.

Parties to a contract face these same challenges regardless of the legal system within which they are operating, although whether a party can make any claim based on the change of circumstances and (if so) what remedies may be available will depend in part on the general, default rules of contract law within the legal system and in part on the extent to which the parties are permitted to override the default rules[5] and have provided for the change of circumstances in the terms of the contract itself. In all legal systems it is advisable for parties to a negotiated commercial contract to make express provision in the contract for changes of circumstances, insofar as this is practicable where the parties are seeking to provide for future circumstances which they are not yet able to foresee in detail. And where the contract is not bespoke and individually negotiated but an industry standard form of contract is used – as in many construction (building and engineering) projects[6] – the standard form may similarly seek to take into account

[4] The contract may provide for events occurring after both parties' primary obligations have been discharged by performance, such as where the seller under a contract of sale has the right to additional payment in defined later circumstances which give the buyer a windfall profit. But in the absence of such contractual provision, any change of circumstances after the contractual relationship has been discharged by performance would normally not give rise to legal consequences.

[5] In European systems, provisions relating to change of circumstances are generally default rules which can be varied by the parties' own allocation of risk in the contract. However, some legal systems may make their legal rules on change of circumstances mandatory: eg, Arab countries which have introduced mandatory hardship rules: see C Seppälä, *The FIDIC Red Book Contract: An International Clause-By-Clause Commentary* (Alphen aan den Rijn, Wolters Kluwer Law International, 2023) 104–05.

[6] eg, the various different forms of contract published by the Joint Contracts Tribunal ('JCT') and by the International Federation of Consulting Engineers ('FIDIC'). The JCT forms are designed for domestic use; FIDIC forms are designed for international use. In the past the FIDIC forms referred to (and defined) 'force majeure'; even if such a form is used for a contract governed by a legal system (such as France: see section III below) in which *force majeure* is a term of art, it will be the contract's

the changes of circumstances that might typically occur within the lifetime of that type of contract, and provide clauses designed to offer a suitable response. However, the drafting of clauses designed to address changes of circumstances is done in the context of the general rules of contract law and the particular rules of the law on change of circumstances, which would apply in default of express provision in the contract. The default rules set the framework for the parties' contract, and, put simply, the less satisfactory the default rules of general contract law are at providing the kind of solution the parties would wish to apply in the event of a change of circumstances, the more important it is for them to make their own, detailed provisions which address the perceived defects in the general law.

Legal systems have very different default rules for changes of circumstances: different rules governing the allocation of risk of such changes and the remedy (or range of remedies) applicable in the event of a legally relevant change of circumstances. A legal system's rules on this issue must not be seen in isolation but will be related to other doctrines within contract law and will reflect broader underlying policies or values in that system's law of contract, including the general notions of contract and of contractual obligation. We shall see that some of the sharp contrasts between English law and modern civil law systems in relation to changes of circumstances flow from their contrasting structures and policies of contract law. Given the range of such differences, it is necessary first to set out a broad overview of the civil law approach, so that we can then compare the approach taken by English law.

III. The Civil Law Approach; the Example of French Law

There are two separate issues to consider for any rule dealing with changes of circumstances: the trigger for the operation of the rule (the definition of a change of circumstances sufficient to give rise to a remedy) and the consequences (the remedy).

A. What Change of Circumstances is Sufficient?

Civil law systems generally draw a distinction between a change of circumstances which renders performance *impossible* and a change which renders performance

definition, not the legal system's own (default) definition that will apply. However, the terminology of the FIDIC forms has now been changed to refer to (and define) an 'Exceptional Event', rather than using the term 'Force Majeure'. See Seppälä (n 5) 1–8, 100–103, 1060–66; W Godwin, *The 2017 FIDIC Contracts* (Chichester, Wiley-Blackwell, 2020) ch 14. The JCT forms still refer to 'force majeure' (without definition) amongst the list of otherwise more precisely defined supervening events: eg, JCT Standard Building Contract With Quantities 2024, conditions 2.29.16 and 8.11.1.1; V Ramsey, S Hughes and P Stansfield, *Keating on Construction Contracts*, 12th edn (London, Sweet & Maxwell, 2024) [21-190]–[21-191].

not impossible but only more *onerous* ('hardship'), and most systems now provide legal mechanisms to respond to cases of both impossibility and hardship.

It is not surprising that the law should provide a remedy for impossibility more readily than for hardship. Most legal systems will say, at least as a starting point, that an event, outside the control and risk of the parties, which renders performance of the contract impossible should have some effect on the binding force of the contract. A tougher line could be taken: that the contractual obligation is absolute and, unless the contract already so provides, a party has no excuse for not fulfilling its contractual undertakings, even if performance has become impossible by reason of some external event beyond its control.[7] However, there seems to be something inherently problematic about a legally binding promise to do the impossible, at least if we take 'impossibility' in an objective sense – not just that the particular party is (subjectively) unable to perform, but that any person in that party's position would be unable to perform. This is generally the starting point for civil lawyers, who see the essential nature of an obligation as the duty to perform, backed up by the primary remedy of enforced performance. This does not mean that the only remedy is enforced performance; there are many situations where damages will naturally be awarded, including cases where the court can no longer order performance. But impossibility of performance goes to the heart of the obligation.

The same cannot, however, be said of hardship. The contract embodies the agreement of the parties, binding them both to its performance, and a change of circumstances which makes performance not impossible but merely more onerous for one of the parties does not undermine the very nature of the contractual obligation, merely the particular bargain that the parties struck. Allowing one party a remedy based on such a change allows the re-writing in its favour of the allocation of (economic) risk – but a primary purpose of the contract, at least in the commercial context, is to establish the risk allocation. And 'hardship' is a question of degree: how significant must the change of circumstances be – how extreme the 'hardship' that it causes?

Civil law systems have long had rules relating to impossibility. The law relating to hardship, however, has been developed over the last century[8] by courts

[7] This was the line once taken in English law: see *Paradine v Jane* (n 43).

[8] The initial point of reference for the modern development of the law relating to hardship (distinct from impossibility) is found in Germany, in decisions of the Reichsgericht (the Imperial supreme court) when the economy suffered from hyperinflation in the 1920s after the First World War: H Kötz, *European Contract Law*, 2nd edn, trans G Mertens and T Weir (Oxford, OUP, 2017) 282–83. The German doctrine of the 'disappearance of the basis of the transaction' was developed by the courts as a particular application of §242 of the German Civil Code which requires the person who has the duty under an obligation 'to perform according to the requirements of good faith, taking customary practice into consideration': see R Zimmermann and S Whittaker, *Good Faith in European Contract Law* (Cambridge, CUP, 2000) 18–32, explaining the significance of §242 generally in the judicial development of doctrines of contract law. The law relating to change of circumstances was eventually codified in a reform of the German Civil Code in 2002 and is now contained in §313 ('Interference with the basis of the transaction'). Impossibility is still dealt with by other provisions; see §275(1), excluding

and legislators in various jurisdictions, a development which has accelerated in recent years. Although it is not now the most recent jurisdiction to reform the law on change of circumstances,[9] French law, which was reformed in 2016,[10] is chosen here as an illustration of the trend in the modern law. In relation to change of circumstances during performance of the contract, French law distinguishes between *force majeure* (for impossibility) and *imprévision* (for hardship).

i. *Impossibility:* Force Majeure

Force majeure is now defined in the Civil Code:

> In contractual matters, there is force majeure where an event beyond the control of the debtor,[11] which could not reasonably have been foreseen at the time of the conclusion of the contract and whose effects could not be avoided by appropriate measures, prevents performance of his obligation by the debtor.[12]

Under this definition the event must render performance of an obligation impossible. In the language of the case law before the 2016 reform, the event must be

a claim for performance to the extent that performance is impossible for the obligor or for any other person. For a broader historical account from the Roman and medieval origins, see A Thier, 'Legal History' in E Hondius and HC Grigoleit (eds), *Unexpected Circumstances in European Contract Law* (Cambridge, CUP, 2011) ch 2.

[9] Most recently, art 5.74 of the new Belgian Civil Code, in force since 1 January 2023, introduced a provision entitled 'change of circumstances' addressing hardship (distinct from impossibility, which remains covered by *force majeure*: art 5.226). There are legislative provisions on hardship in some other European civil law jurisdictions: eg, the Italian Civil Code (of 1942) arts 1467 to 1469; Dutch Civil Code (of 1992) art 6:258. Some other jurisdictions (eg, Spain) have, as originally in Germany, developed a doctrine of hardship by judicial decision without yet, at least, codifying the result. For a general review of the law in European jurisdictions as it stood in 2011, see Hondius and Grigoleit (n 8) ch 4. Legislative texts on hardship are not limited to European jurisdictions: a number of Arab countries have introduced mandatory hardship rules: see Seppälä (n 5).

[10] The current provisions of the French Civil Code ('Cc') dealing with the general law of contract were created by Ordonnance no 2016-131 (10 February 2016) (ratified with some revisions by Loi no 2018-287 (20 April 2018)). In this chapter, English translations of the new French provisions are taken from the translation by J Cartwright, B Fauvarque-Cosson and S Whittaker, commissioned by the Direction des affaires civiles et du sceau, Ministère de la Justice, République française. The French text and translation of the 2016 Ordonnance is printed as the appendix to J Cartwright and S Whittaker (eds), *The Code Napoléon Rewritten: French Contract Law after the 2016 Reforms* (Oxford, Hart Publishing, 2017) 409 ff.

[11] In French law, an 'obligation' (whether contractual or non-contractual) is a legal link between a creditor (*créancier*: the person with the right under the obligation – the *créance*) – and a debtor (*débiteur*: the person with the duty under the obligation – the *dette*). The concept and terminology of 'debtor' and 'debt' is not limited to obligations to pay a sum of money. See S Whittaker and J Cartwright, 'Translating the *Avant-projet de réforme*' in J Cartwright, S Vogenauer and S Whittaker (eds), *Reforming the French Law of Obligations: Comparative reflections on the Avant-projet de réforme du droit des obligations et de la prescription* (Oxford, Hart Publishing, 2009) 425, 437–40.

[12] Art 1218(1) Cc. The term '*force majeure*' was used in the Code in its original form in 1804, but there was no definition until the 2016 reform, although its meaning was well developed by the case law.

'irresistible': if the party claiming *force majeure* could overcome its effects, even with great difficulty or at a high cost, it is not sufficient.[13]

ii. Hardship: Imprévision

Until 2016, the only general doctrine of contract law that could be relied on by a party claiming a change of circumstances was the narrow principle of *force majeure*.[14] Although there could be debate (and some corresponding latitude in the decisions of the courts) about the interpretation of the test for *force majeure* to the facts of the case, the civil courts[15] had refused to develop a general remedy in cases where the effect of the change of circumstances was not on the possibility of performance of the contract, but on its economic balance – even in cases where the disruption to the economy of the contract was very significant. A case from 1876[16] was still routinely cited as authority: the Cour de cassation quashed the decision of the lower court, which had held that in a contract for the supply of water, entered into in the sixteenth century, at a fixed price which had now been made derisory by reason of inflation, the court had the power to adjust the terms of the contract to restore the economic balance. The explanation was firm:

> Under no circumstances is it for the courts, however fair their decision may seem to them to be, to take into account the time and the circumstances in order to modify the parties' agreements and to substitute new terms for those which were freely accepted by the contracting parties.

This strict application of the binding force of the contract has now been consigned to history. In a conscious break from the old law,[17] the 2016 reform introduced a general doctrine of change of circumstances, known (although not so named in the Code) as *imprévision*. This is a radical change, not only in extending the scope of legally relevant changes of circumstances, but also in the remedy it provides. The new provision applies where 'a change of circumstances that was unforeseeable at the time of the conclusion of the contract renders performance excessively onerous for a party who had not accepted the risk of such a change'.[18] This is apparently narrow – it applies only where performance

[13] F Terré, P Simler, Y Lequette and F Chénedé, *Droit Civil: Les Obligations*, 13th edn (Paris, Dalloz, 2022) 844–45.

[14] For an account of the law as it stood before the 2016 reforms, see B Nicholas, *The French Law of Contract*, 2nd edn (Oxford, Clarendon Press, 1992) 200–10; Terré, Simler, Lequette and Chénedé (n 13) 729–36.

[15] In administrative law, the Conseil d'État (the highest tribunal in public law matters) introduced a remedy in 1916 to allow a private party to be awarded a sum beyond that agreed in a concession contract, in order to secure the continued performance of the public service where there was a change of circumstances under which the economics of the contract were absolutely undermined ('l'économie du contrat se trouve absolument bouleversée'): CE 30 March 1916, DP 1916 III 25 ('Gaz de Bordeaux').

[16] Cass civ 6 March 1876, S 1876 1 161 ('Canal de Craponne').

[17] See text to n 32.

[18] Art 1195 Cc. For the full provision, see text to n 27.

becomes 'excessively onerous' for one party, as an exception to the general rule of the binding force of the contract;[19] but it is fundamentally different from the notion of *force majeure*, in that it assumes that it is still possible to perform the contract. Moreover, the notion of onerousness embodied in the new provision is intended to cover a change whose effects are purely economic. It is, though, a new test which will be open to argument as to its interpretation, and its application to the facts of individual cases.[20]

B. What Remedy?

The basis of intervention in the two doctrines of French law which are designed to address changes of circumstances – impossibility (*force majeure*) and hardship (*imprévision*) – is very different, and the remedies differ accordingly.

i. *Impossibility:* Force Majeure

In civil law systems, the obligations within the contract are generally viewed separately; the non-performance of a particular obligation is the basis for the other party having a range of claims (including enforced performance, damages and termination of the whole contract), but the duty to perform an obligation may be excused if its performance becomes impossible. Given that enforced performance is not available in such a case, the focus is on whether the liability in damages which would normally flow from non-performance of the obligation remains in place, and whether the impossibility of performance goes so far as to justify termination. This is the approach taken in French law.

We have seen that the French Civil Code applies the principle of *force majeure* to the case where the party who has the duty to perform an obligation (the 'debtor'[21]) is prevented from performing the obligation.[22] The primary (and automatic) effect of an event of *force majeure* is as a defence to the claim to pay damages for non-performance:

> A debtor is condemned, where appropriate, to the payment of damages either on the ground of the non-performance or a delay in performance of an obligation, unless he justifies this on the ground that performance was prevented by force majeure.[23]

As for the continuing force of the contract itself, the focus on the particular obligation and the impact of the *force majeure* event on its performance allows

[19] Arts 1103, 1193 Cc.
[20] See O Deshayes, T Genicon and Y-M Laithier, *Réforme du Droit des Contrats, du Régime Général et de la Preuve des Obligations: Commentaire Article par Article*, 2nd edn (Paris, LexisNexis, 2018) 448–52; Terré, Simler, Lequette and Chénedé (n 13) 739–44.
[21] See n 11.
[22] Art 1218(1) Cc, quoted in full at text to n 12.
[23] Art 1231-1 Cc.

a nuanced solution: whether the duty to perform the particular obligation is only suspended, or the whole contract is terminated, depends on the effect of the event:

> If the prevention is temporary, performance of the obligation is suspended unless the delay which results justifies termination of the contract. If the prevention is permanent, the contract is terminated by operation of law and the parties are discharged from their obligations under the conditions provided by articles 1351 and 1351-1.[24]
>
> Impossibility of performing the act of performance discharges the debtor to the extent of that impossibility where it results from an event of force majeure and is permanent unless he had agreed to bear the risk of the event or had previously been given notice to perform.[25]

There are some uncertainties in the interpretation of these provisions,[26] but they provide a flexible default solution to the consequences of impossibility where the contract has not provided a different or a more detailed solution.

ii. *Hardship:* Imprévision

The new provision relating to hardship, introduced by the 2016 reform of the French Civil Code, reads as follows:

> If a change of circumstances that was unforeseeable at the time of the conclusion of the contract renders performance excessively onerous for a party who had not accepted the risk of such a change, that party may ask the other contracting party to renegotiate the contract. The first party must continue to perform his obligations during renegotiation.
>
> In the case of refusal or the failure of renegotiations, the parties may agree to terminate the contract from the date and on the conditions which they determine, or by a common agreement ask the court to set about its adaptation. In the absence of an agreement within a reasonable time, the court may, on the request of a party, revise the contract or put an end to it, from a date and subject to such conditions as it shall determine.[27]

This was new in 2016, not simply the enactment of developments already made by the case law – and, indeed, some aspects of the new text were controversial during the parliamentary ratification of the text of the 2016 Ordonnance by a Loi in 2018.[28] The introduction of the new text on hardship was, however, seen as particularly significant by the government in bringing forward the reforms. In its

[24] Art 1218(2) Cc.

[25] Art 1351 Cc. Art 1351-1 Cc addresses the specific case of impossibility of performance as a result of the loss of a thing that is due under the contract (eg, the thing sold under a contract of sale), where the transferor has already been given notice to perform.

[26] See Deshayes, Genicon and Laithier (n 20) 537–40, 912–16; Terré, Simler, Lequette and Chénedé (n 13) 850–55.

[27] Art 1195 Cc.

[28] See n 10. In particular, the Sénat sought by its amendments to remove the remedy of judicial revision of the contract, leaving only termination: Deshayes, Genicon and Laithier (n 20) 468.

Report to the President of the Republic, the Ministry of Justice included a very useful explanation of the purpose of the provision:

> Article 1195 constitutes one of the important innovations of the Ordonnance, because it introduces *imprévision* into French contract law, a notion that is well known in the Administrative Law case-law. It responds expressly to para 6 of the Enabling Law,[29] authorising the Government to provide for 'the possibility for [the parties to the contract] to adapt their contract in case of unforeseeable change of circumstances'. France is one of the last countries in Europe not to recognise the theory of *imprévision* as a ground of moderation of the binding force of contracts. Establishing it, inspired by comparative law such as the European harmonisation projects,[30] facilitates the fight against major contractual imbalance occurring in the course of performance, in accordance with the objective of contractual justice[31] pursued by the Ordonnance. The first paragraph sets out the conditions of this new mechanism: *imprévision* requires an 'unforeseeable' change of circumstances, which must render performance 'excessively onerous' for one party, and the latter must not have accepted this risk. As the drafting shows, this provision is of a non-mandatory character, and the parties may agree in advance to contract out of it by choosing to bear the consequences of the happening of such circumstances which may undermine the economics of the contract. Furthermore, if the aggrieved party asks the other party to renegotiate the contract, he must continue to perform his obligations, in order to avoid this mechanism encouraging disputes designed to cause delay, and to preserve the binding force of contracts. The second paragraph then defines the consequences of a refusal to negotiate or the failure of negotiations: if the parties concur, they may agree on the termination of the contract or apply to the court for the court to adapt the contract. At the end of a reasonable period, one of the parties may similarly apply to the court which may then revise the contract or put an end to it. *Imprévision* is therefore designed to have a preventative role: the risk of destruction or of revision of the contract by the court ought to encourage the parties to negotiate.[32]

[29] Loi no 2015-177 (16 February 2015), authorising the reform of Book III of the Civil Code to be made by Ordonnance, rather than by Loi.

[30] By this expression the Report to the President refers generally to the UNIDROIT Principles of International Commercial Contracts ('PICC'): International Institute for the Unification of Private Law, *Principles of International Commercial Contracts* ('PICC') (Rome, Unidroit, 2004; the current edition is now 2016); the Principles of European Contract Law ('PECL'): O Lando and H Beale (eds), *The Principles of European Contract Law, Parts I and II* (The Hague, Kluwer Law International, 2000); the Draft Common Frame of Reference ('DCFR'): C von Bar and E Clive (eds), *Principles, Definitions and Model Rules of European Private Law: Draft Common Frame of Reference* (Munich, Sellier, 2009); the 'Gandolfi' Code: Academy of European Private Lawyers, *Code européen des contrats: Avant-projet, Livre premier* (revised edn, Milan, Giuffrè, 2004) and the Principes contractuels communs ('PCC'): Association Henri Capitant des Amis de la Culture Juridique Française, *Principes Contractuels Communs: Projet de Cadre Commun de Référence* (Paris, Société de Législation Comparée, 2008). For provisions on hardship, see PICC arts 6.2.1 to 6.2.3 (Hardship); PECL art 6:111 (Change of Circumstances); DCFR art III.–1:110 (Variation or termination by court on a change of circumstances); Gandolfi Code arts 97, 157 (Re-negotiation of contract where performance becomes excessively onerous); PCC art 7:101 (Changement de circonstances). To these provisions could be added the European Commission's Proposal for a Regulation on a Draft Common European Sales Law ('DCESL') COM(2011) 635, where the draft text contained a provision on change of circumstances at art 89.

[31] *cf* n 41.

[32] Rapport au Président de la République relatif à l'ordonnance n° 2016-131 du 10 février 2016 portant réforme du droit des contrats, du régime général et de la preuve des obligations, JORF No 35, 11 February 2016, texte no 25 (author's translation).

This makes clear that France saw itself as catching up with the European trend in introducing such provisions.[33] But it does not simply copy the rules already adopted elsewhere. Each system which has introduced a remedy for a change of circumstances giving rise to hardship, short of impossibility of performance of one or more obligations of the contract, has done so in its own way. The French provision is interesting for a number of points, some of which contrast with the approach in other civil law jurisdictions – even if there is a general trend in favour of introducing some provision along these lines.

Article 1195 starts from the position that the party whose performance has become 'excessively onerous' as a result of the change of position should seek to initiate a renegotiation. This is not a duty to renegotiate; rather, the attempt to open renegotiations is set as the first step to be taken by the party seeking a remedy. However, legal control over contractual negotiations is not alien to the French way of thinking – nor, indeed, to the way of thinking of civil systems generally – since it is now generally recognised that if the parties negotiate, they must do so in good faith.[34]

Under article 1195 no remedy is automatic and, indeed, the party who seeks a remedy has no excuse for non-performance unless and until a solution is found by the parties or by the court. This is different from the remedy for *force majeure* (automatic suspension of the duty to perform and relief from liability to pay damages for non-performance as long as it remains impossible), but the difference is natural: article 1195 presupposes that the obligation can still be performed, but the economic balance of the contract has been (excessively) disturbed. The process envisaged is that the parties should renegotiate the terms of the contract, but if the negotiations fail, the parties may agree to terminate the contract or to leave it to the court to adapt it; and only if there is no such agreement within a reasonable time can the party whose performance has become excessively onerous apply unilaterally to the court to revise or terminate the contract.

There is no indication in the text as to the test to be applied by the court in its decision, and in particular as to the basis on which any revision of the terms of the contract should be established; it is not necessarily to bring the terms into line with what the parties would reasonably have agreed at the time of contracting if they had taken the change of circumstances into account.[35] There are also other

[33] See n 30; see also nn 8, 9.

[34] In France, see arts 1104 ('Contracts must be negotiated, formed and performed in good faith' – a non-excludable duty), 1112 (freedom to negotiate, but negotiations must satisfy the (mandatory) duty of good faith, with liability for fault committed during the negotiations). See also Kötz (n 8) 32–39.

[35] Deshayes, Genicon and Laithier (n 20) 470 (art 1195 is not a *clausula rebus sic stantibus*); Terré, Simler, Lequette and Chénedé (n 13) 745–46. See the different formulations of the court's powers set out in PICC, art 6.2.3(4)(b) ('adapt the contract with a view to restoring its equilibrium'); PECL, art 6:111(3) ('adapt the contract in order to distribute between the parties in a just and equitable manner the losses and gains resulting from the change of circumstances'); DCFR art III.–1:110(2) ('vary the obligation in order to make it reasonable and equitable in the new circumstances'); DCESL art 89(2)(a) ('adapt the contract in order to bring it into accordance with what the parties would reasonably have agreed at the time of contracting if they had taken the change of circumstances into account').

uncertainties as to how the new provision may operate[36] and this, combined with the general process set out in the text (negotiation first, application to the court as a last resort),[37] may lead to it being rarely invoked. Indeed, as the Ministry said in the Report to the President,[38] the risks involved in the court taking the decision on the remedy for hardship ought to encourage the parties to negotiate. They may, of course, exclude the provision in their contract altogether – and it appears that this is likely in commercial contracts, at least, where it is normal to seek to anticipate changes of circumstances in the contract itself.

The notable step taken by the 2016 reform in this area remains, however, the introduction of a regime for judicial control over the consequences of changes of circumstances giving rise to hardship. It was not uncontroversial amongst academics in France,[39] but it is in line with the general development of French contract law in recent years: whilst seeking to strike a balance between fundamental principles – freedom of contract, the binding force of contracts, and good faith[40] – there is a trend to favour 'contractual justice', with some increased powers of the courts over the contract, not only in the consumer sphere but also in contract law generally including commercial contracts.[41]

IV. The Common Law Approach; the Example of English Law

What is the English lawyer to make of the civilian approach to change of circumstances? In the common law, the starting point – and much of the analysis – is simply very different.

[36] For a detailed analysis, see Deshayes, Genicon and Laithier (n 20) 436–74.

[37] The process set out by art 1195 Cc is different from that in other jurisdictions; eg, the German Civil Code does not formally require the parties to negotiate before applying to the court, and appears to give priority to adaptation of the contract (§313(1)), with termination being available if adaptation is not possible or if one party cannot reasonably be required to accept it (§313(3)), although the courts have recognised the duty on the parties to negotiate: M Lehmann, 'Rapport allemand' in P Ancel and A Prüm, *Réformer le droit des contrats? Analyse comparée autour du droit luxembourgeois* (Brussels, Larcier, 2020) 490–91.

[38] See n 32.

[39] eg, Terré, Simler, Lequette and Chénedé (n 13) 736–38.

[40] Arts 1102, 1103 and 1104 Cc respectively.

[41] B Fauvarque-Cosson, 'Does Review on the Ground of *Imprévision* Breach the Principle of the Binding Force of Contracts?' in Cartwright and Whittaker, *The Code Napoléon Rewritten* (n 10) 187, 188 ('Since [1984] the idea of contractual justice has been developing. It can be seen as a manifestation of the development of a wider phenomenon: the taking into account of ethics in the life of business. The traditional conception of the judge, a simple servant of the contract, gives way to a new "contractual morality" based on good faith and fairness'), but concluding at 205 that 'If French courts bear [the] imperative [of legal certainty] clearly in mind this will encourage them to exercise the powers conferred on them by article 1195 with the utmost caution .... Provided that the courts use their powers with foresight and restraint, the "classic and modern philosophy of contract law" will not be overturned.'

In the first place, we do not have an overarching general theory of the law of obligations which sees contractual obligations as inherently carrying the legally enforceable duty to perform, with the associated principle that the law relieves the party from performance (and liability for non-performance) of an obligation which becomes impossible to perform. The common lawyer may see less of an inherent contradiction in a contractual 'duty to perform the impossible' given that the remedy for breach of contract is normally the payment of damages, which is generally still possible despite the change of circumstances affecting the contracted performance.[42] Indeed, English law once took a strict line that a party's non-performance is not excused by reason of change of circumstances,[43] but the courts in the second half of the nineteenth century softened this approach by allowing an exception to the absolute nature of the obligation through the implication of a term,[44] a mechanism which retained the theory that the obligation is strict unless the parties have contracted otherwise, but in effect provided a default rule excusing performance in case of impossibility.[45] The later developments of the doctrine of frustration, as it became known, made more explicit that it is a general doctrine of change of circumstances in English contract law – but still a default rule, since the parties can exclude it by making provision in the contract for change of circumstances – even if the precise theoretical basis of the doctrine has still been debated.[46]

Nor has English law developed an equivalent of the civil law doctrine of hardship – the broader *imprévision* of French law, which softens the very narrow doctrine of *force majeure* (impossibility). It appears (at first sight, at least) that we have a single doctrine: frustration. However, in English law frustration extends beyond the narrow case to which the civil lawyer would limit the doctrine of impossibility – although not as far as the modern European development of hardship. And as there were differences amongst the civil law systems, so there are also differences in the common law, although in general terms the

[42] *Taylor v Caldwell* (1863) 3 B & S 826, 833; 122 ER 309, 312 (Blackburn J): 'There seems no doubt that where there is a positive contract to do a thing, not in itself unlawful, *the contractor must perform it or pay damages for not doing it*, although in consequence of unforeseen accidents, the performance of his contract has become unexpectedly burthensome or even impossible' (emphasis added).

[43] ibid 312; *Paradine v Jane* (1647) Aleyn 26, 27; 82 ER 897, 897 ('[W]hen the party by his own contract creates a duty or charge upon himself, he is bound to make it good, if he may, notwithstanding any accident by inevitable necessity, because he might have provided against it by his contract').

[44] *Taylor v Caldwell* (n 42) 839; 314 ('in contracts in which the performance depends on the continued existence of a given person or thing, a condition is implied that the impossibility of performance arising from the perishing of the person or thing shall excuse the performance').

[45] ibid 839; 314 ('that excuse is by law implied, because from the nature of the contract it is apparent that the parties contracted on the basis of the continued existence of the particular person or chattel').

[46] See J Beatson, A Burrows and J Cartwright, *Anson's Law of Contract*, 31st edn (Oxford, OUP, 2020) 479–84, concluding at 482 that 'there is now general agreement that the appropriate test to apply to determine whether a contract has been frustrated is that of a "radical change in the obligation"' set out by Lord Radcliffe in *Davis Contractors Ltd v Fareham UDC* [1956] AC 696 (HL) 729. See also n 50. For continuing debate about the basis of the doctrine of frustration, see MacMahon, below, ch 2; English, below, ch 8 pp 156–60.

English approach has been followed by the common law jurisdictions: starting with impossibility, extending to a broader doctrine of frustration (including frustration of the purpose of the contract), but not adding a general remedy for economic hardship, either within frustration or as a separate doctrine, nor giving the courts a power to adjust the terms of the contract.[47] Nothing in the nature of a common law contract excludes in principle the introduction of a doctrine of hardship. It is a matter of policy. Once the decision is taken not to insist on a strict view of the binding force of contract, but to allow the contract to be affected by at least some changes of circumstances, the question is how far to go. The English doctrine of frustration is a much more limited response than the civilian doctrine of hardship that has been developed in recent years. This is not to say, however, that the doctrine of frustration is the only tool for the courts to respond to the problems arising by reason of a change of circumstances during performance of the contract, and we shall see some examples of alternative judicial solutions. First, however, we look in outline at the doctrine of frustration to see how it compares with the civilian approach to impossibility and hardship, separating (as in the discussion of French law in section III) the trigger for the operation of the doctrine (the definition of a change of circumstances sufficient to give rise to a remedy); and the consequences (the remedy).[48]

A. The Doctrine of Frustration in English Law

i. What Change of Circumstances is Sufficient?

Some details of the doctrine are debated, but, in outline, frustration occurs where, without default of either party, performance of the contract becomes illegal,[49] impossible or 'radically different'[50] by a change of circumstances not provided for in the contract. Lord Radcliffe referred to a contractual obligation

[47] For Australia, see JW Carter, *Contract Law in Australia*, 8th edn (Sydney, JW Carter Publishing, 2023) chs 33 and 34; for New Zealand, see S Todd and M Barber, *Burrows Finn and Todd on the Law of Contract in New Zealand*, 7th edn (Wellington, LexisNexis NZ, 2022) ch 20; for Canada, see JW Neyers (ed), *Fridman's The Law of Contract in Canada*, 7th edn (Toronto, Carswell, 2024) ch 20; for Singapore, see ABL Phang and Goh Yihan, *Contract Law in Singapore*, 2nd edn (Alphen aan den Rijn, Kluwer Law International, 2021) pt V, ch 2. In the US, there are doctrines of impossibility, impracticability and frustration of purpose, although the courts do not normally excuse a party on the ground of impracticability merely because performance has become more expensive, and they have generally resisted introducing a power to adjust the contract to reflect the economic consequences of changed circumstances: EA Farnsworth, *Farnsworth on Contracts*, 4th edn with updates by Z Wolfe (New York, Wolters Kluwer, looseleaf) §§9.07 (impossibility), 9.08 (impracticability), 9.09 (frustration of purpose), 9.11 (effects of impracticability and frustration).

[48] For further comparative discussion, on which some of the discussion in this chapter is based, see J Cartwright, 'Rapport anglais' in Ancel and Prüm (n 37) ch 4, 'Théorie de l'imprévision', 433, 497–507. Ch 4 of that work also contains reports on Luxembourgish, French, Belgian and German law.

[49] *Fibrosa Spolka Akcyjna v Fairbairn Lawson Combe Barbour Ltd* [1943] AC 32 (HL).

[50] *Davis Contractors* (n 46) 728–29 (Lord Radcliffe).

becoming 'incapable of being performed' as a result of the frustrating event,[51] but 'incapable' does not mean 'impossible' in the sense in which civil lawyers use the word in their doctrines of impossibility.[52] In a number of cases the English courts have held that a contract was frustrated when it was not physically impossible to perform the obligations, but the purpose of the contract could no longer be achieved.[53] This is often referred to as 'frustration of purpose', where the purpose in issue was understood by both parties to be the foundation of the contract, although in reality it is the contractual benefit expected by the party seeking to rely on the frustrating event that is undermined.[54] This is distinct from cases where the burden of one party's performance becomes not impossible but impracticable,[55] or economically burdensome – which are not, in themselves, sufficient to constitute frustration.[56]

In short: the scope of operation of the doctrine of frustration goes beyond the narrow doctrines of impossibility that are generally used in civil law jurisdictions – and certainly beyond the doctrine of *force majeure* in French law.[57] But it does not cover the kind of 'hardship' that many civil law jurisdictions have developed in recent years. Nor has English law developed a general[58] doctrine of hardship alongside frustration: there is no general legislative rule allowing the courts to intervene in the contract on the basis that performance has become onerous for one party as a result of a change of circumstances during performance, and the courts have rejected the argument that they should themselves adopt a power to intervene in the contract on such a basis.

The civilian doctrines of hardship are based on the increased burden on one party as a result of the change of circumstances – or, as the French Civil Code puts it – the change 'renders performance excessively onerous for a party who had not accepted the risk of such a change'.[59] The default position in English law,

[51] ibid.

[52] See section III.A.i above.

[53] For a classic case, see *Krell v Henry* [1903] 2 KB 740 (CA).

[54] E Peel, *Frustration and Force Majeure*, 4th edn (London, Sweet & Maxwell, 2021) ch 7.

[55] ibid [6-001] (noting that impracticability has been accepted under American law: see also n 47) but concluding at [6-027] that 'In England, support for the view that "impracticability" or "commercial impossibility" can, of themselves, be grounds of discharge is confined to dicta and to extra-judicial statements. The English cases do not provide a single clear illustration of discharge on such grounds alone.'

[56] *Davis Contractors* (n 46) 716 (Viscount Simonds, rejecting the argument 'that where, without the default of either party, there has been an unexpected turn of events, which renders the contract more onerous than the parties had contemplated, that is by itself a ground for relieving a party of the obligation he has undertaken'), following *British Movietonews Ltd v London and District Cinemas Ltd* [1952] AC 166 (HL) (see also text to n 60).

[57] See section III.A.i above.

[58] Specific provisions may be introduced, eg, the substantial legislative intervention to address hardship arising from the COVID-19 pandemic. In civil law jurisdictions, the general law on hardship might deal with such matters. For a comparison between tenants' protection in commercial and residential lease contracts in English and Dutch law, see V Mak, 'Covid-19 and Long-Term Contracts' [2022] *European Review of Private Law* 419.

[59] Art 1195 Cc, quoted in full in section III.B.ii above.

by contrast, is that the effect of such changes is inherently within the risk of each party. Viscount Simon said:

> The suggestion that an 'uncontemplated turn of events' is enough to enable a court to substitute its notion of what is 'just and reasonable' for the contract as it stands, even though there is no 'frustrating event,' appears to be likely to lead to some misunderstanding. The parties to an executory contract are often faced, in the course of carrying it out, with a turn of events which they did not at all anticipate – a wholly abnormal rise or fall in prices, a sudden depreciation of currency, an unexpected obstacle to execution, or the like. Yet this does not in itself affect the bargain they have made. If, on the other hand, a consideration of the terms of the contract, in the light of the circumstances existing when it was made, shows that they never agreed to be bound in a fundamentally different situation which has now unexpectedly emerged, the contract ceases to bind at that point – not because the court in its discretion thinks it just and reasonable to qualify the terms of the contract, but because on its true construction it does not apply in that situation.[60]

Viscount Simon's rejection of the argument that the court can intervene appears to be based on two separate points. First, the scope of interference in the contract (the 'trigger') is and should remain narrow. The law should not intervene in the contract on the basis of increased burden of performance (including the increased economic burden), unless that is what the parties have themselves provided in the contract – on a true construction of the contract. The risks said to be normally assumed by the parties include a wholly abnormal rise or fall in prices and a sudden depreciation of currency. Admittedly, we have not in English law had the kind of extreme case of economic change which provoked the German courts to re-think the binding force of the contract and introduce their doctrine of hardship in the 1920s,[61] and we might wonder whether the English courts would re-open this question in such extreme circumstances. But it seems likely that our judges would think that such general change should be made by legislation, not by judicial development of the law of contract;[62] or if they sought a solution, they would find it in the interpretation of the contract. There is, however, no appetite for such an intervention, which would risk undermining the security of contracts.

This links to the second objection which Viscount Simon appears to have had to the development of what we might call a doctrine of hardship: that it would involve the court substituting its notion of what is 'just and reasonable' for the provisions that the parties have themselves agreed in their contract. This goes to the question of the remedy applicable to those changes of circumstances that are recognised by the legal system.

[60] *British Movietonews* (n 56) 185.
[61] See n 8.
[62] *cf* the legislative response to the COVID-19 pandemic (n 58).

ii. *What Remedy?*

The remedy for frustration is termination of the contract. The future, unaccrued obligations of both parties are discharged; obligations already accrued (whether or not already performed) are undisturbed. The remedy for frustration is simple; but it can present practical difficulties for the parties.

Termination for frustration is 'all or nothing': the contractual obligations, on both sides, are discharged in their entirety: there is no 'partial' frustration of only individual obligations within the contract. And the obligations are discharged; the duty of performance is not simply suspended. If the impossibility is likely to be only temporary, there may be no frustration at all. Except in the case of interdependent obligations, where one party may withhold performance of its obligation pending performance of the other party's related obligation,[63] there is no general legal basis for one party to suspend performance.

Moreover, the discharge of the obligations is effected by operation of law, without the intervention of either party or of the court and may have taken effect before even the parties realised that the frustrating event had occurred. There is little scope for judicial discretion – overt discretion, at least. If the issue of frustration is before the court, the court decides whether the alleged event was sufficient in law to frustrate the contract, and the 'radical difference' test[64] may appear rather open-textured, although it is clearly narrowly circumscribed by the case law authorities.[65] And if the test is satisfied, the court does not itself order the termination of the contract: the termination already took effect at the moment of the frustrating event. There is the possibility to make consequential financial orders under section 1 of the Law Reform (Frustrated Contracts) Act 1943, which contains certain structured discretions, but these do not go very deep.[66]

B. Other Judicial Solutions

The limited scope of the definition of frustration, and the limited power of intervention to respond to the consequences of frustration – even if it is found – do not mean that the courts can never find solutions to problems arising from changes of circumstances which do not constitute frustration of the contract.

The tools available to the courts are interpretation of the contract and the implication of terms into the contract. At least in contracts of indefinite duration, the court may be able on the facts to decide by interpretation, or by finding

[63] See Beatson, Burrows and Cartwright (n 46) 441.
[64] See n 50.
[65] See text to n 56.
[66] The heading of s 1 ('Adjustment of rights and liabilities of parties to frustrated contracts') might sound rather more sweeping than the section provides.

an implied term, that one or both parties have the right to terminate on giving reasonable notice.[67] And where, during performance of a long-term contract, there is a change of circumstances which is not sufficient to frustrate the contract but which leaves a gap in the parties' bargain, the courts are reluctant to contemplate the failure of the whole contract, and they may seek to fill the gap using an implied term which best serves the parties' original purpose in the changed circumstances.[68]

However, such cases do not go so far as to create the equivalent of a general doctrine of hardship. Even if the doctrine of frustration might be said to be based on the construction of the contract or the implication of a term,[69] this does not mean that the courts will routinely imply a term covering changes of circumstances outside the scope of frustrating events. For example, there is no basis on which the courts can generally imply a term designed to adjust the parties' bargain in light of the changed circumstances, nor is there a general implied duty on the parties to exercise their contractual rights and remedies in good faith, nor to renegotiate to resolve problems arising from changes in circumstances which fall short of triggering the doctrine of frustration. Even if the parties could – or, indeed, would – have made some provision to address the change of circumstances, the fact that they did not do so does not mean that the courts will do so by implying a term.[70]

[67] *Staffordshire Area Health Authority v South Staffordshire Waterworks Co* [1978] 1 WLR 1387 (CA) (contract in 1929 to supply water 'at all times hereafter' at a fixed price was terminable on reasonable notice (the majority based their decision on the construction of the contract, but Lord Denning MR applied a general principle based on the change of circumstances); *cf* the strictness of the old (pre-2016 reform) approach of the French Cour de cassation in the 'Canal de Craponne' case (n 16)). See also McKendrick, below, ch 7 pp 139–41.

[68] *Standard Chartered plc v Guaranty Nominees Ltd* [2024] EWHC 2605 (Comm), [2025] 2 All ER (Comm) 46 [51]–[52] ('in effect, a form of contractual *cy-près*'). The dividend rate under perpetual preference shares and American depository shares was linked to the London Interbank Offered Rate ('LIBOR'), which ceased to be published. Sir Julian Flaux C and Foxton J held at [66] that it was necessary, in order to give business efficacy to the arrangements, to imply a term to the effect that if the express definition of Three Month LIBOR ceased to be capable of operation, dividends should be calculated using the reasonable alternative rate to three month USD LIBOR at the date the dividend falls to be calculated. This relied on the use of an objective (reasonable) alternative rate, and allowed the parties' agreed bargain to be given effect; *cf* cases where the courts have upheld a contract where the mechanism agreed by the parties for a price to be fixed breaks down, eg, *Sudbrook Trading Estate Ltd v Eggleton* [1983] 1 AC 444 (HL) (option to purchase at price to be agreed by parties' valuers construed as agreement to sell at fair and reasonable price, which the court could determine if the non-essential valuation machinery set by the agreement failed to operate), cited by Sir Julian Flaux C and Foxton J at [48]. For further discussion of the interpretation of long-term contracts as a response to the need to adapt contracts to changes of circumstances, see D Foxton, '"When Everything Changes": Adapting Contracts to Fundamental Changes in Circumstance – the 2024 Jill Poole Memorial Lecture' [2025] *Journal of Business Law* 161, 165–68; and for a broader discussion of the cessation of LIBOR and strategies for dealing with such supervening events, see Braithwaite, below, ch 3.

[69] See MacMahon, below, ch 2, Mitchell, below, ch 5, and English, below, ch 8.

[70] *cf Philips Electronique Grand Public SA v British Sky Broadcasting Ltd* [1995] EMLR 472 (CA) 482 (Bingham MR, approved by Lord Neuberger in *Marks and Spencer plc v BNP Paribas Securities Services Trust Co (Jersey) Ltd* [2015] UKSC 72, [2016] AC 742 at [19]–[21]). See also Braithwaite, below, ch 3 pp 49–50 noting the uncertainty of whether courts will imply a term to 'save' a contract.

The effect of the limited doctrine of frustration, together with the absence of any broader general doctrine of hardship, is to provide an incentive for the parties to include express provision for change of circumstances in their contract.

C. 'Change of Circumstances' Clauses in English Contracts

Clauses are very commonly used in commercial contracts governed by English law to anticipate changes of circumstances, addressing both impossibility and hardship.[71] Such clauses are generally designed to provide certainty for the parties in the event that there should be a change of circumstances affecting one or both parties' performance of the contract, but also to respond to the limitations of the doctrine of frustration: for example, to define more precisely, or more widely, the events that will give rise to a remedy under the clause (eg, a detailed list of possible trigger events tailored to the context of the contract; events short of impossibility – and even including economic changes); to allow for a wider range of remedial responses (eg, suspension as well as termination); and to make the remedy dependent on notice being given to invoke it, rather than it being an automatic remedy. There are, however, some potential pitfalls to watch out for.

There can be difficulty defining precisely the change of circumstances which will trigger the operation of the clause: the context of the contract may allow some degree of tailoring of the clause in setting out the changes that would affect the parties' bargain, but some contracts even refer to 'force majeure'[72] – which will be given effect by the courts although it has no single, definite meaning in English law.[73] The ability to define the operation of the clause with objective clarity is important since even in the modern law, where the courts have moved away from special rules of construction for particular types of clauses in commercial contracts, especially clauses limiting or excluding a party's liability for breach of contract,[74] the Supreme Court still appears to favour a strict construction of 'force majeure' clauses.[75]

There can also be difficulty in defining the consequence of any change of circumstances that might occur, at least if the parties wish not simply to suspend or terminate performance, but to maintain the contractual relationship in the new circumstances. As long as the parties can provide for objectively certain new

[71] See also McKendrick, below, ch 7 pp 127–32.

[72] eg, the JCT contracts which give a list of events which would constitute a change, drawn in relation to the context of the (typical) construction contract, but add 'force majeure' as a final undefined sweeper of last resort: see n 6.

[73] *Thomas Borthwick (Glasgow) Ltd v Faure Fairclough Ltd* [1968] 1 Lloyd's Rep 16 (QB) 28. It is generally interpreted as requiring legal or physical impossibility: *Channel Island Ferries Ltd v Sealink UK Ltd* [1988] 1 Lloyd's Rep 323 (CA) 327.

[74] *Triple Point Technology Inc v PTT Public Co Ltd* [2021] UKSC 29, [2021] AC 1148 at [107]–[108], [111].

[75] *MUR Shipping BV v RTI Ltd* [2024] UKSC 18, [2025] AC 675 at [37].

terms, or at least an objectively certain mechanism to find the new terms, there will be no objection to the clause on the basis of its lack of certainty, and – if necessary – the court can step in and give effect to the clause.[76] For certain types of term, the contract might even provide for one party to have a discretionary power to vary the term; the court cannot itself exercise the power but can control improper exercise.[77] However, the commercial instinct may be for the parties to renegotiate in light of the new circumstances once they are known – which is always possible, of course; the question is whether they can be under an *obligation* to renegotiate. There is no inherent (implied) duty to negotiate or perform a contract in good faith,[78] and therefore no basis on which the parties to a contract governed by English law can be required to renegotiate a contract simply because its performance has become impossible or onerous. The parties may include an express provision in their 'change of circumstances' clause requiring renegotiation, although – unless it is defined in objectively certain terms[79] – it is not certain that such a clause will be enforceable.[80]

V. Some Comparative Conclusions

Circumstances change. The parties to a contract know this, and – given that a contract (in particular, a negotiated, commercial contract) is designed to provide a framework for performance of their obligations and to allocate risks – the parties should generally not be able to complain about the occurrence of matters for which they have not provided in the contract. Sometimes, however, there are such significant changes to the circumstances which prevailed when a contract was entered into that one of the parties claims that the risk allocation is undermined, and the contract should no longer be binding (in whole or in part) or should be binding only with some adaptation to take account of the changed circumstances.

[76] *cf* n 68 above.

[77] *Braganza v BP Shipping Ltd* [2015] UKSC 17, [2015] 1 WLR 1661 (implied term that the discretion must not be exercised arbitrarily, capriciously, or irrationally). See further Foxton (n 68) 175–77.

[78] J Cartwright, *Formation and Variation of Contracts*, 4th edn (London, Sweet & Maxwell, 2024) [2-03]–[2-07].

[79] eg, providing for negotiations on a new price, where the contract indicates that the price is to be reasonable: *Petromec Inc v Petroleo Brasileiro SA* [2005] EWCA Civ 891, [2006] 1 Lloyd's Rep 121 at [86] (setting out cl 12), [118].

[80] The technical objection is the decision of the House of Lords in *Walford v Miles* [1992] 2 AC 128 (HL) 138 (Lord Ackner, rejecting a duty (express, as well as implied) to negotiate in good faith), although there are indications that the lower courts are now more willing to accept a duty to negotiate in good faith, or to use reasonable endeavours to negotiate, at least where it is on some particular, limited matter such as the variation of one of the terms of the existing contract: see, eg, *Petromec Inc v Petroleo Brasileiro SA* (n 79) [121]; *Brooke Homes (Bicester) Ltd v Portfolio Property Partners Ltd* [2021] EWHC 3015 (Ch) at [100]. See further Cartwright (n 78) [2-08], [2-40]; Foxton (n 68) 173–75; McKendrick, below, ch 7 pp 141–44.

Every system of contract law has to provide rules to answer such a claim. The answer given by English law is quite limited: if the facts satisfy the requirements of the doctrine of frustration, the contract will have been terminated by the change of circumstances. But this doctrine has a limited scope: although it extends beyond changes of circumstances which render performance impossible, this goes only as far as changes which render performance 'radically different' – which does not, in principle, cover mere hardship (practical or economic) in performance.[81] And even where frustration applies, the remedy is of limited practical use: automatic termination of the whole contract, with no general remedy of suspension, or severance of the affected part of the contractual performance.[82] Beyond frustration, there is no general doctrine of change of circumstances designed to address lesser changes, and no general power in the courts to adjust the terms of the contract, although there are situations where the courts will apply other tools at their disposal – interpretation, implied terms – in order to resolve the difficulties faced by the parties. Such intervention is, however, at best piecemeal, not based on general principle.[83]

By contrast, modern civil law systems – of which we have seen the example of French law – take a very different approach. The contractual allocation of the risk of the change in circumstances is (as in English law) the natural starting point. But beyond that, two different general doctrines can be invoked. First, impossibility in performance of an obligation as a result of the change of circumstances (in French law, *force majeure*) excuses the liability of the party who has the duty to perform that obligation[84] – a remedy which can be temporary or partial (severing the now-impossible obligation from the rest of the contract), or permanent and total (discharging the whole contract).[85] Second, there is a broader doctrine of hardship (in French law, *imprévision*), which is not easily satisfied, but extends to cases where the effect of the change renders performance 'excessively onerous' – including practical and economic hardship.[86] The operation of this doctrine and its remedies varies from one system to another, but includes the duty to renegotiate, and the court's power to adjust the terms of the contract, as well as termination of the contract.[87]

The differences in approach between the legal systems may be explained by a number of different factors, some reflecting broader structural differences between the systems, others matters of policy.

The response of civil law systems to change of circumstances – and in contract law generally – depends largely on general principles of law, set down in legislation (the natural source of legal principles in codified systems), although sometimes developed by the courts beyond the legislative texts. The general theory of obligations,

[81] See section IV.A.i.
[82] See section IV.A.ii.
[83] See section IV.B.
[84] See section III.A.i.
[85] See section III.B.i.
[86] See section III.A.ii.
[87] See section III.B.ii.

with the primacy of performance of contractual obligations, leads to a natural solution for impossibility in performance;[88] and the general duty of good faith in both negotiation and performance of the contract can form the basis of the parties' duty to renegotiate.[89] The courts have a significant role in controlling many aspects of the contractual relationship,[90] and it is not entirely surprising that the legislator should add a power for them to adjust the contract on a principled basis in light of a change of circumstances.

By contrast, it is significant that the English law of contract has its origins not in legislation but the common law. Although English law has some general doctrines of contract law, such as frustration, which have been developed by the judges,[91] the courts largely resist setting down general principles. There is no general duty of good faith, in either negotiation or performance;[92] the courts find particular, piecemeal solutions, but creating and reasoning from general principles is not how the courts generally work in the application and development of the common law.[93] Unless they can attribute their intervention to the contract itself – to give effect to what the parties intended[94] – the courts are reluctant to intervene on their own motion in the contract.

This leads to a broader question of policy. We have seen that there has been a trend towards 'contractual justice' as a principle of modern French contract law.[95] There is a balance to be struck between the principles of freedom of contract, the binding force of contracts, and good faith,[96] and the courts recognise their power to intervene in the contract. By contrast, English judges exhibit a marked reluctance to intervene in the bargain struck by the parties, except where legislation gives them a specific power – and legislation rarely does so. 'The principle of freedom of contract is fundamental to the English law of contract.'[97] There is no

[88] See section III.B.i.

[89] See text to n 34.

[90] Such control is not limited to consumer contracts, eg, in France, the courts not only have control over unfair contract terms in standard-form contracts (art 1171 Cc), but also have the power to moderate unreasonable penalty clauses (art 1231-5 Cc); nullity of the contract for defects in formation is by court order (art 1178 Cc); and until the 2016 reforms, the Civil Code required a court order for termination of the contract for non-performance, although unilateral termination had become recognised in practice. The general, non-excludable legal duty of good faith in negotiation, formation and performance (art 1104 Cc) provides a potential tool for the courts in their oversight of the contract.

[91] See text to nn 43–46.

[92] See text to nn 78–80.

[93] *Interfoto Picture Library Ltd v Stiletto Visual Programmes Ltd* [1989] QB 433 (CA) 439 (Bingham LJ: 'In many civil law systems, and perhaps in most legal systems outside the common law world, the law of obligations recognises and enforces an overriding principle that in making and carrying out contracts parties should act in good faith. …English law has, characteristically, committed itself to no such overriding principle but has developed piecemeal solutions in response to demonstrated problems of unfairness').

[94] eg, by interpretation of the contract, or implication of a term into the contract: see section IV.B.; see also the particular examples of *Taylor v Caldwell* (nn 44, 45); *Staffordshire Area Health Authority* (n 67).

[95] See n 41.

[96] Arts 1102, 1103 and 1104 Cc respectively.

[97] *MUR Shipping BV v RTI Ltd* (n 75) [41] (Lord Hamblen and Lord Burrows JJSC).

counterbalancing general duty of good faith or fairness, and the courts are clear that matters of policy are for Parliament.[98] This insistence on the parties' agreement as the beginning and (normally) the end of the matter carries through to the law on change of circumstances. The argument that, outside the operation of the doctrine of frustration, the courts have a power to substitute their notion of what is 'just and reasonable' for the contract as it was agreed by the parties, was rejected by the House of Lords in the 1950s,[99] and finds echoes in a Scottish appeal to the Supreme Court in 2013, where Lord Hope rejected the possibility of equitable adjustment by interpretation of the contract where the contract is 'nearly frustrated but not quite': 'To hold otherwise would be to undermine the principle enshrined in the maxim pacta sunt servanda which lies at the root of the whole of the law of contract.'[100]

This general approach to change of circumstances in English law emphasises the significance of the use of clauses in the contract to attempt to address changes which might occur during the lifetime of the contract. Such contract drafting is not, of course, limited to the common law. Civil lawyers also have an interest in providing as fully and clearly as possible in their contracts for possible changes of circumstances. The parties' motivation in different systems may be different: it may be that French lawyers, for example, will draft contract clauses not simply to provide clarity, but in order to exclude the operation of the new doctrine of *imprévision* if they see it as giving too much power to the courts or as containing too much uncertainty in its operation.[101] English lawyers, however, have a different problem: not over-regulation of the contract by the law, but a very limited doctrine of change of circumstances which is inadequate to solve problems the parties may face if circumstances change during performance.

[98] eg, *Pakistan International Airline Corp v Times Travel (UK) Ltd* [2021] UKSC 40, [2021] AC 101 at [26] (Lord Hodge DPSC: 'The courts have taken the position that it is for Parliament and not the judiciary to regulate inequality of bargaining power where a person is trading in a manner which is not otherwise contrary to law').

[99] *British Movietonews* (n 56).

[100] *Lloyds TSB Foundation for Scotland v Lloyds Banking Group plc* [2013] UKSC 3, [2013] 1 WLR 366 at [47].

[101] See text to nn 35–38.

2

Constructing Frustration

PAUL MACMAHON*

The doctrine of frustration is English contract law's most obvious response to the unexpected. Yet it is so narrowly defined that it rarely applies. Despite hopes for a 'mass of litigation' in response to COVID-19,[1] the great upheavals resulting from the pandemic produced precious few attempts to invoke frustration in published decisions.[2]

Frustration is nevertheless worthy of attention. The doctrine is not devoid of all practical significance. Parties to the big-money cases that dominate High Court litigation can realistically make express provision for changed circumstances, but frustration may be more important in the lower-value disputes that make up much of the actual life of contract law. For example, many contracts with wedding venues were certainly discharged because of COVID lockdowns. In those cases, the parties reached consensual solutions; sometimes, at least, the law's solution must have cast a shadow over their bargaining.

Moreover, English law's approach to changed circumstances remains controversial. Like much of the common law, the frustration doctrine has been developed through judicial intuitions. It is thus potentially vulnerable to arguments denying those intuitions. Some heavyweight scholars of English contract law contend that there should be no 'doctrine of frustration'.[3] Conversely, from a civil-law perspective, the doctrine seems too narrow. The French Civil Code was amended in 2016 to include a doctrine of hardship, providing for renegotiation, alteration, or termination of contracts that have unforeseeably become unduly onerous for one party to perform.[4] This amendment brought France broadly into line with

* I am grateful to my commentator Adam Temple and to other participants in the *Contract Law and the Unexpected* conference for thoughts on a previous version. Thanks also to Paul Davies, Elizabeth Howell, Victor Goldberg, and Magda Raczynska for written comments.

[1] C MacMillan, 'Covid-19 and the Problem of Frustrated Contracts' (2021) 32 *King's Law Journal* 60.

[2] See E McKendrick, 'COVID, Contracts, and Change of Circumstances' [2024] *Lloyd's Maritime and Commercial Law Quarterly* 34.

[3] See D Campbell, *Contractual Relations* (Oxford, OUP, 2022) 331; J Morgan, 'Frustration Dissected: Mandatory and Default Rules' in K Barnett, W Day, J Morgan and A Robertson (eds), *Mandatory and Default Rules in Contract and Commercial Law* (Oxford, Hart Publishing, 2026).

[4] *Code Civil*, art 1195. See S Rowan, *The New French Law of Contract* (Oxford, OUP, 2022) ch 9; Cartwright, ch 1 in this book.

other European nations, but English law has no equivalent. And even if one accepts English law's basic approach to changed circumstances, significant uncertainties surround it. '[I]t remains intractably difficult to justify where we place the line separating cases of frustration and cases of absolute obligation',[5] and scholars have criticised the doctrine for its 'inconsistent application'.[6] Courts have not settled on a test for frustration. The roles of fault and foreseeability are contested. The consequences of frustration are the subject of a much-maligned statute.[7] Most fundamentally, the 'juristic basis' for frustration is the subject of an interminable and inconclusive debate: is the doctrine based in some way on party agreement or instead on a sense of justice imposed by law?

These persistent difficulties suggest the need for a fresh perspective. Judges of high authority have said that frustration in commercial contracts 'is almost completely determined by what is ascertained as to mercantile usage and the understanding of mercantile men'.[8] Yet the body of human knowledge whose purpose is to provide insight into the aims and practices of 'mercantile men' and women – economics – is generally kept at arm's length by English contract law scholars. In the US, the topic has been the subject of a line of economics-inspired articles starting in earnest in 1977 with a contribution by Richard Posner and his student Andrew Rosenfield.[9] The leading English treatise on frustration and force majeure refers to some of Judge Posner's judicial remarks, but not to his or to any other economics-inspired scholarship on the topic.[10] Many English judges and scholars would agree with Peter Benson that the economic analysis of frustration doctrine, like economic analysis more generally, is inimical to private law reasoning.[11] Jonathan Morgan, one of the few English scholars to engage seriously with the economic literature, specifically rejects the value of efficiency analysis in understanding frustration.[12]

Seeking to overcome this scepticism, this chapter suggests that English law can learn from economic analysis. Indeed, the chapter aims to show that the logic of current doctrine is already implicitly economic, so that express consideration of ideas developed using economic jargon would do no violence to English law in this area. Crucially, economic analysis can be relevant even if one does not embrace the unrelenting utilitarianism of some of its proponents. Moreover, accepting that economic analysis can provide doctrinal insights does not entail

[5] M Bridge, 'Frustration and Excused Non-Performance' (2021) 137 *LQR* 580, 592.

[6] MacMillan (n 1) 61.

[7] Law Reform (Frustrated Contracts) Act 1943.

[8] *Tsakiroglou & Co Ltd v Noblee Thorl GmbH* [1962] AC 93 (HL) 124; *Pioneer Shipping Ltd v BTP Tioxide Ltd (The Nema)* [1982] AC 724 (HL).

[9] RA Posner and A M Rosenfield 'Impossibility and Related Doctrines in Contract Law: An Economic Analysis' (1977) 6 *Journal of Legal Studies* 83.

[10] EA Peel (ed), *Treitel on Frustration and Force Majeure*, 4th edn (London, Sweet & Maxwell, 2021).

[11] P Benson, *Justice in Transactions* (Cambridge, MA, Harvard University Press, 2019) 155–56.

[12] Morgan (n 3). See also J Morgan, *Great Debates in Contract Law*, 3rd edn (London, Bloomsbury Publishing, 2020) 184–88; J Morgan, *Contract Law Minimalism: A Formalist Restatement of Commercial Contract Law* (Cambridge, CUP, 2013) 119–21.

that first-instance judges should necessarily always deploy economic concepts when resolving cases. English judges have sometimes been receptive to economic insights;[13] Lord Leggatt, for example, has recently invoked the economic analysis of implied terms,[14] and has argued persuasively that the point of commercial law is to facilitate commerce.[15] More specifically, Neil Andrews says that 'Posner's work [on frustration] merits more judicial attention than it has received in the UK'.[16] The aim, however, is to transcend Posner and Rosenfield's account, which is significantly flawed on economic grounds.

It is important not to expect too much. Like English law, economic analysis has struggled with this topic. Economics will not always provide precise solutions in difficult cases, but it can help to provide a more systematic understanding of the issues. If nothing else, it provides a more satisfying basis than judicial intuition for the core assumptions of English law in this area. It can also help to resolve some of the specific controversies that continue to surround the doctrine. It can even help cast some light on the nature of contractual construction, of which the doctrine of frustration is arguably an instance. The chapter starts by surveying the current English approach to frustration and noting some of its difficulties (section I). Readers familiar with the doctrine may wish to skip ahead to section II, which examines economic approaches. Section III explores how English law might benefit from engagement with economics in this area.

I. The Current Doctrine of Frustration

A party subject only to a duty to take reasonable care can avoid liability by showing that it was not at fault in responding to a supervening event. Liability for breach of contract, however, is often strict liability, and where liability is strict, frustration may be the only hope for a party who seeks to avoid liability by invoking a post-contract change of circumstances.

The basic idea is that frustration occurs where 'without default of either party a contractual obligation has become incapable of being performed because the circumstances in which performance is called for would render it a thing radically different from that which was undertaken by the contract'.[17] Frustration is said

[13] Most notably, Lord Mustill invoked the idea of the consumer surplus in *Ruxley Electronics v Forsyth* [1996] AC 344 (HL) 360-61. Lords Hamblen and Burrows have recently stated that '[c]ontract law permits efficient breach'. *King Crude Carriers SA v Ridgebury November LLC* [2025] UKSC 39 [78].

[14] *Barton v Morris* [2023] UKSC 3, [2023] AC 684 [127]–[133] (Lord Leggatt, dissenting).

[15] Lord Leggatt, 'What is the Point of Commercial Law?' [2022] *Lloyd's Maritime and Commercial Law Quarterly* 242.

[16] N Andrews, 'Core Features of Frustration: Legal Basis, Risk Allocation and "Self-Inducement"' in N Andrews, A Tettenborn and G Virgo, *Contractual Duties: Performance, Breach, Termination and Remedies*, 4th edn (London, Sweet & Maxwell, 2023) [16-080].

[17] *Davis Contractors Ltd v Fareham Urban District Council* [1956] AC 696 (HL) 729 (Lord Radcliffe).

to be automatic, and it relieves both parties from their contractual obligations.[18] The doctrine's initial roots lie in cases where the subject-matter of the contract is destroyed.[19] It was extended to cases of frustration of purpose like *Krell v Henry*,[20] where extraneous circumstances deprive one of the parties of its expected benefit, but has almost never been applied in that circumstance since. Attempts to invoke the doctrine by parties contending that performance has become too difficult or expensive generally fail.[21]

More recent cases support a 'multifactorial approach' to determining whether contractual obligations are discharged by frustration.[22] A court should first consider the contract's terms, its context, the parties' knowledge, and their objectively shared assumptions as to risk at the time of the contract.[23] The court should then consider the nature of the supervening event and the parties' 'reasonable and objectively ascertainable calculations as to the possibilities of future performance in the new circumstances'.[24] The doctrine cannot be applied 'without an exercise of judgment', and judges must consider 'the demands of justice'.[25]

Commentators have identified many unresolved questions about the current doctrine.

First, what is the test that courts should apply when faced with a plea of frustration? Many textbooks suggest that frustration operates if performance of the contract becomes impossible, illegal, or radically different.[26] But it is not clear that contractual obligations should end in the event of a radical change, even one rendering performance impossible. English law has long recognised that it is possible to undertake to do an impossible thing, while being answerable for damages for non-performance.[27] Hence, even if the contract's subject matter is destroyed,[28] the obligation to perform is not necessarily discharged.

Second, can a single legal doctrine accommodate all the cases to which 'frustration' applies? English law says 'yes', but this unitary approach has its critics. As Jonathan Morgan argues, cases involving supervening illegality raise distinct concerns relating to third-party effects.[29] Others assert that courts should draw an analytical distinction between cases where the supervening event impedes performance, and those where the supervening event makes the performance less

[18] I will not discuss the fact that frustration operates automatically. Many have argued that English law has taken a wrong turn in this regard. Bridge (n 5) 585–90; J English, *Discharge of Contractual Obligations* (Oxford, OUP, 2025) ch 6; Morgan (n 3).

[19] *Taylor v Caldwell* (1863) 3 B & S 826 (QB) 834.

[20] *Krell v Henry* [1903] 2 KB 740 (CA).

[21] *Davis Contractors* (n 17).

[22] *Edwinton Commercial Corp v Tsavliris Russ (Worldwide Salvage & Towage) Ltd (The Sea Angel)* [2007] 1 CLC 876 (CA) [111].

[23] ibid.

[24] ibid.

[25] ibid [113].

[26] See, eg, A Burrows, *A Restatement of the English Law of Contract* (Oxford, OUP, 2016) s 32.

[27] *Thornborow v Whitacre* (1705) 2 Ld Raym 1164, 92 ER 270 (KB) 271.

[28] *Jackson v Union Marine Insurance* (1874) LR 10 CP 125 (Exch Ch).

[29] Morgan (n 3). I will mostly leave cases of supervening illegality to one side.

valuable for one party.[30] US jurisdictions have developed separate doctrines for 'impossibility' or 'impracticability' on the one hand and 'frustration of purpose' on the other hand;[31] should English law do the same?

Third, can a foreseeable event provide the basis for frustration? Many judicial dicta suggest the answer is 'no'. In *Krell v Henry*, for example, Vaughan Williams LJ stated that '[t]he test seems to be whether the event which causes the impossibility was or might have been anticipated'.[32] New York law agrees; one court concluded that a COVID-inspired closure was not a frustrating event for a lease of retail premises because a pandemic was foreseeable.[33] But the generally prevailing view among English judges – stated most forcefully by Lord Denning[34] – is that foreseeability is not necessarily a bar to frustration.

Fourth, should a party whose faultless choice rendered it unable to perform its obligations be precluded on that ground from invoking the doctrine of frustration? For example, where a party has the option at the time of the contract to perform in two ways, then chooses to disable herself from performing in one of those ways, can she plead frustration if the remaining way of performing becomes impossible? More recent case law rejects the plea of 'self-induced frustration', even where the breaching party is not at fault,[35] but the point is controversial.[36]

Fifth, what should the remedial consequences of frustration be? At common law, a party who has paid money and received nothing in return could seek repayment, and the payee could not reduce the repayment by reference to expenses incurred in furtherance of performance.[37] A provider of services contractually entitled to payment only on completion had no claim at common law if frustration interrupted the work.[38] The law was amended for most contracts by the Law Reform (Frustrated Contracts) Act 1943. Where it applies, the Act provides for: (i) recovery of advance payments subject to a judicial discretion to reduce repayment up to the extent to which the recipient has incurred expenses; and (ii) a judicial (or arbitral) discretion to order payment by a party who has received a non-money benefit up to the value of that benefit, with the decision-maker directed to consider (among other things) the extent of any expenses incurred by the recipient of the benefit. The 1943 Act has been criticised from

[30] For a recent defence of this distinction, see J Nadler, 'Impossibility and Frustration' in M Chen-Wishart and P Saprai, *Research Handbook on the Philosophy of Contract Law* (Cheltenham, Edward Elgar, 2025). See also Peel (n 10) [2-061].

[31] See Restatement (Second of Contracts) (1981) s 261 (impracticability) and s 265 (frustration of purpose).

[32] *Krell v Henry* (n 20) 752.

[33] *The Gap, Inc. v Ponte Gadea New York LLC*, 524 F Supp 3d 224 (SDNY 2021).

[34] *Ocean Tramp Tankers Corp v V/O Sovfracht (The Eugenia)* [1964] 2 QB 226 (CA) 234.

[35] *J Lauritzen AS v Wijsmuller BV (The Super Servant Two)* [1990] 1 Lloyd's Rep 1 (CA).

[36] For criticism see, eg, E Peel (ed), *Treitel: The Law of Contract*, 16th edn (London, Sweet and Maxwell, 2025) [19-095].

[37] *Fibrosa Spolka Akcyjna v Fairbairn Lawson Combe Barbour Ltd* [1943] AC 32 (HL).

[38] *Appleby v Myers* (1866-67) LR 2 CP 651 (Exch Ch).

various perspectives, and is said to combine 'complexity, lack of principle, and uncertainty'.[39]

Sixth, how, if at all, can the doctrine be squared with wider ideas about contracts? In other words, what is the 'juristic' or 'juridical' basis of frustration? The most extensive recent discussion of this issue in the case law concludes that the notion of 'radical difference' best encapsulates the doctrine,[40] but that is more a test for frustration rather than a juridical basis.

Judges consistently state that frustration is tied in some way to justice; it applies where 'it would be unjust to hold [a party] to the literal sense of its stipulations in the new circumstances'.[41] Characteristically, this idea was embraced by Lord Denning, who claimed that 'the court really exercises a qualifying power – a power to qualify the absolute, literal or wide terms of the contract in order to do what is just and reasonable in the new situation'.[42] A judicial discretion unmoored to the parties' agreement is bound to seem unattractive and out of keeping with the rest of contract law. Moreover, on closer inspection, even Lord Denning did not envisage a judicial power to impose a solution on the parties. His discussion is based on the idiosyncratic premise that the unqualified written words of the contract constitute its terms. He posited a power to bring the literal words of the contract (the 'terms') into line with the 'intent' of the parties' agreement. Now that it is more clearly understood that the construction of the parties' agreement requires attention to context and commercial common sense as well as the contractual text, the necessity of an extra-contractual solution falls away.

If so, the juristic basis of frustration lies in the 'construction' theory. Though out of vogue among some judges,[43] some version of the construction theory is supported by the most satisfying academic discussions of the question.[44] One variant considers frustration to be an aspect of the interpretation of express terms.[45] As Lord Radcliffe put it, with a paraphrase of Virgil, '*Non haec in foedera veni*. It was not this that I promised to do'.[46] If, on a true construction of the agreement,

[39] R Stevens, *The Laws of Restitution* (Oxford, OUP, 2023) 137.

[40] *Canary Wharf (BP4) T1 Ltd v European Medicines Agency* [2019] EWHC 335 (Ch).

[41] *Hirji Mulji v Cheong Yue Steamship Co Ltd* [1926] AC 497 (PC) 510 (Lord Sumner). See also *The Super Servant Two* (n 35) 8.

[42] *British Movietonews v London and District Cinemas* [1951] 1 KB 190 (CA) 200.

[43] See, eg, *Canary Wharf* (n 40) [26] fn 38: 'The weakness of the construction approach is that it assumes – wrongly – that construction or interpretation of the contract can resolve every problem.' But see *Bunge SA v Kyla Shipping Co Ltd* [2012] EWHC 3522 (Comm), [2013] 1 Lloyd's Rep 565, [70].

[44] Bridge (n 5); English (n 18); Morgan (n 3).

[45] Some English lawyers consider 'construction' a synonym for 'interpretation'. See, eg, *Arnold v Britton* [2015] UKSC 36, [2015] AC 1619, [14]. American sources, however, have long drawn a distinction between interpretation (determining the meaning of the parties' communications) and construction (determining the legal effect of those communications). See G Klass, 'Contracts, Constitutions, and Getting the Interpretation-Construction Distinction Right' (2020) 18 *Georgetown Journal of Law and Public Policy* 13.

[46] *Davis Contractors* (n 17) 729. This phrase has long been used by English judges in contract disputes and can be traced to Lord Mansfield. See *Hoare v Dawes* (1780) 1 Douglas 371, 99 ER 239 (KB).

the party is not liable in the circumstances that have eventuated, there is no need to add a term. And if, on a true construction of the agreement, the parties have agreed to maintain liability despite a change of circumstances, there is no room for the doctrine of frustration to operate. The construction idea fits well with the multifactorial approach: in the same way that a judge construing the words of the contract takes account of a variety of textual and contextual factors, so must a judge consider a variety of factors when deciding whether a party should be relieved of liability.[47]

Another version of the construction theory justifies cases where an obligation is discharged by positing an implied term to that effect.[48] Initially, the operation of the doctrine was justified in *Taylor v Caldwell* by reference to an implied condition that the parties would be excused if performance became impossible due to the destruction of the subject matter through neither party's fault.[49] In some twentieth-century cases, the notion that the doctrine was based on an implied term was subjected to severe judicial criticism. Lord Radcliffe saw it as an illustration of 'the tendency of English courts to refer all the consequences of a contract to the will of those who made it'.[50] This criticism, however, misses the mark; implied terms are not based on a concurrence of the parties' subjective wills. Indeed, in *Taylor v Caldwell*, Blackburn J said that '[t]he parties when framing their agreement evidently had not present to their minds the possibility of such a disaster'.[51] Rather, the point was the (objective) *appearance* that the parties to this kind of contract proceed on the basis that the subject matter will continue to exist.

The problem with construction theories is that many think there is not much more to be said about an idea once it is classified as involving construction. In chapter eight of this book, Jordan English says that 'the doctrine of frustration is simply a question of construction',[52] but there is little that is simple about contractual construction. As Dr English himself says in his book on contractual discharge, the implied condition view is 'not a panacea' for the 'difficult questions of construction' courts face.[53] On a simple view, the construction of contracts is synonymous with interpretation, and requires asking what a reasonable person would believe the particular parties to that contract meant by the words they chose.[54] On a more sophisticated view, the construction of contracts also involves supplying answers when meaning runs out, whether by

[47] See PS Atiyah, *Essays on Contract* (Revised edn, Oxford, OUP, 1988) 270–72; see also W Day, 'Isn't Brexit Frustrating?' (2019) 78 *CLJ* 270, 271.

[48] For a recent defence, see A Kramer, 'Contractual Interpretation: Meaning, Intention, and Disembodied Spirits' in E Peel and R Probert (eds), *Shaping the Law of Obligations: Essays in Honour of Professor Ewan McKendrick KC* (Oxford, OUP, 2023).

[49] *Taylor v Caldwell* (n 19).

[50] *Davis Contractors* (n 17) 728.

[51] *Taylor v Caldwell* (n 19) 833.

[52] See Jordan English, ch 8, p 146 in this book.

[53] English (n 18) 211.

[54] *Arnold v Britton* [2015] UKSC 36.

finding implied terms or giving meaning to express terms. In *Arnold v Britton*, Lord Neuberger acknowledged that sometimes 'an event subsequently occurs which was plainly not intended or contemplated by the parties'; in such cases the court should give effect to what the parties *would* clearly have intended their words to mean.[55] Complicating matters further, courts sometimes apply general interpretive presumptions that are not based on the apparent intentions of particular parties but a more generalised sense of what parties to contracts would want.[56] And if an implied terms analysis is correct, a court must judge what the parties would have wanted in the circumstances that have transpired.

As noted below, economic analysis seeks to answer questions of central importance to orthodox accounts of contractual construction: what are the parties' purposes when entering into contractual arrangements? What would they have agreed if they had turned their minds to the eventuality in question? To the extent 'construction' includes the process of finding implied terms, what is necessary to give business efficacy to an agreement? Ironically, the word 'construction' is itself ambiguous between 'construing' and 'constructing'. In contract law, we generally use the word 'construction' to refer to the process of construing contracts. Yet these words share the same Latin root: *construere*, to pile together or build up. My suggestion in this chapter is that in building up the terms of contracts, judges should often use economic bricks.

II. Economic Approaches to Frustration

The economic analysis of contract law started in earnest in the US in the 1970s, but it had some precursors. In one early attempt to apply economic thought to frustration doctrines, Edwin Patterson made the crucial point that the question is one of risk allocation.[57] The economic approach is committed to a forward-looking or ex ante perspective on contracts in general. From the ex post perspective, a court is asked to decide where to allocate a loss. From the ex ante perspective, however, the question is how to allocate risk to provide the parties with the right incentives. Where parties have agreed to allocate the risk in a certain way, law-and-economics scholars advocate enforcing the parties' agreement because they assume that parties who have explicitly chosen how to allocate risk have a better chance of getting the incentives right than courts do. But what should the courts do when the parties have not clearly agreed how to allocate risk?

[55] ibid [22].

[56] See P MacMahon, 'The Costs of Contractual Certainty: *RTI v MUR Shipping*' (2025) 88 *MLR* 404, 410–11.

[57] EW Patterson, 'The Apportionment of Business Risks through Legal Devices' (1924) 24 *Columbia Law Review* 335.

A. Selecting the Superior Risk-Bearer

The first systematic attempt to develop a risk-allocation approach was that of Posner and Rosenfield (P&R). Reflecting different doctrinal labels in the US, P&R refer to three doctrines that are equivalent to the English doctrine of frustration: impossibility, impracticability, and frustration of purpose. P&R frame the issue as deciding 'who should bear the loss resulting from an event that has rendered performance uneconomical'.[58]

The article is relatively accessible for a law-and-economics piece, but it nevertheless makes some quick moves that are worth dwelling on. I will extract three of P&R's core propositions.

> *P&R Proposition 1*: The purpose of this area of law is to reduce the costs of contract negotiation by supplying contract terms that the parties would have adopted explicitly had they negotiated over them.[59]

P&R assume (realistically) that the parties cannot and will not expend the resources necessary to write a fully complete contract; the law provides a service by giving an answer after the fact even though the parties have not provided for the eventuality that has occurred. While the economic perspective on contracts is often criticised for approaching the parties' relation from an exogenous standpoint, P&R invite courts to take up the parties' own perspective on the terms of their exchange. In directing the law to supply the terms the parties would have adopted, P&R leave third-party effects to one side. P&R also eschew any concern for the distributive fairness of the allocation of risk as such, as is characteristic in economic analysis of contract law. Nevertheless, asking what the parties would *jointly* have agreed allows both parties' interests to be represented.

The next move in P&R's argument is crucial:

> *P&R Proposition 2*: Had they negotiated over the terms, the parties would have agreed to maximise the value of the exchange.[60]

In P&R's article, economic efficiency (here, conceived as maximising the value of the exchange) is justified *because* it accords with the parties' hypothetical choices.[61] This ordering might seem out of character; Posner is famed for subordinating other concerns to efficiency.[62] But in this article, at least, hypothetical agreement justifies efficiency, rather than the other way around. P&R say that the parties would agree to maximise the overall value of the exchange at the time of the contract.

[58] P&R (n 9) 86.
[59] ibid 88.
[60] ibid 89.
[61] On the complexities of arguments from hypothetical bargains, see D Charny, 'Hypothetical Bargains: The Normative Structure of Contract Interpretation' (1991) 89 *Michigan Law Review* 1815.
[62] David Campbell sees in P&R's article 'the equivocation between giving effect to the choices of individuals and devising objective welfare maximising rules to be imposed on them that came to dominate Posner's thinking'. Campbell (n 3) 330, fn 60.

They would simultaneously agree to share the surplus they have created by setting a price, though the precise division of the spoils will depend on the parties' relative bargaining power.

P&R's article is largely concerned with *how* contracting parties would maximise the value of the exchange had they negotiated over what should happen in the events that have occurred. Here is the core of P&R's answer:

> *P&R Proposition 3*: To maximise the joint surplus, the parties would allocate a risk to the party best able to guard against the risk and/or to minimise its consequences.

If the promisee is the superior risk bearer, the contract should be discharged. If the promisor is the superior risk bearer, non-performance should be treated as a breach of contract.

Note that Proposition 3 sets forth two fundamentally different ways that a party could be the superior risk bearer. First, a party might be better able to *reduce* the risk by taking precautions against the occurrence in question, thereby lessening its likelihood and/or diminishing its severity if it does occur. It is usually not cost-justified to eliminate a risk entirely, so the ideal contract would incentivise the correct level of precaution, ideally by holding a party liable if it could have prevented the loss at a lower cost than the expected cost of the event. Where a promisor could have prevented the risk from materialising at a lower cost than the expected cost of the risky event, the promisor should be held liable.

But, P&R continue, it does not follow that the promisor should be discharged if it could not have prevented the loss at a reasonable cost; that would mean liability in contract was always fault-based. Contract law is often strict liability, they say, because of the second way that a party might be a superior risk bearer: one or other of the parties might be better able to *absorb* the economic dislocation that an unavoidable loss brings about.[63] Some parties are less able to deal with losses than others; these less-able parties are hence likely to be 'risk averse'. As insurance contracts show, risk-averse parties may wish to pay a fixed and certain amount of money to shift the risk to someone else, even if that sum is greater than the expected cost of the risk. They may be willing to trade (say) a 1 per cent chance of a £100,000 loss for a certain loss of (say) £2,000.

One party to a contract may be the cheaper 'insurer'. This might be because it can buy an insurance policy from a third party, or it might be because it can 'self-insure' against the loss by, for example, charging a higher price for a good or service to reflect the risk and thereby spreading it among its customers. The ability of a party to insure against loss depends on its ability to ascertain the probability and the magnitude of losses and the costs of arranging an insurance policy or

[63] 'Residual risk management' is a helpful term to describe what the parties wish to do with those risks that cannot be avoided by the exercise of due care. See GG Triantis, 'Contractual Allocations of Unknown Risks: A Critique of the Doctrine of Commercial Impracticability' (1992) 42 *University of Toronto Law Journal* 450, 454.

self-insuring. Knowing that it is serving as insurer, the cheaper insurer can then decide how much to charge the other party for serving as the insurer, by raising or lowering the price.

Having stated these propositions, P&R look to US law, which is broadly similar to English law, and find it to be largely in accord with their approach. They agree with the law's position that a promisor whose inability to perform is due to her own fault should be disentitled from escaping her obligation.[64] And they applaud the stance of US courts in upholding express allocations of risk agreed by the parties.[65] They apply their framework to a broad range of hypothetical and real cases. Where an employee dies, for example, they say the contract should generally be discharged because neither party is generally better able to predict life expectancy, and the employer is in a better position to know the extent of any loss and to self-insure against it.[66] The closure of the Suez Canal was rightly held not to discharge a voyage charter because the shipowner was better placed to estimate the probability of the canal being closed and the likely length of the delay resulting from taking an alternative course.[67] A supplier who fails to deliver a specified quantity of an agricultural product should be discharged if the supplier is a farmer whose own crop was destroyed by an unexpected flood or drought; the buyer is better placed to bear this risk because it can diversify its purchases geographically.[68] Where the seller is a wholesaler, however, there is no reason to think that it is less well able than the buyer to achieve this form of self-insurance, and the contract should not be discharged.[69] And so on.

P&R also discuss the remedial consequences of frustration.[70] They support a general rule of restitution of benefits conferred by each party on the other, with the caveat that payments should not be recoverable if their purpose was to compensate the recipient for bearing risk. They reject the recovery of reliance losses and criticise the idea of loss-splitting in the aftermath of frustration; each of these solutions would, they say, undermine incentives to reduce and manage risk.

B. P&R Criticised on Economic Grounds

Though P&R's article is often taken in England to be the definitive economic contribution to this topic, the methodology it proposes that courts should follow has in fact found few defenders in the ensuing decades, even within economic analysis. Critics of P&R have pointed out that the courts do not usually seek out

[64] P&R (n 9) 98.
[65] ibid 98–99.
[66] ibid 100.
[67] ibid 104. P&R discuss *Transatlantic Financing Corp v United States*, 363 F2d 312 (DC Cir 1966) where (rarely for a judge) Judge Skelly Wright adverted explicitly to insurance considerations.
[68] P&R (n 9) 106.
[69] ibid 106–07.
[70] ibid 112–17.

the best absorber of risk and have provided reasons why they should not seek to do so.

As explained below, P&R are guilty of taking an idea that makes sense in theory and applying it despite insuperable practical obstacles. Guido Calabresi has contrasted 'Economic Analysis of Law' with 'Law and Economics'.[71] In the spirit of its great precursor Jeremy Bentham, Economic Analysis of Law examines the legal world from the standpoint of economic theory and rejects those aspects of legal practice that do not fit the theory. Richard Posner has often been accused of economic imperialism, and his work on frustration provides an example. Some critics have seen the failure of P&R's analysis as a reason to doubt economic analysis of contract law in general.[72] But there is more to the economic analysis of frustration than P&R. The later literature shows that economics can illuminate law without seeking entirely to replace legal reasoning. A 'Law and Economics' perspective, in Calabresi's typology, follows the example of Mill rather than Bentham, and is willing to recognise a bilateral relationship between the two disciplines, so that economic theory may sometimes need to be revised to take account of wisdom developed in the legal world. In this vein, later contributions to the economics of frustration have worked harder to understand the economic logic of the current law, modifying P&R to take account, in particular, of the limitations of courts' capacities.

i. *The Difficulty of Finding the Party Better Placed to Absorb the Loss*

P&R admit that sometimes it is difficult to say who the superior risk bearer is. In the coronation cases, for example, were the owners or the renters the superior risk bearers? Neither party was better than the other at predicting the King's incapacity. The owner, say P&R, was better able to calculate the loss and could (if renting multiple apartments) have bought a single insurance policy to cover various apartments.[73] On the other hand, leaving losses to fall on individual renters would have spread the losses among various renters rather than leaving them all to fall on an owner with multiple apartments. P&R admit that their analysis is inconclusive. That is not a fatal objection to their theory. No theory can avoid borderline cases, and the English judiciary considered this case close to the line. In the coronation cases, only contracts whose performance was effectively useless to the recipient of performance were discharged,[74] and *Krell v Henry* was criticised by some later judges.[75]

[71] G Calabresi, *The Future of Law and Economics* (New Haven, Yale University Press, 2016).

[72] Morgan (n 3). See also EA Posner, 'Economic Analysis of Contract Law after Three Decades: Success or Failure?' (2003) 112 *Yale Law Journal* 829, 848–49; S Bayern, *The Analytical Failures of Law and Economics* (Cambridge, CUP, 2023) 145–48.

[73] P&R (n 9) 110. P&R make the dubious assumption that the owners in the coronation cases owned multiple apartments.

[74] *Herne Bay Steam Boat Co v Hutton* [1903] 2 KB 683 (CA).

[75] *Larrinaga & Co Ltd v Société Franco-Américaine des Phosphates de Medulla* [1923] Lloyd's Rep 457 (HL) 460; *Maritime National Fish Ltd v Ocean Trawlers Ltd* [1935] AC 524 (HL) 528–29.

Yet critics of P&R's approach have shown that the problem with finding the best risk bearer goes deeper.[76] P&R are realistic in their assumptions about the parties' inability to provide specifically for risks. But they are unrealistic in overestimating the capacity of courts to make judgments about the parties' relative ability to deal with risk. Moreover, risk-management considerations often point in different directions. The performing party is usually more likely to be able to estimate the likelihood of loss, while the receiving party is more likely to be able to estimate its magnitude. In practice, courts do not have the information to decide who is the superior risk-handler. In the Suez cases, for example, are owners necessarily better placed than shippers to insure against risk? And isn't there a strong case that the grower of crops is better placed than the buyer to predict droughts or floods, and to buy insurance against these risks? Many of P&R's rationalisations of the cases seem ad hoc and unconvincing.

ii. Allocating the Risk to the Party Best Placed to Prevent the Loss

P&R's analysis seems to require courts to decide routinely on the better risk-absorber in the event of changed circumstances and to excuse performance when the non-performing party is the better insurer. But if that were the right approach, discharge by supervening event would be much more common than it currently is in US and English law. Again, a more accurate economic analysis explains what is wrong with P&R's approach.

Economic analyses of the issue after P&R have tended to downplay insurance considerations and to focus instead on incentives to reduce risk.[77] Contrary to what P&R seem to say initially, risk-reduction is not only relevant when it can be proved that the performing party was at fault in failing to prevent the loss. Liability for breach of contract is typically strict, but not only because of insurance considerations. The reasons for strict liability are better understood in tort law. Posner himself was a staunch defender of a negligence standard in tort law,[78] but others in the law-and-economics tradition have provided justifications for strict liability. One such justification is provided by Calabresi.[79] A negligence standard may work well when the court can decide whether the defendant was, on the facts of the case, the cheapest cost-avoider. But where courts lack information and expertise, it may make better sense for courts to identify and make liable the 'best decider' – the party systematically likely to be

[76] MJ Trebilcock, 'The Role of Insurance Considerations in the Choice of Efficient Civil Liability Rules' (1988) 4 *Journal of Law, Economics, and Organization* 243.

[77] Trebilcock (n 76). See also A Sykes, 'The Doctrine of Commercial Impracticability in a Second-Best World' (1990) 19 *Journal of Legal Studies* 43.

[78] RA Posner, 'A Theory of Negligence' (1972) 1 *Journal of Legal Studies* 29.

[79] G Calabresi and JT Hirschoff, 'Toward a Test for Strict Liability in Torts' (1972) 81 *Yale Law Journal* 1055.

in a better position to make the cost-benefit analysis and to act on it by taking precautions.[80]

In fact, despite initially downplaying the relevance of risk-reduction considerations, P&R do fall back on these considerations during their discussion of particular cases.[81] Indeed, P&R eventually state that '[t]he performing party to a contract is generally the superior risk bearer'.[82] If they had said this at the beginning of their discussion, P&R would probably have received much less criticism in the ensuing decades. The performing party is generally the superior risk bearer in significant part because the performing party is in the best position to decide on precautions, even if it is not possible to demonstrate fault in the particular case. P&R accept that in 'doubtful cases' the strict liability solution is the correct one in contract cases.[83] But, at least in their initial discussion, P&R seem to underestimate the universe of 'doubtful cases'.

iii. The Economic Value of Rules

One source of concern about P&R's approach is that it seems to require courts to make case-by-case determinations of the superior risk-bearer. Yet doing so would be a bad idea on economic grounds. From an economic standpoint, the purpose of the law is to provide incentives. If courts were simply to seek to find the better risk-bearer in each case, the law would be so unpredictable that the parties would find it difficult to know what the terms of their contract were and would hence be unsure what risks they needed to guard or insure against. A case-by-case approach would also increase the costs of dispute resolution when compared with a rule-based framework. Parties value predictability, so courts should develop rules for broader classes of cases.

P&R do recognise this point,[84] and stress administrative costs when rejecting a loss-splitting rule in the aftermath of discharge.[85] Still, their discussion tends to downplay the importance of rules. They stress the danger that judges will prematurely declare bad rules that will then ossify[86] and envisage that the law should develop fairly loose categories – personal service contracts, transportation contracts, agricultural product contracts, and so on – with plenty of scope for argument about whether a particular case falls within one of their categories. Later analyses suggest

[80] Calabresi and Hirschoff (n 79) 1075–76.

[81] As Trebilcock says, 'it is sometimes difficult to be sure whether [P&R's] analysis turns on least-cost insurer or least-cost avoider considerations'. Trebilcock (n 76) 252–53.

[82] P&R (n 9) 110.

[83] ibid. Posner maintained his attachment to a fault standard in tort cases on the ground that it is necessary to incentivise both parties to an accident to take precautions. In contract law, however, it is often only the performing party who could realistically prevent the relevant mishap, and the rules on mitigation and remoteness already provide incentives for the receiving party to minimise the extent of the loss.

[84] P&R (n 9) 95–96.

[85] ibid 114.

[86] ibid 96, fn 31.

that P&R's general presumption that the performing party is the superior risk bearer should instead have the status of a rule with limited or no exceptions.[87]

iv. The Potential Value of Non-Majoritarian Defaults

One of the most obvious ways that P&R's approach is dated is in its commitment to Proposition 1: that the law should always seek to supply contract terms the parties would have adopted explicitly had they negotiated over them. Economic analysis of contract law has progressed since P&R wrote. Since the 1980s, economic analysis has recognised the idea of 'penalty default': a rule deliberately set at what the parties would *not* want, so as to encourage them to reveal information to each other and to the courts.[88] The most commonly cited example of a penalty default is the rule of remoteness of damage as set forth in *Hadley v Baxendale*,[89] according to which a breaching party will not be liable for losses arising from the victim's special circumstances unless the victim had communicated the special circumstance to the breaching party at the time of the contract. Where both parties had perfect information, they would agree to make the breaching party liable for the extra loss to induce the taking of reasonable precautions to avoid it and would price the relevant goods or services accordingly. But prospective breaching parties do not have perfect information about the consequences of breach. A rule denying liability for undisclosed special vulnerabilities assists the bargaining process by providing an incentive for the prospective victim to disclose the relevant information.

The idea of a penalty default has potential implications for frustration doctrine. These naturally went unmentioned by P&R, given the state of the art in the 1970s. In particular, the penalty default notion provides further support for the idea, discussed in the last section, of a general rule that risk should be allocated to the performing party. Such a rule puts the onus on the performing party to negotiate an express allocation of risk that would relieve it of liability in specified circumstances.

III. Economic Analysis and English Law

Economic scholarship after P&R, then, supports the general rule that risk should be placed on the performing party, supports a restrictive approach to pleas of frustration, is sceptical of the ability of judges to discern which party is better able to absorb risk, stresses the value of rules, and suggests that the burden of carving out exceptions to performance obligations should often be placed on the parties.

[87] This point is stressed by Triantis (n 63) 476–77 and Sykes (n 76) 70–72.

[88] I Ayres and R Gertner, 'Filling Gaps in Incomplete Contracts: An Economic Theory of Default Rules' (1989) 99 *Yale Law Journal* 87.

[89] *Hadley v Baxendale* (1854) 156 ER 145, 9 Ex Ch 341 (Exch).

Though each discipline uses different jargon, there is in fact a considerable affinity between English law and post-P&R economic approaches to frustration.[90] Admittedly, there is little in economic analysis to support judicial statements that the frustration is based on a standard of fairness that is external to the parties' agreement, but these statements are difficult to square with other aspects of English law anyway. Like the economic approach, English law insists on returning to the time the contract was made to determine the appropriate allocation of risk.[91] Like the economic approach, English law takes no notice of third-party effects when deciding whether or not a contract is frustrated, except in cases of supervening illegality, which do raise third-party concerns.[92] And English courts do not seem to be motivated by considerations of distributional fairness. Like the economic approach, English law recognises that the parties should be free to expand or constrict the circumstances in which the parties are relieved of liability in the event of changed circumstances.[93] Like the economic approach, English law declines to allow frustration of contract where one of the parties was at fault. As in economic analysis, foreseeability is not as such a bar to the operation of the doctrine, but it sometimes provides a reason to conclude that the parties have deliberately allocated a foreseeable risk. Additionally, leaving supervening illegality to one side, the economic analysis of these problems supports English law's single idea of frustration of contract; though most economics-inspired scholarship focuses on US law, which distinguishes between impossibility, impracticability, and frustration of purpose, economic analysts usually stress the unity of these doctrines as responses to the same basic issue.[94] And English law, of course, stresses the value of certainty, for quintessentially economic reasons.

What ties law and economics together in this field are the assumptions that the parties to contracts want to increase the value of their exchange and that the main role for courts is to help them to do so. These assumptions are not stated in terms by the English courts but are implicit in the English tests for interpretation of express terms and the finding of implied terms. If granted, these assumptions

[90] In his excellent recent article, Jonathan Morgan criticises P&R on similar grounds to those canvassed above and purports to reject economic analysis entirely. Morgan's suggested approach involves giving separate treatment for supervening illegality, upholding a strict approach to frustration with no general default rule that a radical difference should discharge contracts, and treating the question as a matter of construction. Morgan (n 3). This approach is in fact highly consistent with a more sophisticated economic analysis of the problem. It is unsurprising, then, that Morgan cites remarks by Judges Posner and Easterbrook with approval.

[91] See, eg, *The Sea Angel* (n 22) [111].

[92] See *Islamic Republic of Iran Shipping Lines v Steamship Mutual Underwriting Association (Bermuda)* [2010] EWHC 2661 (Comm).

[93] The ability to do so may be limited by the Unfair Contract Terms Act 1977 or Consumer Rights Act 2015.

[94] P&R (n 9) 86. Givati and Kaplan criticise P&R for failing to distinguish more cleanly between impossibility, impracticability, and frustration of purpose, contending that P&R fail to 'take law seriously'. Y Givati and Y Kaplan, 'A New Theory of Impossibility, Impracticability, and Frustration' (2023) 52 *Journal of Legal Studies* 377. In England, however, 'taking law seriously' would seem to mean defending a single doctrine.

provide a way to achieve a rapprochement between economists and those who believe contract law's ultimate touchstone is autonomy. Hence, even those who are generally sceptical of essentially utilitarian approaches to ultimate normative questions can find common cause with economic approaches when it comes to interpreting and filling gaps in contracts.[95] The dominant mode of justification in English contract law is by reference to the agreement of the parties, or by an extension of that agreement that is fundamentally in keeping with the agreement itself; economic analysis can give content to these ideas.

There is, as we have seen, no consensus among economic analysts about exactly how to go about promoting the joint value of the exchange. Despite its mathematical pretensions, economic analysis cannot provide precise answers because the costs and benefits of different rules are not practically quantifiable. Even if economic efficiency were the only value to which contract law should answer (which it is not), judgments about the correct legal response would still depend in significant part on conjecture. That might seem disappointing, but it also shows a congruence between economic and legal reasoning; current judicial practice likewise involves intuitive judgments.

Economic reasoning, then, will not produce easy answers. But it can provide a more systematic account of the relevant considerations. In what follows I will look for economic justifications for English law's current stance, without saying that English law could not be improved.

A. Precaution and the Doctrine's Narrowness

From an economic perspective, the strictness of the English doctrine may be justified on the basis that risks should fall on the performing party as the party with the greater ability to affect whether the risk eventuates, whether or not there is proof of fault in the particular case. Regardless of fault, for example, it is up to a builder to determine the expected costs of work, and the builder 'takes the risk of the cost being greater or less than expected'.[96] Likewise, a supplier of generic goods cannot generally plead frustration even if it is impossible to source goods meeting the contract description; the source of the goods is the seller's, not the buyer's, concern.[97] This economic rationale was stated explicitly in *CTI Group Inc v Transclear SA (The Mary Nour)*: 'there is always a risk of supplier failure and as between the buyer and the seller it is the seller who is in a position to guard against the risk'.[98]

[95] For arguments along these lines, see C Fried, *Contract as Promise: A Theory of Contractual Obligation*, 2nd edn (Oxford, OUP, 2015) 138–41; H Dagan and M Heller, *The Choice Theory of Contracts* (Cambridge, CUP, 2017) 52–55.

[96] *Davis Contractors* (n 21) 709.

[97] See *Blackburn Bobbin Co Ltd v TW Allen & Sons Ltd* [1918] 2 KB 467 (CA).

[98] *CTI Group Inc v Transclear SA (The Mary Nour)* [2008] EWCA Civ 856, [2008] 2 Lloyd's Rep 526, [8] (quotation from Field J at first instance).

The same rationale appears in Bingham LJ's justification for rejecting self-induced frustration in *The Super Servant Two*:

> [T]he real question … is whether the frustrating event relied upon is truly an outside event or extraneous change of situation or whether it is an event which the party seeking to rely on it had the means and opportunity to prevent but nevertheless caused or permitted to come about.[99]

Though, as noted above, the exclusion of 'self-induced frustration' is considered harsh, it fits well with the economic rationale for disregarding questions of fault. The question is not whether the performing party was at fault for the obstacle to performance but whether that party was, in a broader sense, responsible for it.

This risk-reduction-focused economic analysis casts doubt on the presumptive rule of discharge in cases of impossibility or radical difference. And it might lead English law to revise some of its outcomes, even that in *Taylor v Caldwell*. The owner was in possession of the music hall, and the fire was caused by plumbers whom the owner had hired.[100] Even if it could not be established that the owner was at fault, there are good reasons for the parties to prefer to place this risk on the owner as the party generally in a better position to decide on appropriate precautions. Or, at the very least, it makes economic sense to place the burden on the music-hall owner to prove the absence of fault; that is arguably not where the burden lies in English law.[101]

B. The (Limited) Relevance of Risk Management

P&R's focus on risk-management considerations does not find many echoes in the English case law. In this regard, English law aligns with the many post-P&R economists who doubt the capacity of courts to discern the parties' comparative abilities to bear and spread losses.

Still, a generalised scepticism about courts' capacities does not justify eliminating risk-absorption considerations from the doctrine. There is nothing in English law's tests for frustration to exclude risk-management concerns. Under the multifactorial approach, courts are directed to consider the contract's 'matrix or context, the parties' knowledge, expectations, assumptions and contemplations, in particular as to risk, as at the time of the contract'.[102] In *The Sea Angel*, Rix LJ stated that the parties' attitudes to risk were relevant 'so far as these can be ascribed mutually and objectively'.[103] The parties' attitudes to risk might well be influenced by their respective risk-absorbing or spreading capacities. When considering

[99] *The Super Servant Two* (n 35) 8.

[100] C Macmillan, '*Taylor v Caldwell*' in C Mitchell and P Mitchell (eds), *Landmark Cases in the Law of Contract* (Oxford, Hart Publishing, 2008) 179.

[101] Peel (n 10) [14-034].

[102] *The Sea Angel* (n 22) [111].

[103] ibid.

whether, properly construed, the performing party's undertaking extends to the circumstances that have transpired, it may be obvious that one party is better placed to deal with a loss. In such cases, considerations of risk management are relevant, and the construction approach to frustration allows their retention. Accordingly, an express term requiring one party to insure against a loss is sometimes taken as a signal that the parties have allocated the risk, such that the contract should not be considered frustrated.[104]

C. Frustration and the Value of Rules

With its multifactorial approach and direct appeals to justice, the contemporary English doctrine of frustration sounds vague. But this vagueness does not in reality pose a significant threat to the 'commercial certainty' so prized by English lawyers. The general rule that changes of circumstances have no effect on contractual obligations is subject only to small exceptions. That is due to a collective judicial sense that the doctrine 'must not be lightly invoked and must be kept within very narrow limits'.[105] Most obviously, the requirement of a 'radical difference' has been strictly applied, making clear that there will be no frustration in all but the most extreme cases. As aspects of this general requirement, courts continually reiterate that increased cost of performance never (or almost never) suffices, and that frustration of purpose will only suffice if the purpose is totally frustrated. Accordingly, English law does not resemble P&R's approach. Given these large oceans of clarity, the multifactorial approach creates only a small area of uncertainty, and the doctrine is thus generally clear enough to provide the incentives to guard and insure against risk required by the economic approach.

Another economic reason to provide a clear default rule is to facilitate the process of contracting around it.[106] This idea from economics has been mentioned by two leading English contract law scholars, though with little enthusiasm. Hugh Beale suggests that English law's insistence on holding liable a party whose performance is delayed by matters beyond his control is intended to provide a solution 'so unattractive that it will encourage the parties to devise a force majeure clause'.[107] David Campbell also reaches the conclusion that frustration of contract is an accidentally created penalty default,[108] though his view is that frustration of contract is unattractive because it is too generous. The economic approach provides reasons

[104] eg, *Bunge SA v Kyla Shipping Co Ltd* [2012] EWHC 3522 (Comm), [2013] 1 Lloyd's Rep 565.

[105] *The Super Servant Two* (n 35) 8.

[106] On the other hand, it is possible to make economic arguments for uncertainty. US law is less predictable in this area than English law; its uncertainty has recently been defended on the ground that it facilitates risk-sharing renegotiation. Y Givati, Y Kaplan, and Y Listokin, 'Excuse 2.0' (2024) 109 *Cornell Law Review* 629.

[107] H Beale, *Mistake and Non-Disclosure of Fact: Models for English Contract Law* (Oxford, OUP, 2012) 111–12.

[108] Campbell (n 3) 330.

to value a restrictive default rule, at least where the parties can reasonably be expected to opt out of that rule where it does not suit their purposes. English law's strict approach provides a clear signal to parties who wish to excuse themselves to explicitly stipulate for it via a force majeure clause.

D. The Consequences of Frustration

Admittedly, economic analysis does not justify the Law Reform (Frustrated Contracts) Act 1943. Victor Goldberg has heavily criticised the Act in the most extensive analysis of the consequences of frustration from an economic perspective.[109] Economic scholarship also provides no support for those who contend that the Act should be replaced by a more general power to share or otherwise allocate losses between the parties; the economic purpose of the law in this area is to allocate risk ex ante rather than to share losses ex post. Economic scholarship can, however, suggest how the 1943 Act might best be interpreted if courts get the opportunity to shape its meaning further. The economic focus on the risk-allocation and the value of rules militates against a reading of the statute that gives judges a general discretion to share losses as they see fit between the parties,[110] and would tend to prefer Robert Goff J's relatively predictable analysis that the Act requires restitution subject to a change of position defence.[111]

E. The Juristic Basis of Frustration

Though in theory economists may be willing to subordinate party agreement to efficiency, in practice economic analysts are committed to the parties' perspective on contracts and are sceptical of any idea that frustration flows from an extra-contractual standard of justice. Economic analysis thus tends to provide support for the construction theory. Economists might find it difficult to choose between 'interpretation' and 'implied term' variants but would agree with Lord Hoffmann that the distinction between these processes is not as significant as sometimes thought.[112]

There are, of course, several economic approaches to contract construction. P&R's approach is to supply the terms the parties would have chosen had they negotiated over the contingency in question, though they admit that this approach

[109] VP Goldberg, 'After Frustration: Three Cheers for *Chandler v. Webster*' (2011) 68 *Washington & Lee Law Review* 1133.

[110] See *Gamerco SA v ICM/Fair Warning (Agency) Ltd* [1995] 1 WLR 1226 (QB) 1237 ('a very broad discretion').

[111] *BP (Exploration) Libya Ltd v Hunt (No. 2)* [1979] 1 WLR 783 (QB) 800.

[112] *Attorney General of Belize v Belize Telecom Ltd* [2009] UKPC 10, [2009] 1 WLR 1988 [16]–[27]; RA Posner, 'The Law and Economics of Contract Interpretation' (2005) 83 *Texas Law Review* 1581, 1586: 'Gap-filling and disambiguating are both "interpretive"'.

may need to be modified so that the analysis takes place at the level of categories of contract rather than the individual case. Blackburn J seemed to defend a similar search for a generalised hypothetical intention in *Taylor v Caldwell*, justifying the finding of an implied condition on the ground that 'in the course of affairs men in making such contracts in general would, if it were brought to their minds, say that there should be such a condition'.[113] Despite Blackburn J's dictum, the English courts tend to agree with subsequent economic analysts who are sceptical that the courts should try to mimic what the parties would have decided if they had written a complete contract. English law's test for terms implied in fact is more restrictive than the hypothetical bargain approach; courts ask not what the parties would have agreed but whether the proposed term was necessary to give business efficacy to the contract, or whether they would both have said the term was so obvious that it was unnecessary to include it. The parties themselves would not want the courts to undertake the task of guessing what the parties would have agreed, in part because it is expensive and in part because it entails a danger that the courts will overturn a deliberately chosen allocation of risk.

IV. Conclusion

Any attempt to draw on economic analysis to illuminate English contract law doctrine is certain to be met with the response that judges 'want legal reasoning … not reasoning from another discipline'.[114] But the process of construction requires attention to context and the parties' purposes; economics can help illuminate these crucial elements of the background to the law's task in responding to changed circumstances. When met with pleas of frustration, English courts stress the benefits of clear rules and the importance of allocating risks to the party generally better able to reduce those risks. They downplay risk-management concerns. And they tend to push the burden of providing exceptions to performance obligations onto the parties. In doing all these things, they align with the greater weight of opinion in law-and-economics scholarship.

[113] *Taylor v Caldwell* (n 19) 834.

[114] Lord Burrows, 'Judges and Academics, and the Endless Road to Unattainable Perfection' (2022) 55 *Israel Law Review* 50, 55.

3

Managing Unexpected Events in Global Markets: Lessons from LIBOR

JO BRAITHWAITE*

I. 'Unexpected Events' and Global Markets

The theme of this volume is 'unexpected events' and their impact on contracts. The last five years have provided numerous reminders that unexpected events (and the unexpected effects of events that may, at a general level, be expected) are inevitable and have the potential to disrupt the global economy. Beyond the harm to contracting parties themselves, the inter-connectedness of global markets means that disruption to the performance of certain types of contracts may be amplified, including in ways that caught financial regulators by surprise in 2008. Contracts in highly concentrated markets such as those in certain commodities,[1] or that are building blocks in a larger transaction,[2] or written on widely used terms,[3] or which are designed to provide back-to-back agreements[4] are all means by which contagion can spread. This topic therefore not only involves considering how exogenous events can disrupt contracts, but also how disrupted contracts can generate significant externalities.

* I am grateful to Professor Paul S Davies and Dr Magda Raczynska of UCL Faculty of Laws for the opportunity to present a draft of this chapter at their May 2025 conference on 'Contract Law and the Unexpected' and for their and other conference participants' comments. Particular thanks to Kate Gibbons of Clifford Chance for acting as discussant. Thank you also to LSE Law School colleagues Dr Elizabeth Howell and Dr David Murphy for their expert feedback. The usual disclaimers apply.

[1] eg, Financial Stability Board, *The Financial Stability Aspects of Commodities Markets* (20 February 2023).

[2] eg, the network of contracts of 'purgatorial complexity' behind the notes in *Belmont Park Investments Pty Ltd v BNY Corporate Trustee Services Ltd* [2011] UKSC 38 [138] and [112].

[3] As Lord Diplock observed in *The Nema*: 'Business on the Baltic, the insurance market and the commodity markets would be impracticable without the use of standard terms to deal with what are to be the legal rights and obligations of the parties upon the happening of a whole variety of events which experience has shown are liable to occur, even though it be only rarely, in the course of the performance of contracts of those kinds.' *Pioneer Shipping Ltd v BTP Tioxide Ltd (The Nema)* [1982] AC 724, 737.

[4] eg, the international 'back-to-back' swaps discussed in *Banco Santander Totta SA v Cia Carris de Ferro de Lisboa SA* [2016] EWCA Civ 1267.

Contracts can, of course, go a long way towards allocating the risks of supervening events, by including so-called force majeure clauses, 'fallback' drafting, or other types of express provisions (and also, of course, by the parties entering into third-party contracts[5] such as insurance), but myriad cases demonstrate the limits of such drafting in practice.[6] In extreme circumstances, frustration may 'bring a contract prospectively to an end because of the effect of a supervening event'[7] but, as the effect is, as Bingham LJ memorably put it in *The Super Servant Two*, 'to kill the contract', English authority is clear it is not to be lightly invoked.[8] Recent cases relating to Brexit and the COVID-19 pandemic have confirmed the complexities and limitations of the doctrine.[9]

With these issues forming the background, the aim of this chapter is to suggest how innovative strategies can help to prevent or mitigate disruption to contracts from supervening events. In order to develop the argument, the chapter draws upon a case study, namely, the successful worldwide project which ran between 2013 and 2024 to reform and replace 'LIBOR' (the London Interbank Offered Rate) interest rate benchmarks. LIBOR had, at one point, been calculated daily in London for five currencies and seven maturities, and as of mid-2018, it was embedded in diverse contracts around the world, worth an estimated $400 trillion.[10] However, as the risks around the LIBOR-setting process grew, regulators sought to reform the benchmark and, later on, decided to replace it entirely. The culmination of this project was the cessation of LIBOR, the final settings of which were closed down in September 2024.[11] Given the value, reach and diversity of the contracts affected, the cessation of LIBOR without causing widespread market disruption was a remarkable accomplishment.

The LIBOR case study has much to offer in terms of this topic. While some civil litigation has emerged now that LIBOR has been phased out,[12] vast numbers of consumer, commercial and financial contracts referencing LIBOR in core economic terms have been amended or otherwise managed in order to phase in new ways of calculating contractual interest. This unprecedented reform involved more than a decade of carefully co-ordinated work across private and public stakeholders: as the US working group recorded in its closing report, 'the transition from LIBOR involved billions of dollars and millions of hours of work

[5] This aspect of contractual planning is outside the scope of the chapter, but for analysis, in the context of a risk-based account of financial law, see J Benjamin, *Financial Law* (Oxford, OUP, 2007).

[6] See section II below and as discussed in-depth elsewhere in this volume.

[7] *Canary Wharf (BP4) T1 Ltd v European Medicines Agency* [2019] EWHC 335 (Ch) [21] (Marcus Smith J).

[8] *J Lauritzen AS v Wijsmuller BV (The Super Servant Two)* [1990] 1 Lloyd's Rep 1, 8 under 'Question 2: general'.

[9] eg, respectively, *Canary Wharf (BP4) T1 Ltd* (n 7); *Salam Air SAOC v Latam Airlines Group SA* [2020] EWHC 2414 (Comm).

[10] A Schrimpf and V Sushko, 'Beyond LIBOR: A primer on the new benchmark rates' (March 2019) Bank for International Settlements Quarterly Review, 29.

[11] 1-, 3- and 6-month US dollar LIBOR settings were the final settings to be published, ending on 30 September 2024. See further section II.B below.

[12] *Standard Chartered plc v Guaranty Nominees Limited & Ors* [2024] EWHC 2605 (Comm).

by the private sector, active involvement by the U.S. official sector, and ultimately even legislation by Congress'.[13] As such, the case study offers several innovative strategies from which general lessons may be drawn. Importantly, the LIBOR case study also highlights legal issues arising from cross-border contracts which are threatened by supervening events. In summary, although this global reform project has been squeezed out of the wider debates by concurrent events relating to Brexit and the COVID-19 pandemic, the chapter argues that it has much to offer the topic in hand.

The chapter proceeds as follows. Section II explores the limitations of ex ante contractual planning, even in contracts between sophisticated parties, and explains why the strategies adopted in the run-up to LIBOR cessation may usefully be considered in this context. Section III explores strategies which proved effective in minimising the disruption caused by phasing out LIBOR rates and replacing them with so-called 'Risk-Free Rates'. Section IV explores the idea that the approach of a legal system to unexpected events should 'fit' the risk profile of the particular jurisdiction and proposes some general lessons.

II. The Limits of Contractual Planning

There are several reasons why even the most sophisticated commercial contracts will never be able to plan completely for supervening events. This section explores some of these reasons, before suggesting that strategies on the lines of those deployed in the build-up to LIBOR cessation can usefully contribute to the management of such events.

A. Risks and Contractual Planning

While there is a broad spectrum of situations which might result in disruption to dealings between contracting parties, a useful starting point is to distinguish between events that are unexpected and events that are unprovided for in contracts. Businesses have regulatory, commercial and operational incentives to minimise the first; various legal requirements may also be relevant, depending on the nature of the business in question.[14] For example, the risk analysis undertaken by the 'systemically significant' financial market infrastructure company LCH Ltd is overseen by the Bank of England, in line with global standards.[15] LCH Ltd, in

[13] The Alternative Reference Rates Committee (ARRC), *ARRC Closing Report: Final Reflections on the Transition from LIBOR* (November 2023) 4.

[14] eg, the UK Corporate Governance Code, s 4 on 'Audit, Risk and Internal Control', provision 28: 'The board should carry out a robust assessment of the company's emerging and principal risks' (footnote omitted): Financial Reporting Council, UK Corporate Governance Code (January 2024).

[15] The Bank of England, *The Bank of England's supervision of financial market infrastructures Annual Report 16 December 2023-17 December 2024* (18 December 2024) chs 3 and 4.

turn, has several different risk committees reporting to the company and group boards and a detailed 'Risk Governance Framework' in place.[16] Ideally, through these types of reviews, a company can identify, analyse and then mitigate relevant risks (or, conversely, pursue them) in line with its business model.

Bilateral drafting and third-party contracts[17] can both be used to allocate the risks of supervening events; however, the capacity of contracts to do so remains limited. The first problem is, of course, that 'risk transfer' terms, however framed, do not always work smoothly when tested. Legal issues relating to scope, coverage and interpretation can arise both in relation to bilateral risk allocation and third-party contracts. In terms of the former, there was a surge of litigation involving the very widely used risk allocation terms of the ISDA Master Agreement in the wake of the 2008 crash, including around its vital 'close-out' provisions, and valuation mechanisms requiring the exercise of contractual discretion.[18] For the same reasons, arrangements involving third parties may also fail to operate smoothly when needed. For instance, in contrast to the AELTC's experience, the COVID-related coverage of the business interruption insurance policies considered in *FCA v Arch* was only resolved after a test case proceeded to the UK Supreme Court.[19] Other insurance and reinsurance disputes relating to businesses' pandemic coverage continue in the English courts.[20]

Furthermore, there will always be risks which even the most sophisticated organisations do not foresee. Nassim Nicholas Taleb's study of our persistent inability to predict 'black swan', or low probability, high impact events, famously explores some of the reasons why this is the case.[21] International connectedness further increases exposure to risk; Apple Inc., for example, reports that thousands of businesses across 50 jurisdictions are involved in its supply chain.[22] Moreover, the way that different risks interact with one another can also complicate planning. Following on from the COVID-19 pandemic, Veerle Heyvaert has developed a

[16] The LCH Ltd Risk Management webpage provides a chart of the Risk Governance Committee structure and for the LCH Risk Governance Framework, under the sub-heading 'Risk Classification' in the 'Risk Governance and Framework' section of the LCH Ltd Risk Management webpage, at www.lseg.com/en/post-trade/clearing/risk-management/ltd-risk-management.

[17] In a well-known example, drawing on the experience of the SARS outbreak in the early 2000s, the All England Lawn Tennis Club (AELTC) purchased annual pandemic insurance, which, in 2020, reportedly paid out £114 million for losses relating to the COVID-19 pandemic: C Ruel, 'Wimbledon set for coronavirus windfall in huge pay-out from pandemic insurance' *Insurance Times* (14 April 2020).

[18] J Braithwaite, *The Financial Courts: Adjudicating Disputes in the Derivatives Markets* (Cambridge, CUP, 2021) chs 3 and 7. 'ISDA' refers to the International Swaps and Derivatives Association.

[19] *Financial Conduct Authority v Arch Insurance (UK) Ltd & Ors* [2021] UKSC 1. On the AELTC's insurance coverage, see n 17.

[20] eg, interpreting the meaning and relevance of 'damage' in a licensed premises insurance policy: *Bellini N/E Trading Ltd (t/a Bellini) v Brit UW Ltd* [2024] EWCA Civ 435; interpreting 'Property Catastrophe Excess of Loss Reinsurance' in *Unipolsai Assicurazioni Spa v Covéa Insurance plc* [2024] EWCA Civ 1110.

[21] NN Taleb, *The Black Swan: The Impact of the Highly Improbable* (London, Penguin, 2007).

[22] Apple Inc., *People and Environment in our Supply Chain: 2025 Annual Progress Report* (2025) 4 and 8.

valuable framework for better understanding how globally significant threats can interact with one another. She suggests that risks from climate change and zoonotic disease should in fact be understood as what she calls 'intersystemic systemic risks', because both 'come with major threats of spilling over and triggering additional – and potentially equally systemic – risks in other social systems'.[23] Amongst other shared features, she identifies how both types of 'intersystemic' risks are, to an extent, 'already inescapable', because damage is already 'locked in'[24] and likely to compound once it materialises.[25] While Heyvaert uses her model to explore the implications for health and environmental regulation, it also raises questions about the preparedness of commercial and financial contracts for the spillover effects of intersystemic risks.

In response, contracts routinely include terms designed to operate as a 'back-stop' for more bespoke risk management provisions. Force majeure clauses and 'fallback' provisions are just some of the ways that commercial contracts expect the unexpected. Up to a point, these clauses are valuable and effective; in *Canary Wharf*, the judge observed that in 'the vast majority' of cases, 'the construction of the contract will resolve the issue between the parties'.[26] However, as disputes about contractual performance following in the wake of various shocks demonstrate, 'back-stop' clauses are themselves open to challenge around the interpretation of the language used by drafters,[27] or sometimes on the basis of a broader argument about the future of what has been called 'the parties' "common purpose"'.[28]

Even back-stop drafting, therefore, can be found to have gaps once it is tested, no less so when professionally drafted and in contracts between experienced parties. In *Canary Wharf*, the judge also noted that 'even a sophisticated contract which, on its face, *appears* to make provision for all subsequent vicissitudes may find itself defeated by the truly unforeseen'.[29] As the courts and the literature both recognise, gaps are especially likely to emerge in long-term contracts.[30] Parties can face great uncertainty as a result, which can quickly present a risk to other entities using the same or similar terms. Some recent examples include an ISDA collateral agreement which failed to address what should happen when the relevant interest rate became negative;[31] syndicated loan agreements which did not

[23] V Heyvaert, 'Governing Intersystemic Systemic Risks: Lessons from Covid and Climate Change' (2022) 85(4) *MLR* 938, 944.

[24] ibid 950.

[25] ibid 963.

[26] *Canary Wharf* (n 7) [29] (Marcus Smith J).

[27] *RTI Ltd v MUR Shipping BV* [2024] UKSC 18, on the concept of 'reasonable endeavours'.

[28] *Canary Wharf* (n 7) [29] (Marcus Smith J), describing how to identify the nature of the contractual promise.

[29] ibid, fn omitted; emphasis in the original.

[30] eg, *Teeside Gas Transportation Ltd v CATS North Sea Ltd & Ors* [2019] EWHC 1220 (Comm) [37] (Butcher J), considering it 'unrealistic' that a contract intended to last 28 years would cover 'every possible factual scenario', cited in *Standard Chartered* (n 12) [45], which itself considered a contract which was perpetual, in line with regulatory requirements for a bank's 'Tier 1' capital, ibid [44].

[31] *Netherlands v Deutsche Bank AG* [2019] EWCA Civ 771.

provide for what should happen when a *lender* failed;[32] a New York-law-governed syndicated loan made to the cosmetics firm Revlon Inc., which did not address what should happen when the agent accidentally overpaid lenders and some of that group refused to return the money;[33] and a bank's equity capital which failed to provide for the cessation of the relevant interest rate benchmark.[34] When such circumstances are not expressly provided for by the parties' contracts, the outcome can be difficult to predict. If the matter is litigated, the courts may eventually conclude that a term should be implied in order to 'save' a contract;[35] but might also reach a conclusion which causes 'Shockwaves' and 'alarm' in the markets.[36] In the meantime, affected parties can be left in an uncertain position for a considerable period of time.

B. LIBOR Cessation

The policy of 'LIBOR cessation' was announced in July 2017, in a speech by the then-Chief Executive of the UK Financial Conduct Authority.[37] This unprecedented reform involved phasing out the daily publication of LIBOR interest rate benchmarks, with market participants being expected to transition to using so-called 'Risk-free Rates' (RFRs) in their contracts instead.[38] After much co-ordinated work by public and private sectors to manage the process, cessation was phased in from end-2021 until the final settings (1-, 3- and 6-month US dollar LIBOR) ceased on 30 September 2024.

The wider context for the announcement of LIBOR cessation was an ongoing, multi-jurisdictional project to reform financial benchmarks, in order to make them more reliable, robust and representative.[39] In the case of LIBOR, reforms

[32] Discussing the introduction of Defaulting Lender and Impaired Agent provisions into the Loan Market Association's finance agreements in 2009, described as 'The Lehman Effect', see R Oman et al, 'What does lender insolvency mean for your loan facilities?' *Addleshaw Goddard LLP, Insights & Briefings* (13 March 2023).

[33] C di Vito Piscicelli and S Haddad, 'Erroneous Payments in Syndicated Loans: The Future of the "Revlon Blockers"' ([2022] *Butterworths Journal of International Banking and Financial Law* 723, which also addresses the relevant trade associations' circulation of terms for parties to add to loan agreements in response to the first instance NY court's ruling.

[34] *Standard Chartered* (n 12).

[35] ibid [78], with the decision ultimately implying a term as to a replacement rate for three-month USD LIBOR.

[36] di Vito Piscicelli (n 33) 723. See also the discussion of implied terms in Professor John Cartwright's contribution to this volume in ch 1.

[37] Andrew Bailey (Chief Executive of the FCA), 'The Future of LIBOR' (speech at Bloomberg London, 27 July 2017) at www.fca.org.uk/news/speeches/the-future-of-libor.

[38] In April 2017 the UK's Working Group on Sterling Risk-Free Rates recommended the Bank of England's SONIA (Sterling Overnight Index Average) as the replacement 'risk-free rate' for GBP and in June 2017, the Working Group published a document explaining this decision and marking its new focus on 'successful adoption' in the markets: UK Risk-Free Rate Working Group, 'SONIA as the RFR and approaches to adoption' (June 2017) 1.

[39] On the LIBOR-setting scandal, not covered here, see L Vaughan and G Finch, *The Fix: How Bankers Lied, Cheated and Colluded to Rig the World's Most Important Number* (Chichester, Wiley, 2017).

to the rate-setting process began in 2014 but these did not address underlying problems, including the illiquidity of inter-bank lending markets that LIBOR was meant to represent, as well as the growing reluctance of banks to participate in the LIBOR-setting process.[40] By 2017, regulators had reached the view that LIBOR was unsustainable. Consequently, the policy shifted to phasing out LIBOR entirely, with participants across diverse domestic and global markets expected to transition to using RFRs in new and extant contracts before cessation came into effect.

The challenges around LIBOR cessation were immense. LIBOR was set in London, but even as late as mid-2018, it featured in $400 trillion of contracts worldwide.[41] Markets in over-the-counter (OTC) and exchange-traded derivatives, bonds, loans ('including syndicated and bilateral corporate loans, commercial and residential mortgages and [in the US in particular] consumer credit, including student loans credit cards and auto loans') and securitisations, amongst others, all routinely referenced LIBOR, as did some corporate valuation exercises.[42] It was used in so many diverse settings that in 2017 the Chief Executive of the Financial Conduct Authority (FCA) stated that 'LIBOR is a public good'.[43] Indeed, the potential implications for financial stability of disruption to LIBOR were so significant that the Bank of England's Financial Policy Committee held back publication of the minutes of its March 2017 discussion of the topic for six months, on the grounds of public interest.[44] In the US, a joint statement from the main financial market regulatory bodies observed that 'Failure to prepare for disruptions to USD LIBOR, including operating with insufficiently robust fallback language, could undermine financial stability and banks' safety and soundness.'[45]

LIBOR cessation was not, therefore, a supervening event which could be left to play out in the standard ways described in the preceding section. To complicate

[40] Dave Ramsden (Deputy Governor for Markets & Banking, The Bank of England) 'Last Orders: Calling Time on LIBOR' (speech at the Bank of England, 5 June 2019) at www.bankofengland.co.uk/news/speeches 2.

[41] Schrimpf (n 10) 29. The same figure is provided in the Bank of England's Financial Policy Committee's Financial Stability Report (August 2020), Box 10.

[42] See Market Participants Group on Reforming Interest Rate Benchmarks: Final Report, (March 2014), [1.1: Background and Objectives]. This group was established by the Official Sector Steering Group set up by the Financial Stability Board in June 2013, with the aim of making recommendations about transition away from LIBOR.

[43] Andrew Bailey (n 37).

[44] The Bank of England, *Record of the Financial Policy Committee Meeting on 20 Sept 2017* (3 October 2017) 19. These minutes were then published in ibid, Annex 2. The March 2017 text includes the statement that 'As the FPC had observed in 2013, the disruption to financial stability could be large in the event that Libor became unavailable, given both the scale of contracts in which Libor was still used as a reference rate and the lack of clarity on the legal position of contracts should Libor or other benchmarks become unavailable. The Committee agreed that market reliance on the Libor benchmark created a financial stability risk.' ibid, para 57.

[45] Board of Governors of the Federal Reserve System, Federal Deposit Insurance Corporation and Office of the Comptroller of the Currency, *Statement on LIBOR Transition* (30 November 2020) 1, fnn omitted, but one adds that 'For example, a disorderly transition away from LIBOR could pose consumer protection, litigation and reputational risks.'

matters, the legal risks were amplified by the inconsistent ways in which participants, even within the same markets, had responded to earlier phases of LIBOR transition. For example, some contracts had long included some version of interest rate 'fall-back' drafting which, if found to apply in the circumstances, sought to provide an alternative basis for calculating contractual rates. Many contracts, however, did not include these types of provisions, or did not include versions which would work in these unprecedented circumstances. There were also fears about the implications of LIBOR cessation for inter-connected and/or cross-border contracts, about the risk of frustration, and about the concurrent legal risks associated with Brexit, as considered by the UK Financial Markets Law Committee (FMLC) in its October 2020 report, for instance.[46] The reform therefore raised many of the risks identified earlier in this section, alongside economic and operational complexities, all on a vast scale.

Attempting to identify and address these complex risks generated years' worth of work for financial regulators working closely with expert groups such as the UK's Risk-Free Rates Working Group (RFRWG),[47] and, in the US, the Alternative Reference Rates Committee (ARRC). The archived website of the UK's RFRWG makes available large numbers of detailed publications and consultations generated by this group alone, including those specifically focusing on derivatives, cash markets, infrastructure and pension funds.[48] Furthermore, as identified at the beginning of the chapter, inter-connected markets presented additional risks: for example, there was serious concern that inconsistent approaches to LIBOR cessation in different sectors would undermine hedging arrangements. These factors all help to explain why LIBOR cessation took some seven years to implement in full. As the following section considers, such multifaceted and global risks required a broad range of strategies in response.

III. Strategies for LIBOR Cessation

If contracts have limited capacity to plan for unexpected events, what other approaches might help? This section explores various strategies which helped to prepare diverse commercial and financial sectors for the phased-in cessation of LIBOR, ultimately contributing to the successful implementation of this policy across major economies worldwide.[49] Section IV then considers the more general implications of these strategies.

[46] FMLC, *LIBOR Transition: Issues of Legal Uncertainty* (October 2020).

[47] The Bank of England and FCA were ex officio members of the RFRWG, and provided administrative support, while the LMA and ISDA were members: details at Bank of England, Working Group on Sterling Risk-Free Reference Rates webpage, at www.bankofengland.co.uk/markets/transition-to-sterling-risk-free-rates-from-libor/working-group-on-sterling-risk-free-reference-rates.

[48] ibid.

[49] The organisation of this section is thematic and is not to suggest a chronological order, etc. In practice, there were various interconnections between the developments addressed here, but space precludes discussion of this context.

A. Clearing by a Central Counterparty

The preceding section observed that LIBOR was routinely used in the global derivatives markets, in which the largest market is that in interest rate derivatives.[50] After the 2008 global financial crisis, clearing certain types of OTC derivatives was made mandatory across major G20 jurisdictions, with the aim of making these vast, global markets more transparent, robust and resilient.[51] Important categories of standardised interest rate derivatives are amongst those which are now subject to mandatory clearing,[52] and it has been reported that 76.9 per cent of interest rate derivatives by notional value (ie, totalling $445 trillion) were cleared in the first half of 2024.[53] With reference to the LIBOR case study, this section explains how the entities at the centre of a cleared market can manage the impact of unexpected events on contracts, both ex ante and ex post.[54]

In a cleared market, central counterparties (CCPs) act as buyer to every seller and seller to every buyer, with the result that participants contract with the CCP and not with each other, so that cleared markets take the form of networks with the CCP at the hub.[55] While clearing has a long history, the policy of *mandating* clearing for certain contracts, implemented after the global financial crisis, was a significant reform, which was linked to the 'shock absorber' function of CCPs.[56] This term refers to a CCP's capacity to mitigate disruption affecting one or more of its members' positions through a combination of collecting initial and variation margin from members, building up mutualised default funds, and extensive powers contained in its membership terms.[57] One well-known example of this function in action was the UK central counterparty LCH Ltd's successful

[50] Bank for International Settlements, OTC derivatives statistics: Tables and dashboards, eg, showing that, by notional amounts outstanding, interest rate contracts have a value of $579 trillion as at S1-2024: data.bis.org/topics/OTC_DER/tables-and-dashboards/BIS,DER_D7,1.0.

[51] Described in J Braithwaite, 'The Inherent Limits of Legal Devices: Lessons for the Public Sector's Central Counterparty Prescription for the OTC Derivatives Markets' (2011) 12(1) *European Business Organisation Law Review* 87.

[52] On the position in the EU: European Securities and Markets Authority (ESMA), Clearing obligation and risk mitigation techniques under EMIR, Classes of OTC derivatives subject to central clearing obligation at www.esma.europa.eu/post-trading/clearing-obligation-and-risk-mitigation-techniques-under-emir.

[53] ISDA, *Key trends in the size and composition of OTC derivatives markets in the first half of 2024* (December 2024), Chart 11: Global IRD Notional Outstanding by Counterparties.

[54] The cessation of LIBOR and shift to the use of RFRs is said to have had other important effects on the structure of the OTC interest rate derivatives markets, as discussed in W Huang and K Todorov, 'The Post-Libor World: A Global View from the BIS Derivatives Statistics' [2022] *BIS Quarterly Review* 19.

[55] On the role and operation of CCPs see D Murphy, *OTC Derivatives: Bilateral Trading and Central Clearing: An Introduction to Regulatory Policy, Market Impact and Systemic Risk* (Basingstoke, Palgrave MacMillan, 2013).

[56] Discussed in detail in n 57 below and more recently: 'CCPs … [act] as a dampener of shocks, mitigating contagion in the financial markets' The Bank of England, *The Bank of England's approach to cost benefit analysis: Statement of policy* (12 December 2024).

[57] J Braithwaite and D Murphy, 'Got to be certain: The legal framework for CCP default management processes' (2016) *Bank of England Financial Stability Paper* 37.

handling of the $9 trillion notional position in interest rate swaps (some 66,000 trades) held by Lehman Brothers when the bank collapsed in 2008.[58] Famously, as regards these cleared positions, the default was resolved within three weeks, with no loss to other clearing members, which contrasted with the complexities, years of delay and long-running litigation associated with closing out some of Lehmans' uncleared derivatives.[59]

The LIBOR case study demonstrates how CCPs can not only manage shocks ex post but can also help to strengthen contracts to withstand supervening events, ex ante. As noted above, the build-up to LIBOR cessation involved parties to contracts which referenced this benchmark being warned to replace it with reference to the 'Risk-Free Rates' (RFRs) approved by national regulators, such as SONIA for UK sterling. This change affected both new and extant contracts. This exercise represented an unprecedented challenge for regulators and for contracting counterparties, not only because of the scale, number and diversity of the contracts affected, but also because of the technical nature of the changes required. This change went to the core economic terms of parties' bargains and gave rise to significant legal, operational and economic complexities, for example, relating to differences between the methodologies underlying the two types of benchmark. Where clearing was used, however, the centralised market structure, alongside the consistency of terms across clearing services, and powers in the membership agreements between CCP and market participants, all greatly facilitated the shift to referencing RFRs.

By way of example, LSEG's[60] publications set out some of the steps involved in LCH Ltd's transition of contracts cleared in its services away from various settings of LIBOR (in USD and other currencies) to RFRs. This process involved initial consultations between CCP and members; the CCP providing precise details about the contractual implications of official regulatory announcements about the status of LIBOR; the launch of RFR clearing services; dress rehearsals ahead of the so-called 'conversion date',[61] and ultimately, a clear deadline when 'clearing eligibility' for the LIBOR-based would be withdrawn, whereupon remaining positions would be converted to RFR referencing ones[62] (18 December 2021, in the case of sterling LIBOR contracts, and in April and May 2023 for USD LIBOR, USD LIBOR being phased out later than sterling).[63]

[58] Discussed by LCH in its company history, at www.lseg.com/en/post-trade/clearing/about-lch/our-history.

[59] ibid. The contrast is made in Sir Jon Cunliffe, Deputy Governor Financial Stability, Member of the Monetary Policy Committee, Member of the Financial Policy Committee and Member of the Prudential Regulation Committee, 'Central Clearing and Resolution: Learning some of the lessons of Lehmans' (speech, 5 June 2018), 2.

[60] LSEG, the global infrastructure group of which LCH Ltd is a part: see www.lseg.com/en.

[61] eg, LCH, *SwapClear USD LIBOR Conversion Quick Guide* (2023) 3.

[62] See LSEG and LCH, *RFR transition in cleared swap markets* (2024), available on the webpage 'LCH and Benchmark Reform' at www.lseg.com/en/post-trade/clearing/lch-services/swapclear/benchmark-reform. ibid, under the heading 'LCH resources', see contract conversion guides and risk notices for clients.

[63] Bloomberg, *LIBOR transition: Expert views* (2021), Interview with Philip Whitehurst, LCH, 13–14; the overview of transitioning USD and non-dollar LIBOR contracts set out in LSEG and LCH, *SwapClear consultation: CAD CDOR contract conversion* (August 2023).

CCPs may therefore be best known for their 'shock absorber' function, but this aspect of the build-up to LIBOR cessation shows how this market structure also offers the means to update contracts centrally, to address supervening risks ex ante. As a result, in cleared markets, benchmark transition could be co-ordinated centrally and implemented consistently across clearing services, which enabled important sectors of the OTC derivatives markets, like the interest rate swaps cleared on LCH's SwapClear service, to be shifted to RFR-based contracts. This was a major, but presumably unforeseen, benefit of the post-global financial crisis policy of mandatory clearing for eligible OTC derivatives. By contrast, in sectors such as uncleared derivatives, along with syndicated loans, bonds and consumer contracts, LIBOR cessation meant that, potentially, each contract had to be considered in turn. However, as the following section shows, strategies to facilitate benchmark transition emerged in this context too.

B. 'Centralised' Contractual Amendments

The preceding section explored how a CCP can centrally manage cleared contracts. This is, however, a solution with limits. CCPs will only ever offer clearing services for certain types of standardised contracts because, for clearing to be available, there must be a liquid market, where a CCP has concluded there is a business case, for which it has been duly authorised. However, LIBOR cessation demonstrates how similar strategies can, in some circumstances, be applied across cleared *and non-cleared* markets, despite their structural differences.

Throughout the benchmark reform process, major market participants and trade associations co-operated very closely with public sector regulators, to the extent that there have been several official references to 'public-private partnership' in the context of delivering LIBOR reform.[64] This term highlights the significance of this type of co-operation over the different phases of LIBOR reform, to which the working groups were central. One important aspect of this 'partnership' saw trade associations put forward model contracts and contractual amendments intended for widely used standard contracts in order to facilitate firms' preparations for LIBOR cessation, as regulators were phasing in this part of the reforms. The technical objectives and approaches of these different amendments varied, and evolved over time, but the overall goals were to encourage market participants to update existing

[64] eg, S Boyce, Chair of the Working Group on Sterling Risk-Free Reference Rates, quoted in FCA, Bank of England and Working Group on Sterling Risk-Free Rates, 'The end of LIBOR' (Joint press release, 1 October 2024) at www.fca.org.uk/news/press-releases/end-libor. Also, The Bank of England, Finalising LIBOR transition – achievements in sterling markets and what remains to be done (Joint press release from the Bank of England, Financial Conduct Authority and the Working Group on Sterling Risk-Free Reference Rates, 9 February 2022) fn 2, stating that:

> 'This transition was delivered through *a partnership between public and private sectors*, initiated through the creation of the Working Group on Sterling Risk-Free Reference Rates (the "Working Group"), which has facilitated the transition in UK markets.' (Hyperlinks in the original omitted; emphasis added).

contracts so they would operate in a legally certain way across the various phases of LIBOR reform and, later, to accommodate the incoming RFRs. The UK Loan Market Association (LMA),[65] for instance, had a documentation committee which produced 'significant volumes of educational material' for its members to guide them during the different phases of LIBOR reform. It also offered RFR Agreements and amended terms in relation to its syndicated lending documents.[66] Market participants considering LMA's IBOR transition documents and RFR Agreements[67] were further supported in adapting these terms for their own use by extensive guidance published by the Association of Corporate Treasurers (ACT). By way of example, the 2022 version of the ACT's guide offers some 50 pages of guidance about the implications of adopting RFRs in the LMA's loan and hedging documentation,[68] including commentary to support users as they worked out the specific RFR-related drafting most appropriate for their deal.[69]

The global trade association with the most prominent role on the private side of this 'partnership' was the International Swaps and Derivatives Association (ISDA), the major trade association for participants in the OTC derivatives markets, with over 1,000 members worldwide.[70] In the years leading up to LIBOR cessation, ISDA disseminated many different educational and practical resources, and published numerous sets of contractual terms tailor-made to amend, repair or otherwise adjust its various standardised documents in readiness for different phases of benchmark reform.[71] Reflecting the expectation around the use of ISDA's documents generally, these amendments were designed to be adopted in a standardised way. This aim was reflected in the centralised technique by which parties could agree on the relevant variation, which was as notable as the drafting itself.

ISDA's 'Protocol' mechanism was designed to catalyse the adoption of ISDA amendments, and, according to the trade association's website, it has been adopted for different purposes since 1998.[72] The process works as follows: an ISDA Protocol sets out contractual amendments as they relate to a specific set of ISDA standard terms, and also provides terms about the mechanical details of the amendment (eg, when the changes will be implemented). The Protocol opens for users of the

[65] The LMA describes itself as 'the authoritative voice of the loan market in EMEA' with 'over 880 members across 69 jurisdictions', see LMA, About Us, at www.lma.eu.com/about-us.

[66] The Association of Corporate Treasurers, *A Borrower's Guide to the LMA's Investment Grade Agreements*, 6th edn (Slaughter & May, November 2022) 20-21, and commentary on LIBOR transition is the subject of ibid, Part II (the 'ACT Guide').

[67] Including full sets of terms for loans referencing SONIA, SOFR, €STR, SARON, ibid 51.

[68] ibid Part II.

[69] eg, ibid, Part IV, s 5: Costs of Utilisation.

[70] ISDA's website states that it has over 1,000 members from 76 countries; see ISDA, About ISDA at www.isda.org/about-isda/.

[71] The ISDA 'InfoHub' on Benchmark Reform and Transition' sets out in 11 sections ISDA publications and information on financial benchmark reform and LIBOR transition, at www.isda.org/2022/05/16/benchmark-reform-and-transition-from-libor/.

[72] ISDA, *ISDA Protocol Overview and Refund Policy*, at www.isda.org/protocols/isda-standard-adherence-refund-policy/.

relevant documents to sign up to (or 'adhere' to, in the term used in this context). If both parties to a transaction governed by the relevant documents adhere, the Protocol is binding, removing their need to reach agreement bilaterally. As ISDA puts it, '[t]he fundamental benefit to an adhering party to a protocol is that it eliminates the necessity for costly and time-consuming bilateral negotiations'.[73]

This process offers significant efficiency in a sector where a single participant might have thousands of ISDA Master Agreements with different counterparties across dozens of jurisdictions.[74] Furthermore, it also offers a way of amending contracts with consistency and legal certainty, both across the market, and across a portfolio, which is of particular importance given derivatives' routine use in hedging and as elements of complex financial structures. While Protocols have been used to respond to different types of supervening events since 1998, the benefits of this centralised, trade association-led approach are particularly valuable in the context of interest benchmark reform, because the necessary amendments in this case are technical, relate to core economic terms, and, in many cases, need to work cross-border. To put it another way, Protocols help to achieve outcomes in the bilateral markets which are comparable to the effects of the centralised changes in a cleared market, enabled by the CCP's role as a contracting party.

There are various ISDA Protocols relating to benchmark reform and LIBOR cessation, and space precludes a comprehensive discussion here. By way of example, however, in September 2018, ISDA published a 'Benchmark Supplement' which amended certain ISDA documents to address the discontinuation of the 'Relevant Benchmark' where this referenced LIBOR. In October 2020, ISDA published terms which parties could use to incorporate new floating rate options into legacy contracts, which would apply where IBORs become 'non-representative' or discontinued (the 'Fallbacks Protocol'). This language, if adopted by counterparties, became effective on the later of 25 January 2021, or when both parties to a document in scope signed up. Later Protocols have addressed the phasing out of other IBORs, such as EONIA.[75] According to the Director of Markets and Wholesale Policy at the UK FCA, adherence to this Fallbacks Protocol meant that contracts 'will have safely transitioned to compounded risk-free rates (RFRs)'.[76] The ISDA 2020 IBOR Fallbacks Protocol has over 16,300 adherents signed up at the time of writing.[77] The scale of this take-up demonstrates the mechanism's

[73] ibid.

[74] By way of illustration, at the time of its collapse, the London-based entity, Lehman Brothers (International) Europe Ltd was said to have 134,000 bilateral OTC derivatives outstanding governed by approximately 2,000 MAs: *Lomas v JFB Firth Rixson Inc* [2010] EWHC 3372 (Ch) [29].

[75] See ISDA, Open Protocols at www.isda.org/protocols/ including the ISDA 2021 EONIA Collateral Agreement Fallbacks Protocol (Open from 18 August 2021).

[76] E Schooling Latter, FCA Director Markets and Wholesale Policy, 'Maintaining Momentum' (December 2020) 7(3) *ISDA: IQ* 18.

[77] As of 15 August 2025, there are 16,346 adherents to the ISDA 2020 IBOR Fallbacks Protocol, listed on the ISDA Protocols website at www.isda.org/protocol/isda-2020-ibor-fallbacks-protocol/adhering-parties.

impact right across the markets, far beyond the pool of the trade association's 1,000 members.

A further, important point relating to jurisdiction needs to be emphasised. In the cleared markets, discussed above, a CCP's ability to manage risks depends, to a large extent, on privity of contract between the CCP and member. In relation to the ISDA Protocols, however, the mechanism facilitates amendments to contracts between market participants, to which ISDA is not a party. As a result, ISDA Protocols have the potential for much greater reach across a market. Similarly, the amendments available through the Protocols have the potential to make a broader impact than other types of legal strategies which may seek to bring about change in the markets, including case law or legislation, because they are designed to work across traditional jurisdictional boundaries. Specifically, the Protocols are expressly designed for use in any covered contracts and by any parties who can validly sign up, without limitation in either case by applicable jurisdiction or governing law. Looking at the 2020 Fallbacks Protocol, for example, adherents can come from any jurisdiction as long as they have status, powers and consent to sign.[78] The terms around the use of the Protocol are governed by the law of England and Wales, but the amendments will apply to a 'Protocol Covered Document' according to the governing law of that agreement.[79] 'Protocol Covered Documents' are, in turn, defined broadly, and include the 2002 or 1992 ISDA Master Agreement (regardless of whether the parties have selected New York or London governing law in those documents); ISDA's versions of its Master Agreement governed by French or Irish law;[80] and non-ISDA 'Additional Master Agreements' set out in an Appendix to the Fallbacks Protocol,[81] which include Spanish, Swiss, Austrian, Korean and Japanese Master Agreement documents for use in the OTC derivatives markets, Master Agreements published by other trade associations, and those published for use in markets such as bullion, power and repos. As such, the ISDA Fallbacks Protocol is designed to enable the broadest possible take-up, including by entities which are not ISDA members who wish to use it to amend non-ISDA contracts being used in markets which are not OTC derivatives markets. This highly flexible design means that the reach of the ISDA Protocols is even broader than might be assumed and, in this context, more sweeping than that of any regulator or CCP. One consequence was that regulators embedded ISDA's contractual amendment processes into their own recommendations, leveraging the greater reach of this private mechanism. For example, the FCA and PRA emphasised to market participants the value of signing up to the contractual amendments provided by ISDA.[82]

[78] ISDA, ISDA 2020 IBOR Fallbacks Protocol (23 October 2020) section 2.

[79] ibid s 3(e).

[80] ibid s 4, definition of 'ISDA Master Agreement'.

[81] ibid s 4, definition of 'Additional Master Agreement' and Additional Documents Annex, Part 1: Additional Master Agreements.

[82] eg, the Dear CEO letter of 26 March 2021, which imposed the 'expectation' on regulated firms to comply with the Working Group's milestones in relation to transition away from LIBOR. D Bailey and S Breeden, Prudential Regulation Authority and D Geale and E Schooling Latter, Financial Conduct Authority, 'Dear CEO letter: Transition from LIBOR to Risk Free Rates' (26 March 2021).

Similarly, the FSB's 2021 Global Transition Roadmap for LIBOR recommended that firms should already have '[a]dhered to the ISDA Protocol, subject to individual firms' usual governance procedures and negotiations … Adherence to the protocol is strongly encouraged …'[83]

As this section has shown, trade associations played a vital role in the 'public-private partnership' which sought to prepare markets for LIBOR cessation. Trade associations' input took different forms, but this section has focused on how they were able to facilitate amendments to bilateral contracts in ways that transcended jurisdictional borders. Put another way, the strategies deployed by trade associations, most notably seen in ISDA's Protocol mechanism, were vital to preparing markets for LIBOR cessation because they closely matched how these rates had been used in the first place.

C. Legislative 'Safe Harbors'

In this context, the term 'tough legacy' contracts refers to contracts which provide for interest to be calculated with reference to LIBOR, but which lack effective 'fallback' provisions defining rates to use instead of LIBOR, and which were not amended to prepare for benchmark transition. The topic of what would happen to 'tough legacy' contracts post-LIBOR cessation was a long-standing concern across multiple jurisdictions, and this section considers legislation introduced in response.

In the US, as already noted, LIBOR was widely referenced in consumer and student debt, as well as in the wholesale financial markets, and these more diverse uses of LIBOR as a benchmark presented particular risks in terms of 'tough legacy' contracts. Alongside the many initiatives which sought to push US parties to amend their own contracts in readiness for LIBOR cessation, which followed the patterns already discussed, the risks from 'tough legacy' contracts were directly addressed by federal legislation. The 2022 Adjustable Interest Rate (LIBOR) Act[84] (the 'LIBOR Act') provided a sweeping plan for USD LIBOR-referencing[85] contracts, broadly defined,[86] which 'do not provide for the use of a clearly defined or practicable replacement benchmark rate when LIBOR is discontinued'.[87]

[83] FSB, *Global Transition Roadmap for LIBOR* (2 June 2021) 2.

[84] Adjustable Interest Rate (LIBOR) Act, Division U of Consolidated Appropriations Act, 2022 H.R. 2471 (LIBOR Act).

[85] LIBOR is defined for this purpose as 'overnight and 1-, 3-, 6-, and 12-month tenors of U.S. dollar LIBOR (formerly known as the London interbank offered rate) as administered by ICE Benchmark Administration Limited (or any predecessor or successor administrator thereof)' but 'does not include the 1-week or 2-month tenors of U.S. dollar LIBOR.' LIBOR Act § 103(15).

[86] ibid § 103(16), as 'any contract, agreement, indenture, organizational document, guarantee, mortgage, deed of trust, lease, security (whether representing debt or equity, including any interest in a corporation, a partnership, or a limited liability company), instrument, or other obligation or asset that, by its terms, uses LIBOR as a benchmark.'

[87] ibid § 102(a)(2).

Specifically, the LIBOR Act provides that, at a set date (set by the Act as the first London 'banking date' after 30 June 2023, subject to an earlier date provided by the contract)[88] the 'Board-selected benchmark replacement shall be the benchmark replacement for any LIBOR contract',[89] without consent being required from 'any other person'.[90] This mandatory switch is subject to alternative provisions in the contract[91] and to specific phasing-in provisions for contracts the Act defines as 'consumer loans'.[92] The Act expressly overrides any conflicting provision of 'State or local law'.[93]

The replacement rate provided for in this measure, the 'Board-selected benchmark', is defined as 'a benchmark replacement identified by the [Board of Governors of the Federal Reserve] that is based on SOFR, including any tenor spread adjustment [as provided for in the Act]'.[94] In other words, for tough legacy contracts in scope, references to LIBOR are automatically replaced by the officially selected RFR for the US dollar market, and consequential amendments necessary to make the substituted rates work are deemed to be made accordingly.[95] This legislative provision therefore cleanly and consistently addresses the 'tough legacy' problem for contracts in scope; one law firm describes it as 'a clear and uniform solution for transitioning legacy contracts'.[96] It is, however, a remarkable official intervention into the core economic terms of private contracts which are already in force, albeit one that could be avoided by parties agreeing on their own, workable alternative to LIBOR. Furthermore, as well as imposing a mandatory switch from LIBOR to the prescribed alternative for contracts in scope, the LIBOR Act also makes express provision that this mandated change to contractual interest rate provisions is deemed to be 'commercially reasonable' and that it cannot be grounds for a party to make a claim against the other, on any of a long list of grounds, or otherwise seek to suspend or terminate performance (the so-called 'continuity' and 'safe harbor' provisions).[97]

Though there was much debate about the risks arising from 'tough legacy' contracts,[98] the UK did not pass legislation with the sweeping effects of the US

[88] ibid § 103(17); § 104(c)(2)(B). The former section gives the Federal Reserve Board the power to replace 30 June 2023 with another date in certain circumstances.

[89] ibid § 104(a).

[90] ibid § 104(d)(2).

[91] ibid § 102(b)(1), § 104(f).

[92] ibid § 104(e)(2).

[93] ibid § 107.

[94] ibid §103(6). SOFR stands for the approved RFR for USD, ie, the Secured Overnight Financing Rate and is calculated by the New York Fed.

[95] So-called 'Conforming Changes' to the contract are described in the LIBOR Act as 'technical, administrative or operational' and may be imposed either by the Federal Reserve Board or, in a non-consumer contract only, when judged to be 'necessary or appropriate' by the interest rate 'calculating person' identified in the contract. ibid § 103(4).

[96] Mayer Brown, 'A deeper dive into the US Adjustable Interest Rate (LIBOR) Act' (Insights, 4 April 2022) available at www.mayerbrown.com/en/insights/publications/2022/04/a-deeper-dive-into-the-us-adjustable-interest-rate-libor-act#five.

[97] LIBOR Act § 105.

[98] eg, running through the numerous publications on LIBOR transition by the UK Financial Markets Law Committee, available at fmlc.org/publications/?_filter_search=LIBOR%20Transition.

LIBOR Act. UK legislation did, however, pursue two of the same strategies in less ambitious ways. First, the Critical Benchmarks (References and Administrators' Liability) Act 2021 (the 'UK Act') included the provision that references in 'a contract or other arrangement' to LIBOR would be read 'for all purposes' as including the so-called 'synthetic' LIBOR.[99] Synthetic LIBOR in this context was a rate calculated by the regulated benchmark administrator not on the basis of panel submissions, but rather, in line with a 'synthetic' methodology imposed by the regulator, as a temporary measure in the lead-up to cessation.[100] Second, the UK Act provides certain immunities from litigation for private sector stakeholders associated with a designated 'Article 23A' benchmark.[101] Under this provision of the UK Benchmarks Regulation, regulators may designate certain 'critical benchmarks'[102] as permanently unrepresentative of the market that they reference[103] so that they then have special powers to phase out such benchmarks. The UK Act backs up these special powers by providing that the private sector administrators of benchmarks, their officers and employees have what is effectively a 'safe harbor' from claims for damages relating to their actions or inactions while fulfilling regulators' orders.[104] While this is obviously far narrower than the 'safe harbor' supporting the core measures in the US LIBOR Act, it remains an unusual approach for this jurisdiction, and it speaks to the concerns about litigation risk which recurred throughout this reform. Finally, this provision also highlights another example of the close interaction between public and private sectors in the course of mitigating legal risks relating to LIBOR cessation.

IV. Implications

Given that certain types of 'intersystemic risks' are said to be inevitable, and that the highly connected global economy has a proven capacity to spread

[99] Critical Benchmarks (References and Administrators' Liability) Act 2021, s 1 inserting a new Art 23FA into the UK's retained EU legislation on benchmarks, namely: Regulation (EU) 2016/1011 of 8 June 2016 on indices used as benchmarks in financial instruments and financial contracts or to measure the performance of investment funds and amending Directives 2008/48/EC and 2014/17/EU and Regulation (EU) No 596/2014 (Retained EU Legislation) ('UK BMR').

[100] ICE Benchmark Administration® Ltd (IBA)'s role in relation to LIBOR-setting and LIBOR Cessation is outlined on its website at ICE, LIBOR®, LIBOR Cessation & 'Synthetic' LIBOR, at www.ice.com/iba/libor.

[101] The relevant provision is: Critical Benchmarks (References and Administrators' Liability) Act 2021, s 2 inserting a new Art 23FC into the UK BMR.

[102] As defined under UK BMR, Art 20, taking into account factors including the size of the markets where it is used and impact on the UK if the benchmark were to cease or no longer be representative of its underlying 'market or economic reality' (UK BMR, Art 20(3)). Designation means that regulators have certain powers and responsibilities in relation to the benchmark, eg, a biennial review by the FCA, under UK BMR, Art A20.

[103] UK BMR, Art 23A, added by the Financial Services Act 2021.

[104] Under UK BMR, Art 23D regulators have sweeping powers to impose requirements on benchmark administrators in relation to 'orderly cessation' of an Art 23A benchmark.

disruption, there is a special urgency around the topic explored in this volume. This section considers the broader implications of the case study, considering if lessons from LIBOR might improve how the law responds to, or, as one scholar has put it, 'fits', the complex risks discussed earlier in the chapter.

In work on force majeure in the Louisiana Civil Code, Vernon Palmer has explored the 'fit'[105] between this area of law and the particular risks in that jurisdiction. Applying this framework, Palmer identified a 'striking anomaly'.[106] On the one hand, he showed that Louisiana 'has taken the precept of *pacta sunt servanda* very far', with one of the 'most rigorous' approaches in the world, which is even more 'unyielding' than that in English, US federal, or French law.[107] This rigidity was the result, he showed, of legal history; law inherited 'from Rome and France' had remained frozen, even while civil law systems themselves had adopted a more flexible approach, for example, with the addition of the defence of '*imprévision*' in France.[108] On the other hand, Palmer observed that Louisiana

> has to be regarded as one of the world capitals of *force majeure*, as shown by its recurrent subjection to hurricanes, epidemics, floods and other disasters that repeatedly interfere with the ability of obligors and debtors to perform their contractual promises … Diseases and epidemics have been frequent visitors as well.[109]

As a result of this 'paradox', Palmer argued, there were 'extreme hardships and financial burdens caused by supervening events' in Louisiana.[110] Even while expressing pessimism for its prospects, Palmer builds on this insight to propose an amendment to the relevant part of the state's Civil Code, which, he argued, would better fit the risk profile of the jurisdiction.[111]

The idea of testing a legal regime for supervening events against the relevant risks is a promising one, beyond the case of Louisiana. As discussed, the risks to the performance of commercial and financial contracts can be complex, contagious and cross-border in their effects. What kind of legal regime 'fits' with risks of this nature? In the English legal context, Palmer's approach would be a valuable way of opening up questions about whether certain legal rules risk falling out of date, as in the Louisiana example, and about the substantive implications of English law's use in cross-border, international, and standardised contracts. Palmer's approach also offers a useful way of thinking about the limitations of the law more generally, and about risks which test those limits. As we have seen, even in sophisticated,

[105] V Palmer, 'The Sanctity of Promises in a Capital of Force Majeure: Hurricanes, Pandemics and the Doctrine of Impossibility under Louisiana Law' (2023) 10(1) *Journal of International and Comparative Law* 45, 52.
[106] ibid 46.
[107] ibid 47.
[108] ibid 52–54.
[109] ibid 47.
[110] ibid 56.
[111] ibid Part IV.

professionally drafted agreements, express provision for unexpected events can fall short when tested. Similarly, even dispute resolution which consistently takes account of the 'interests alike of justice and of the conduct of commercial transactions'[112] cannot be a complete answer to risks of the kind explored in this chapter. As such, the strategies highlighted by the LIBOR case study should be considered as a way of broadening the available legal response to better fit the risks of disruption in today's global markets.

Three such strategies emerge from this case study. The first is leveraging public and private sector co-operation in order to make new and extant contracts more robust in light of supervening events. In the LIBOR context, this type of co-operation went far beyond the usual type of one-off consultation, extending to years' worth of collaborative work around assessing risk, market robustness, and technical amendments. At the same time, the involvement of international firms and global trade associations, some of which were active in parallel working groups in other jurisdictions, also helped to ensure that UK initiatives were informed by cross-border insights. In other contexts, such public-private working groups could usefully consider the technical implications of supervening events which threaten the performance of extant contracts, for example, relating to climate risks, and/or work on proposals to 'repair' contracts in light of developments which are not robustly addressed by existing terms. The LIBOR case study from the uncleared derivatives markets helpfully shows how a co-ordinated 'repair' can be implemented where contracts are on standardised terms, which would also potentially apply to many consumer contexts, as well as the insurance and shipping sectors, for example. The 'Revlon blocker' case study, noted above, shows how suggested amendments can also be circulated around less standardised and less centralised markets for parties to adapt as needed.

A further suggestion would be to formalise working groups' role as a part of the legal response to supervening events. This could involve appointing some members with legal as well as market expertise and, as in the UK RFR Working Group's case, ensuring that terms of reference included the objective of enhancing the robustness of relevant legal arrangements.[113] Working groups would also be well-positioned to monitor litigation risks and, potentially, also to co-ordinate appropriate test cases, which are now provided for in the UK's Financial List.[114] This type of specialist test case has been available since October 2015, for a claim started in the Financial List 'which raises issues of generally importance in relation to which immediately relevant authoritative English law guidance is needed'.[115] It

[112] *The Nema* (n 3) 737F (Lord Diplock), addressing the importance of interpreting standard terms in a uniform way.

[113] Working Group on Sterling Risk-Free Rates: Terms of Reference Updated April 2022. These ToR include numerous objectives relating to financial contracts, including 'Identifying and promoting best practices and association product conventions to ensure that financial contracts are resilient to the cessation or material alteration of LIBOR ....'

[114] Civil Procedure Rules, PD 63AA, para 6.

[115] ibid para 6.1.

offers a valuable way of clarifying the impact of supervening events on commercial and financial contracts, though, to date, it seems underused, with only two test cases brought so far. Ten years on, it would be valuable to revisit this scheme to consider how it could be promoted.

The LIBOR case study suggests that a second strategy involves facilitating market participants' incorporation of recommended contractual changes, in a way that is convenient, consistent and legally certain. Depending on the relevant market's structure, there are various possibilities, but the case study showed how different types of centralised entities are able to facilitate efficient, timely and legally certain changes, without necessarily being a party to the contracts in question. As a backstop, but with more limited jurisdictional reach, the case study also highlights the potential for legislation to impose changes on private contracts, but the potential risks are indicated by the safe harbor arrangements which were designed to block litigation which might otherwise follow.

A final, related observation relates to jurisdiction. For decades, LIBOR was administered in London, and, as a result, its cessation was, as a technical matter, brought about by UK regulators. As we have seen, however, the contracts threatened by LIBOR cessation were entered into by parties all over the world, in other countries' domestic markets as well as in many cross-border settings. These contracts were not limited to a particular jurisdiction, nor to a specific choice of governing law, and nor were parties using LIBOR subject to a specific regulatory regime. To put it another way, neither the UK regulators, nor any other lawmaker or regulator had jurisdiction over the contracts and other arrangements which were vulnerable to disruption from this policy. To exacerbate the problem, the nature of the benchmark meant that there were no centralised data about where, or by whom, or how LIBOR was being used. As a result, the threat of disruption from LIBOR cessation was far more diffuse than, say, the threat posed by the failure of a globally used IT system, which could still affect contracts in dozens of jurisdictions and be subject to diverse governing laws, but in this case, the software would be licensed from the relevant IT company to each customer.[116] There is no single solution for managing interconnected risks which, as with LIBOR cessation, expose the limits of national law and regulation. Instead, this scenario underlines the importance of both cross-border co-operation and market participants' involvement in risk mitigation. Returning to Palmer's insights into the relationship between legal rules and relevant risks, the LIBOR case study demonstrates that in global markets it is necessary, but not sufficient, to consider the ways in which supervening events are dealt with by the formal rules of a particular legal system. Consequently, the challenge is to consider which combination of legal strategies will be best placed to manage the risks ahead of us and, then, to plan accordingly.

[116] eg, the 2024 disruption caused by CrowdStrike's antivirus software update: M Shlangestein 'Delta expects $380 million in lost sales from the CrowdStrike outage that forced it to cancel thousands of flights' *Forbes* (9 August 2024).

4

Smart Contracts and the Unexpected

SARAH GREEN

> Do conventional legal principles work, or may they need to adapt, when traders hand their affairs to computers operating by algorithm?[1]

Such was the question posed by Mance IJ, sitting in the Singapore Court of Appeal and deciding how the doctrine of mistake should be applied to smart, as opposed to conventional, contracts. The same question, in broader terms, formed the basis of a Law Commission project in 2021. That project found, in its Advice to Government published in 2021, that conventional legal principles do indeed work in relation to agreements that are formed by algorithms.[2] Its ultimate conclusion was that it is not the legal principles themselves that need to change, but the manner in which they are applied, or the means by which the questions to which they give rise are answered. For instance, it is clear that an enforceable legal contract will require an offer that is accepted and an intention on the part of both parties that legal relations be created, regardless of whether that agreement is made by humans communicating directly with one another, or by computers, instructed by those parties, interacting with one another. What might not yet be clear is what those elements might look like, and where a court might find them, in the smart contract context. Whereas a conventional offer will often be found in a letter or email, a smart contract offer is more likely to be found in computer code (which means that, to a human who is not code-literate, it might not look much like the sort of offer with which lawyers are currently familiar). In any event, the point is that enforceable contracts have the same legal requirements, regardless of their factual form: they are all objectively recognisable agreements between parties that meet the law's criteria for validity and enforcement.

This chapter considers the question of mistakes made during the process of reaching an agreement. This issue is a thorny one even in the conventional context. It is complicated further by the fact that contracts made by means of

[1] Mance IJ in *Quoine Pte Ltd v B2C2 Ltd* [2020] SGCA(I) 02 at [152].
[2] *Smart Legal Contracts: Advice to Government* (Law Com No 401, 2021).

automated processes based on code are formed in a way that is remote from the parties to them. In other words, parties set out the parameters of their agreements unilaterally and in advance of knowing what their counterparties' parameters are. The machines that they instruct then do the work of matching compatible expectations. The mischief addressed by unilateral mistake remains relevant here; a mutual choice to automate the ultimate formation of agreements is no more a licence knowingly to take advantage of another's error than is the choice to use conventional means.

Smart contracts[3] are formed by the interaction of one software program with another. The idea is that both of these software programs will have been coded so as to propose and to agree to terms within a certain set of parameters, meaning that the formation of any contract between them will occur in an automated way, with no human involvement beyond the coding and deployment of each separate program.[4] The fact that the making and performance of such contracts is automated raises distinct and novel questions about how they will be analysed and treated in the event of a dispute. Essentially, when parties engage in smart contracting, what they are really doing is issuing a set of conditions under which they are willing to transact. The computers to which those instructions are given then make and execute any contracts that result from the conditions of any two pieces of software being compatible at a given time. So, to take a very simple example, A (or maybe rather, A's coder) has written a program that will purchase up to 100 tokens of a security (let's call it SmartShare) whenever SmartShare is available at the market price or below.[5] B has written a program that will sell as much of SmartShare as it has available at the market price or above. Where B has, say, 75 units of SmartShare available when the price reaches its market level, the software will form and execute a contract between A and B for the sale of those 75 units of SmartShare from B to A. So far, so simple. (And so convenient – in principle, this sort of trading is frictionless, efficient and immune from human fallibility in its execution.[6]) There are, however, at least two features of this arrangement that present reasons for asking the question posed by Mance IJ above. First, there is the fact that the contracting party, whose mind is the one contract law expects to meet another's, is not usually the same person as the one writing the code. Second, the contract that was in fact concluded and performed is not the only one that can, will or might have resulted from the coded instructions that were written. And until it

[3] 'Smart contract' is a term applied by non-lawyers to all sorts of automated algorithms, many of which would not meet the requirements of a legal contract. For the purposes of this chapter, the term will be used to refer only to 'smart legal contracts' – the subset of those algorithmic transactions that do fulfil the criteria of a legally enforceable contract.

[4] Such transactions have facilitated the development (and swift growth) of decentralised financed (De-Fi) and are now a common means of executing several different types of commercial agreement, including the trading of securities.

[5] In reality, such programs will of course be much more complicated than this and will nearly always include instructions both to buy and to sell a variety of different tokens and assets. The granular example highlighted here, however, remains a helpful illustration of the relevant forensic issue.

[6] Although not necessarily of course in its design; more of which below.

was concluded or performed, the parties to the contract will not have known for sure in advance that it would be so concluded, with whom it would be made and what its precise terms would be.

This challenges several areas of conventional contract law analysis. Specifically, it will cause (and to some extent already has caused) courts to reconsider the application of the doctrine of mistake. Not only does the law need to identify for these purposes *whose* mind – the contracting party's or coder's – needs to have been mistaken, but also to revisit the knowledge element of the doctrine of mistake. It is on one view (more on this below) well-established in common law that in order for a unilateral mistake to be operative in vitiating a contract, the non-mistaken party must have actual knowledge of their counterparty's error. There is of course nothing novel about the phenomenon of parties agreeing to contracts containing terms of which they were unaware, or whose likely future effect they did not understand (or could not predict). In a smart contracting context, however, parties consciously and deliberately operate on a speculative basis by setting out parameters that identify an acceptable range of future agreements. At the time these instructions are written, and a fortiori at the time that their content is communicated to a coder for translation into machine language, it is therefore neither possible nor constructive to ask what a contracting party knew or did not know about the state of mind of their future counterparty. First, they would not at the relevant time even necessarily know who that future counterparty would be. Second, any such counterparty would have engaged in a similar exercise, making speculative arrangements based on a range of conditions. On this set of facts, asking questions about knowledge of other parties' states of mind is therefore as inauthentic as it is irrelevant.

This poses a serious challenge to the conventional application of the doctrine of mistake, depending as that concept does on the condition of *knowing* something about another's current beliefs and understandings. In a smart contracting context, in which agreements are formed at a point that is temporally distinct from the one at which parties made their decisions, and in which those decisions have multiple potential outcomes, and interact with potentially unknown counterparties, the relevant analytical concept would seem to be something closer to intention rather than to knowledge. After all, knowledge can only pertain to an existing fact or state of affairs, and a person can have no more than intention in relation to a future conditional state of affairs. Given that unilateral mistake in its current form arguably requires the non-mistaken party to have actual knowledge of the mistaken party's intention as to the terms of the contract, it is difficult to see how parties to a smart contract will ever be able to meet this threshold. As already established, such parties will not necessarily know at the time they code their own instructions who their future counterparty or counterparties will be. Neither will they necessarily know what contractual parameters those parties will have set out in their own code. Indeed, some potential future counterparties will not even at the relevant time have made any decisions or issued any coded instructions. Obviously, on such facts (which are likely to be common in the smart contracting world), it is impossible for any party to have any form of *knowledge* about what their counterparties' (perhaps as yet non-existent) instructions might contain.

I. The Nature of Computer Code

It is not only the substantive process of smart contracting that presents a challenge to established principles of English contract law, but also the technological means by which such contracts are formed. A significant difference between the mechanics of conventional agreements made between humans and those smart contracts formed between machines is that certain results in the latter case, rather than being *expected* at the point of coding, can in fact be *determined* at that point. Coded instructions to a computer are in a sense deterministic in a way that agreed obligations between humans are not. In other words, most computer programs currently used for smart contracting, certainly in the De-Fi context,[7] given the same input and conditions, will always produce the same outputs. If, for instance, a program mandates the sale of tokens at a given price, a sale at that price will always take place where the relevant conditions are met (eg, the availability of tokens and the existence of an offer at the right price). There is no room in such a situation for discretion, nuance, judgement or dereliction. In this sense, there is therefore no room for the unexpected. As already established, however, it is not true to say that a particular contractual outcome is determined at the moment that a contracting party runs its smart contract-forming software. That outcome will depend on the conditions and circumstances that the program encounters because, unlike the incredibly simple example given here, it is more likely to have been written to accommodate a variety of factual situations, and to respond to each in a given way. So, whilst any particular element of a program could well be described as deterministic – say, tokens will always be sold where they are available and there is an offer at market price or above – as a whole, smart contracting programs are better described as stochastic.[8] In other words, the formation of any particular resultant contract can only be predicted in a probabilistic sense at the time the software is coded, which is the last time at which there will be any human involvement in the process.

This is significant for any analysis of such contracts in terms of mistake because the knowledge of any contracting party will be more limited than it would be in the context of conventional contract formation. In the latter, parties interacting directly with one another can choose, and can therefore *know*, which of the terms acceptable to them will be the ones that make it into the contract. Those making a smart contract, by contrast, will only know the range of terms that might make it into any future contract made on the basis of their code. Such parties can only

[7] Most notably, those not based on generative Artificial Intelligence – software that can 'learn' to produce novel and/or different outcomes.

[8] With thanks to Adam Sanitt for drawing my attention to the significance of this.

intend to have an agreement fall within a certain range of outcomes, but cannot know exactly what they will end up agreeing to in each and every agreement that is formed by their contract-forming software. The implications of this were given their first significant judicial consideration by the Singapore Court of Appeal in *Quoine v B2C2 Ltd*.[9]

II. Mistake and Smart Contracts in the Singapore Court of Appeal – *Quoine v B2C2 Ltd*

In *Quoine Pte Ltd v B2C2 Ltd*, the claimant company (B2C2) had traded cryptocurrencies, including Bitcoin and Ethereum, on the defendant Quoine's platform, QUOINExchange. That platform enabled parties like B2C2 to trade cryptocurrencies for other cryptocurrencies or for fiat currencies. On 19 April 2017, owing to an operational oversight by Quoine, the platform was not able to access external market data to generate new orders, resulting in the trading software having no or insufficient input for its trades. This is precisely the sort of event that smart contract programs have to accommodate, and that programmers have therefore to anticipate. In the case of B2C2's software, this absence of data triggered a default calculation in the software to come into effect, referred to as a 'Deep Price'. At first instance, this was described by the judge as follows:

> The B2C2 trading software ('the Software') is largely deterministic; it produces the exact same output when provided with the same input … this was a benefit as it makes testing easier and the behaviour of the system is easier to understand, reason about and validate … as might be expected, [it] had been the subject of a number of changes during the course of time. When the software was originally written, [the coder] included a number of routines designed both to maintain the integrity of the system and to ensure that it continued to operate in circumstances when there was insufficient liquidity in a given market for the system to operate normally.
>
> The way in which the software determines what are appropriate prices at which to place Bid or Ask quotes is controlled by a strategy known as the PureQuote Strategy. For present purposes the effect of this strategy can be summarised relatively briefly. The software evaluates the first 20 price levels on a given platform on both the Bid and Ask side. It then excludes from that evaluation any price levels that relate to an order of a specified low volume. It then calculates an appropriate price at which to quote on either the Bid or Ask side as the case may be. However, it is accepted that there may be occasions when either the order book is empty or where it is populated by a large number of low-volume orders within the first 20 that the strategy is unable to determine a price. One way to cater for this would be to introduce a circuit breaker so

[9] *Quoine* (n 1).

> that the system would 'error out', ie, stop working. But this is undesirable in a program that is designed to work continuously without human oversight, so [the coder] built into the software the requirement that at all times there should be added two 'deep prices' to both the Bid side and the Ask side of the software's internal representation of the order book. By this means there would always be prices which the software could draw upon so that the system would not error out. These prices have to be chosen in a manner such that on the Ask side it is sufficiently large that the prospect of a trade at that level is both unlikely and, if it occurs, will adequately protect B2C2 against the risk of any adverse consequences of such a trade. Conversely, the chosen price on the Bid side needs to be low.[10]

On the date in question, the rate at which these deep prices were calculated was approximately 250 times the going rate of about 0.04 Bitcoins to one Ethereum. All of the trades in question had been executed as a result of automated programming with no human intervention:

> As is typical of algorithmic trading, the buy and sell contracts on the Platform were concluded without any direct human involvement, save that involved in the creation of the algorithmic processes leading to their formation. Algorithmic trading has been described as follows (see Alain Chaboud et al, 'Rise of the Machines: Algorithmic Trading in the Foreign Exchange Market', International Finance Discussion Papers, 29 September 2009 www.federalreserve.gov/pubs/ifdp/2009/980/ifdp980.pdf at 1):
>
>> In algorithmic trading … [traders'] computers directly interface with trading platforms, placing orders without immediate human intervention. The computers observe market data and possibly other information at very high frequency, and, based on a built-in algorithm, send back trading instructions, often within milliseconds …[11]

Quoine subsequently cancelled these trades on the basis that they were such a significant deviation from market value that they triggered the platform's Aberrant Value Clause, which, if applicable, would indeed have permitted cancellation under the contract. That clause was, however, found by the Court of Appeal to have been drafted too narrowly to apply to these particular transactions on the basis that it referred to aberrant values caused by 'emergency system maintenance or a system failure', neither of which had occurred on the instant facts because orders had in fact been made. It is significant that, on these facts, although the price was abnormal, it was the one intended by B2C2 in accordance with its coded instructions. In turn, the disputed trades were concluded based on prices correctly quoted by the trading software for B2C2, and market orders that were correctly placed by the platform for the counterparties. B2C2 subsequently commenced proceedings against Quoine for breach of contract (and/or breach of trust), arguing that usage of the platform was governed by a user agreement, and that Quoine had breached a provision of it which disallowed an order from being cancelled once fulfilled

[10] *Quoine* in the HC at [82]–[85].

[11] *Quoine* (n 1) at [1].

(the 'Irreversible Action Clause'). Quoine's defence was that the contracts between B2C2 and the counterparties to the aberrant trades were void or voidable due to mistake (Singapore still recognises equitable mistake), and that therefore it was entitled to cancel the trades. The Singapore Court of Appeal held that the trades were valid and binding contracts, finding that the purported mistake was not sufficiently fundamental to void the contracts.

Notably, one of Quoine's arguments was that if the parties had met on the trading floor face-to-face, they would never have agreed to the price of ten Bitcoins to one Ethereum: the mistaken price would never have been accepted, and the trades therefore never made. The Court found this analogy unhelpful, taking the view that, since the parties had chosen to engage in an automated form of contracting, arguments as to how they would have acted if they had instead chosen to transact between humans were redundant. It was therefore material that the parties' instructions to their computers were for the relevant purposes deterministic:

> It should be noted that the Trading Software's algorithm is deterministic ... [so] will always produce precisely the same output given the same input. To put it another way, the Trading Software will do just what it was programmed to do and does not have the capacity to develop its own responses to varying conditions. Hence, faced with any given set of conditions, it will always respond to that in the same way.[12]

As explained above, however, the fact that the code is internally deterministic (meaning that it will always respond consistently to similar conditions) needs to be set against the fact that it will not respond at all except to those conditions and that neither the contracting parties nor the coders could know when the software was coded which conditions it would encounter and with which parties it would transact. As the Court put it in *Quoine*:

> The complexity arose because the defence of unilateral mistake was being raised for the first time, as far as we are aware, in the context of algorithmic trading and the formation of contracts by such means. B2C2 and the Counterparties had entered into the Trading Contracts by means of B2C2's and Quoine's deterministic algorithms. B2C2 and the Counterparties therefore did not know until after the Trading Contracts had been entered into, whether an offer would be made or accepted, or the terms on which a contract would be concluded. How then could the doctrine of unilateral mistake apply in this situation, where the contracting parties did not know the specific terms on which the Trading Contracts would be entered into?[13]

In answering this question in *Quoine*, the Court considered the state of mind of the controller of the platform; the person responsible for the instructions that gave rise to the aberrant price generation.[14] On the facts in *Quoine*, the Court found that the coder responsible for the default price generation programming did not have

[12] *Quoine Pte Ltd v B2C2 Ltd* [2020] SGCA(I) 2 at [15].
[13] ibid at [78].
[14] In this case, a Director of B2C2, who also designed its Trading Software.

sufficient knowledge of the other parties' mistaken belief that 'the trades were … being transacted under normal market conditions, meaning at prices which accurately reflected or did not deviate significantly from the true market value and/or price of ETH relative to BTC on 19 April 2017'.[15] Given that smart contracting operates on the basis of pre-programmed instructions that are not reviewed before individual agreements are made on the basis of them, and since machines do not (yet) have minds of their own, the question of the coder's state of mind in formulating those instructions will often be a crucial one. Not only does unilateral mistake at common law require the non-mistaken party to have actual knowledge that the other party is mistaken as to the terms of the contract but,[16] as is well illustrated by a long line of cases involving conventional contracts, this is a high threshold. It is going to be an even more difficult standard to reach for parties who set out the parameters of their agreements in the abstract and in advance of knowing what the parameters (and maybe also the identity) of their counterparty might be. They are not therefore only anticipating what they might and might not want to agree to, but also what their counterparties might and might not want to agree to. In the conventional contracting context, of course, parties do this in advance of negotiation, but they then have an opportunity to tailor their final agreements in light of what they learn as a result of interaction with their counterparty. They also have the chance to identify their counterparty and to gauge that party's intentions and beliefs as to the terms of the agreement between them. In the smart contracting context, by contrast, there is no such facility: agreements will be formed in a way that is remote from the contracting parties' final decision-making opportunity. Given that that is the case, it is often going to be very hard, if not impossible, to establish what a party writing smart contracting instructions knows about the state of mind of an as yet unidentified potential counterparty as the latter wrote their instructions. Where the future counterparty does not write their instructions until after the non-mistaken party has written theirs (a scenario likely to be common, given that such contract-forming software is programmed and then left to run on and make repeat agreements on a platform over time), it will certainly be impossible to consider what the non-mistaken party can have 'known' about code that did not even exist at the relevant time.

In *Quoine*, the Singapore Court of Appeal noted that the judge at first instance, had

> refused to consider the matter by reference to what the position would have been and what the contracting parties were likely to have known, intended and agreed had they had face-to-face negotiations at a hypothetical meeting on the 'floor of the exchange' to enter into the Trading Contracts, at the time these were entered into, because this was simply not how they had agreed to form their contracts. Instead, they had decided to form contracts using the relevant deterministic algorithms ….We agree with this characterisation of the parties' method of contracting and we think it would be wholly

[15] *Quoine* (n 1) at [44].

[16] *Agip SpA v Navigazione Alta Italia SpA (The Nai Genova and the Nai Superba)* [1984] 1 Lloyd's Rep 353; *Commission for New Towns v Cooper (Great Britain)* [1995] Ch 259 and H Beale, *Chitty on Contracts*, 35th edn, (London, Sweet & Maxwell, 2024) [5-072].

> artificial to recast the relevant matrix of fact, which was one where the contracting parties did not in fact know beforehand that they were going to enter into the Trading Contracts or their terms, and were content to abide by what the relevant algorithms did at least as long as this was within the ambit of their programmed parameters. We also agree with the Judge that it follows from this that in cases where contracts are made by way of *deterministic* algorithms, any analysis concerning knowledge of a mistake or unconscionably taking advantage of one must be done by reference to the state of mind of the programmers of the algorithms at the time of the programming … a deterministic computer program or algorithm is bound by the parameters set by the programmer, and can (and generally will) only do what the programmer has programmed it to do. Given a particular input, it will produce a particular output; on each occasion, the output should and will be the same if the former does not change. *Therefore, when it comes to assessing the state of knowledge that is to be attributed to the parties at the time of a contract made by way of deterministic algorithms, the relevant inquiry cannot be directed at the parties themselves, who had no knowledge of or direct personal involvement in the formation of the contract. Rather, working backwards from the output that emanated from the programs, we are driven to assess the relevant state of knowledge by examining that of the programmers … Apart from determining whose knowledge is relevant, it is also important to consider the relevant time for assessing that person's knowledge. In our judgment, the relevant time frame within which we should assess the knowledge of a programmer or the person running the algorithm would be from the point of programming up to the point that the relevant contract is formed* … The question can first be framed in this way: if the algorithm was programmed to produce a particular output, *why* was this done? But the inquiry cannot end there and must extend past that point of time because there may be situations where a programmer or the person running the algorithm who did not contemplate the relevant mistake at the point of programming came to learn of it subsequently *before* the contract had been formed, and yet allowed the algorithm to continue running, intending thereby to take advantage of the mistake. In such a case, it would be wrong to ignore the subsequent acquisition of knowledge. This is why it is appropriate to have regard to the state of knowledge up to the time of the contract.[17]

The Court then referred to an academic analysis of the judgment whose appeal they were hearing:

> An issue to which the case gives rise is an apparent timing mismatch: the traders' mistakes must necessarily have arisen, or at least have been continuing, at the point of the original trades, whereas the last human input into the programming must by practical necessity have occurred *before* those trades. How then could the state of mind of the programmer when originally programming B2C2's 'deep price' methodology ever include knowledge of the relevant mistake? … the law might need to recognise *that so long as the knowledge or intention of the original programmer* was that there ought not to be the sort of mistake which subsequently arose, then it does not matter for the rules of unilateral mistake if the particular instantiation of that mistake post-dates the last act of a human being, so long as the programmer's state of mind could be said still to be extant at the time the mistake is made (in other words, that the code has not changed by then in a way which would be inconsistent with that state of mind).[18]

[17] *Quoine* (n 1) at [97]–[100] (emphasis added).

[18] N Yeo and J Farmer, 'Mapping the Landscape: Cryptocurrency Disputes under English Law (Part 2)' (2019) 5 *Journal of International Banking and Financial Law* 290, 291 (emphasis added).

But this, a programmer's belief that 'there ought not to be the sort of mistake which subsequently arose' when she writes her smart contract-forming code, is the highest at which her level of cognitive awareness of future terms can be put. It is not controversial to assert that this does not amount to actual knowledge. The Singapore Court of Appeal continued its analysis along similar lines:

> [T]he relevant inquiry in this case could be framed thus: when programming the Trading Software with the deep prices, was the programmer doing so with actual or constructive knowledge of the fact that sell orders at those prices would only ever be accepted by a party operating under a mistake and was the programmer acting to take advantage of that mistake? In our judgment, this was the essential methodology applied by the Judge at [229]–[230] of the Judgment and which led him to conclude that Mr Boonen neither had such knowledge nor programmed the Trading Software to take advantage of any such mistake:
>
> > *229 It is next necessary to determine whether Mr Boonen had actual knowledge of the mistaken belief at the time he inserted the deep prices … Can it be said that Mr Boonen knew that 'it was never contemplated by [any trader] that any trades would be transacted on the Platform at prices which deviated so substantially from the actual market prices'? This amounts to a belief held by Mr Boonen at that date* ***that the price was so abnormal that no trader would trade at that price otherwise by way of a mistake****.*
> >
> > *230 … I have concluded on the basis of those findings of fact that Mr Boonen did not insert the deep prices with that belief. He foresaw that a number of factors might arise which would cause the deep prices to be inserted and the overriding reasons for them being inserted was to protect B2C2 in the event of the unexpected happening. He did not exclude the possibility of trades at those prices being executed. Whilst he was aware that one possible cause was that it could be the result, wholly or in part, of some error or omission on the part of someone, including himself, he did not turn his mind in any detail to the circumstances that might lead to such trades being executed. He knew that the Platform was an automated system and that therefore no opportunity would arise for any particular trade to be reviewed by the parties in advance. In the circumstances of this case, in order for him to have actual knowledge that other traders believed that in no circumstances would a trade be transacted on the Platform at prices which deviated so substantially from the actual market prices, I consider that it would be necessary for it to be demonstrated that he held that belief himself, which he did not …*
> >
> > [bold emphasis added]
>
> We have also observed above … that the programmer's knowledge, or indeed the knowledge of anyone running the algorithm, is relevant *past* the point of programming, and up till the Disputed Trades occurred.[19]

The relevant mistaken belief alleged by Quoine was that 'they were buying ETH for BTC under contracts at prices which accurately represented or did not deviate significantly from the true market value and/or price of ETH relative to BTC

[19] *Quoine* (n 1) at [124]–[125].

on 19 April 2017 ('the Second Mistaken Belief').'[20] As to this belief, the Singapore Court of Appeal stated:

> [I]t is apparent to us that Mr Boonen did not have actual or constructive knowledge of the Second Mistaken Belief. Mr Boonen would have had to foresee a perfect storm of events that began with the problems with the Quoter Program and ended with the Disputed Trades being concluded at the deep price for him to have had, or be taken to have had, the Second Mistaken Belief.[21] Despite Quoine's considerable efforts to mount a case suggesting even a hint of this, there was simply no evidence to suggest that Mr Boonen had ever contemplated anything of the sort. We therefore reject Quoine's case on this aspect of the appeal.[22]

Even had Mr Boonen foreseen the 'perfect storm of events' referred to here and therefore known that the deep price was going to be triggered, this is not the same as saying that he had either actual (or even constructive knowledge)[23] of Quoine's state of mind in relation to that situation. Unilateral mistake is concerned with an asymmetry of understanding in relation to the terms of the contract – not in relation to future facts, which, if they are ever to be relevant in vitiating an agreement, could do so only as the basis of a common mistake.[24] In order to have the requisite knowledge for unilateral mistake, Mr Boonen (as the non-mistaken party) would not only have had to foresee this chain of events as a matter of future fact (or another that culminated in the application of the deep price) but also somehow be aware of what Quoine, when coding its own smart contract-forming software, intended in relation to a price formulation of which it was at the material time unaware. The first of these, the chain of events leading to the trigger of the deep price, does not present too great a forensic hurdle. After all, anticipating future commercial and technological events and preparing a response to them could be said to be the very essence of a coder's role in this context. It is difficult, however, to regard the ability of a party in Mr Boonen's position to have an awareness of a future counterparty's state of mind in relation to the effect of his code as anything other than illusory.

III. Unilateral Mistake: The Knowledge Requirement

Given that the *Quoine* scenario is a fairly standard and typical illustration of how smart contracting operates, it is hard to see how unilateral mistake in its current form could often arise, or be of use, in the smart contracting context. The state of

[20] *Quoine* (n 1) at [38]. The 'First Mistaken Belief' was that it was necessary to close out their positions in response to the margin calls which the platform made on them – in other words, the process that led to the trades being made at the Deep Price in the first place.

[21] Presumably intended to say knowledge of that belief.

[22] ibid at [126].

[23] Although constructive knowledge is, *semble*, in any event relevant only to equitable mistake (see *Quoine* (n 1) at [89]), which is no longer a live issue in English law.

[24] *Bell v Lever Bros* [1932] AC 161 at [225].

mind of those engaging in smart contracting will simply not be something that others can know about at the relevant time. As established above, whilst the relevant time in question is not limited to the point at which the code is written, but continues until the mistake itself is made, this is unlikely to make much difference in practice. The point at which the mistake is made will be the time at which the agreement is formed, and, as the absence of the meeting on the trading floor on the facts of *Quoine* demonstrates, this is hardly likely to give parties any greater opportunity to learn anything about their counterparty's knowledge or intentions than they had at the time when their own code was written.

Significantly, were the requirement to be that of constructive knowledge, the applicability and relevance of unilateral mistake to smart contracting would be greatly increased. Constructive knowledge – knowledge that a person is presumed to have if, on an objective assessment of the situation, they should have had it – is far more apposite to the automated agreement situation than actual knowledge. The material distinction between the two types of knowledge lies, of course, in the hypothetical dimension; constructive knowledge bridges the gap between what was and what ought to have been. But in doing so, it allows for more than a normative judgement to be made. It also allows for multiple potential factual situations to be accounted for. In the context of criminal law, constructive knowledge plays an important role in establishing culpability, by allowing for the evaluation of individual behaviour against normative societal standards.[25] Its role in contract law, by contrast, is to assess the extent to which interactions between individuals have objectively common, and therefore agreed, elements. Where parties form their intentions and conditions unilaterally, as they do in most smart contracting cases, the only authentic question that can be asked about their knowledge of potential counterparty's states of mind is what they *should* have known about how any future contracting party might respond to the content of their own smart contract-forming code. In other words, a contractually relevant question would be something along the lines of 'What are the objectively reasonable contractual outcomes from a particular set of offer or acceptance parameters in a given market environment?' Therefore, if unilateral mistake is going to continue to serve contracting parties and to remain relevant in a world in which automated contracting is increasing in both importance and popularity, it would benefit from a reconsideration of its requisite knowledge element.

At first blush, this might appear to suggest a dramatic overhaul. As it happens, however, the question of what standard of knowledge is required for unilateral mistake in English law has not for a while had a particularly clear-cut answer. Although there appears very recently to have been more support, both judicial and academic, for the actual knowledge requirement, the question of whether constructive knowledge can suffice could not be said to be conclusively settled.

[25] See, eg, RG Sullivan, 'Knowledge, Belief and Culpability' in S Shute and A Simester (eds), *Criminal Law Theory: Doctrines of the General Part*, (Oxford, OUP, 2002).

The learned editors of *Chitty* take the view that there is as yet no determinative answer in English law:

> Whether A is actually bound by an acceptance of his apparent offer depends on the state of mind of the alleged offeree (B); to this extent, the test of agreement can be said to be not 'wholly objective'. If B actually and reasonably believes that A has the requisite intention, the objective test is satisfied so that B can hold A to his apparent offer even though A did not, subjectively, have the requisite intention. However, if B knows that, in spite of the objective appearance, A does not have the requisite intention, A is not bound; the objective test does not apply in favour of B as he knows the truth about A's actual intention. There are other permutations. If B does not know, but ought to have known that A does not have the requisite intention, English law gives no clear answer. However, there are suggestions that B will not be able to hold A to his apparent offer.[26]

In his *Restatement of the Law of Contract,* Lord Burrows sets out the following rules, appearing in 4(b)(i) to allow for constructive knowledge to suffice:

> (4) A mistake in entering the contract renders the contract void (or, to put it another way, there is no acceptance of an offer and hence no contract) if –
>
> (a) the parties are at cross-purposes such that there is a central objective ambiguity as to what has been agreed; or
>
> (b) one party is mistaken and –
>
> (i) the other party knows, or ought reasonably to know, of that mistake;
>
> (ii) the mistake is as to the terms of the contract or as to the identity of the other party; and
>
> (iii) it is the mistaken party who is alleging that the contract is void.[27]

Professor Cartwright says the following:

> **13-21 Mistake of one party known by the other**
>
> Under this test a party cannot enforce a contract on his own terms, even if it appears on the objective evidence to have been concluded, where he knows that the other party was mistaken about the terms. [...] This is the basis on which it is sometimes said that a party will not be allowed to 'snap at' an offer: that is, if he receives an offer which he knows contains a mistake about a term – for example, the price stated in the offer is lower than the offeror intended the contract to prescribe – he cannot by accepting the offer before the offeror has discovered his mistake conclude a binding contract at a lower price. The fact that he knew that the offeror made a mistake in his letter of offer means that he cannot show that he in fact believed that it reflected the offeror's true intentions.
>
> **13-22 Mistake of one party that the other should have known about**
>
> Similarly, a party cannot enforce a contract on terms which he should have known did not reflect the other party's true intentions. In this case, [...] a reasonable person in his position would not have believed that the other party was agreeing to those terms.

[26] H Beale, *Chitty on Contracts,* 33rd edn, (London, Sweet & Maxwell, 2019) [2-004].
[27] A Burrows, *Restatement of the English Law of Contract,* 2nd edn (Oxford, OUP, 2020) section 35(4).

> In practice, it may be easier to rely on this ground to avoid the contract, rather than proving that the party actually knew about the mistake, because it is easier to prove what a reasonable person would have understood than what the other party actually did understand.[28]

These were the accounts drawn by counsel to the attention of Ellenbogen J in *Longley v PPB Entertainment Services Ltd*,[29] who, in *obiter dicta*, went on to conclude that 'constructive knowledge does not suffice for the purposes of unilateral mistake':

> Lord Burrows cites no authority for the proposition set out at section 35(4)(b)(i) and Professor Cartwright refers to the authorities which I have considered above.[30] The editors of Chitty, rightly, observe that English law gives no clear answer on the point. I have been referred to no reasoned analysis of the issue (obiter or otherwise) by the courts of England and Wales, in particular post-dating *Digilandmall.com*. In my judgment, such an analysis leads to the conclusion that actual knowledge by B of A's relevant mistake is required and that a consideration of that which the reasonable person in B's position ought to have known is merely one means by which to ascertain, on the balance of probabilities, whether B in fact possessed the requisite actual knowledge.[31]

In reaching this conclusion, Ellenbogen J reasons that 'a mistake of which the offeree ought to have been, but was not in fact, aware does not lead to the conclusion that, subjectively, the parties were not ad idem; it points to the opposite conclusion'.[32] This rings true in relation to agreements made between humans in real time. In that context, where both parties have the opportunity to find out what their counterparty thinks and indeed know that they have this opportunity, asking what they could (and should) have known does not address the status of their agreement in the same way as asking what they did in fact know. Where, however, that opportunity is not available to either party, and where they both know that this will be the case – that is, where there is no 'meeting on the trading floor' and no intention of there being – asking about what they should have thought about their counterparty's position in response to their own *does* say something worthwhile about the status of an agreement formed in this way. Requiring actual knowledge for unilateral mistake here amounts to a denial that the parties to smart contracts can ever avoid them as a result of being mistaken as to their terms. This does not intuitively feel like the right answer; to choose an automated procedure for reaching agreements that is *for both parties* capable of achieving a range of outcomes is not to declare oneself open to any suggested terms, no matter how

[28] J Cartwright, *Cartwright on Misrepresentation, Mistake and Non-disclosure*, 7 edn (London, Sweet & Maxwell, 2025) [13-21]–[13-22].

[29] *Longley v PPB Entertainment Services Ltd* [2022] EWHC 977 (QB) at [94].

[30] Footnote inserted. *Chwee Kin Keong v Digilandmall.com Pte Ltd* [2006] 1 LRC 37, *Smith v Hughes, Hartog v Colin & Shields, Centrovincial Estates, Merril Lynch, OT Africa Line* and *Statoil*, none of which Ellenbogen J regarded as having settled the matter.

[31] *Longley* (n 29) at [94.10].

[32] ibid at [94.6].

obviously unreasonable they would be to the objective observer. It goes without saying that there should be an onus on those engaging in smart contracting to ensure, insofar as is possible, that their smart contract-forming code is capable of limiting the terms to which it will agree. But not only is it obvious to anyone who has ever done any coding (or indeed any contracting) that it is simply not possible for this to be an infallible exercise, neither is it inconsistent with the requirement for constructive knowledge on the part of the non-mistaken party. Programmers who know that they will be held to the standard of what a reasonable coder would expect in response to the conditions they set out will be more, rather than less, likely to take care with their code than they would be under a system in which their terms could never be avoided by another party, no matter how objectively unreasonable, simply because they could never be said actually to know that that other party was mistaken in relation to them.

In a world in which the automated formation of agreements is increasingly available and appealing to parties, allowing a doctrine as fundamental to the essence of contract as unilateral mistake to develop in a way that accommodates it seems sensible. Particularly given that English law is apparently at something of a crossroads in terms of its approach to the knowledge element of mistake, the time seems ripe to clarify the requirements of the doctrine. Conventional contracts left an open question in the law, largely because of the tension in contract law between the subjective expectations of parties (catered for by an actual knowledge requirement) and the need to find a common ground between those subjective positions (which is where the concession to constructive knowledge comes in). Smart contracts could be the reason why the law chooses now to answer that question definitively because objectivity is baked into their formation: the parties to such contracts choose to relinquish their subjective control over the terms of their future agreements (the absence of 'meeting on the trading floor') in favour of producing objectively and publicly verifiable parameters with which other similar parameters can interact. Subjective intention is left behind at the keyboard because coded instructions to computers are, at the most, deterministic and, at the least, stochastic.

This gives rise to the somewhat inevitable question of the extent to which rules for conventional contracts should be determined, or even influenced, by a novel contractual process that in some respects could be said to bear no resemblance to the core situations for which the law of contract was fashioned. Such an argument might have more force were it to be the case that the rules for those conventional contracts were either certain or long-established. But this, as we have seen, is not the case. The objective consistency that a constructive knowledge requirement aims for is as pertinent for contracts written on parchment as it is for those etched onto a hard drive. Objective assessments are, for good reason, a mainstay of English contract law. Suggesting that the possibility of one be made a certainty is hardly a tale of the unexpected.

5

Interpreting the Contract in the Light of Unexpected Events

CATHERINE MITCHELL*

I. Introduction

Contract interpretation has an obvious role to play when considering the effects of unexpected events on contract performance. When disputes arise over unexpected events, the first (and perhaps the only) step in resolving the dispute is to examine the contract to discover if the terms allocate the risk of the event to one of the parties. The finding that a contract is frustrated, and the parties excused from further performance, can follow only after it is first determined that the risk has not been allocated under the contract and the 'circumstances in which performance is called for would render it a thing radically different from that which was undertaken by the contract'.[1] In addition, courts may have to interpret general exculpatory contract provisions around force majeure, material adverse change and hardship in order to decide if they furnish an escape from the consequences of unexpected events. This chapter has a slightly different focus, however. We are not concerned with the interpretation of contract terms or contract doctrines specifically directed to the occurrence of unexpected events (frustration, force majeure and discharge of the contract are not dealt with in any detail here), but rather with the more general use of contract interpretation where the contract is silent or equivocal over the effect of those events.

When courts attempt to address unexpected events within the scheme of existing contract terms, one of two interpretative strategies will typically be relied upon. Both strategies are evident in the case law, though, as we will see, usually in different types of contracting context. The first strategy is the bad bargain approach. Here, subsequent events are deemed irrelevant to the question of what the contract means, even where the event has changed the performance environment

* Thanks to Paul Davies, Magda Raczynska and Andrew Twigger for helpful comments on an earlier version of this chapter.

[1] *Davis Contractors Ltd v Fareham UDC* [1956] UKHL 3, [1956] AC 696, 729 Lord Radcliffe.

significantly. This approach often leads to the extant contractual obligations being upheld, notwithstanding that the event has not been precisely identified or the risk of it unambiguously allocated to one of the parties in their agreement. The loss lies where it falls.[2] Upholding the contract in changed circumstances is usually justified by an appeal to the principle of *pacta sunt servanda* and the desire to prevent a party escaping the consequences of what has become a bad bargain. The bad bargain outcome generally follows from the application of plain meaning interpretation methods to the contract language and a finding that the contract is relatively complete. The bad bargain approach to unexpected events is amply demonstrated in the contract litigation arising from the COVID-19 outbreak. This is examined in section II.

The second strategy involves interpreting the contract to avoid the operation of the contract's ordinary meaning, effectively rescuing the party who would incur the loss from the unexpected event. When identifying party intentions in the face of the unexpected, courts often take their lead not from the language of the contract but from elements of the context, such as the contract's purposes, contractor-type and so on. This more contextual interpretative enquiry may result in a court reallocating a risk away from where it would otherwise fall. The use of contract interpretation to shift risk may be castigated as illegitimately changing the bargain, but it is sometimes necessary to achieve broader contract law aims, such as protecting the reasonable expectations of the parties or ensuring the underlying principles of contract are maintained. This is considered in section III. Section IV reflects on this divide between the bad bargain approach (following plain meaning interpretation) and the rescue (following contextual interpretation). It considers why contract interpretation appeals as a mechanism to resolve problems around unexpected events, and whether, given the recent pivot back to plain meaning interpretative approaches in courts, rescue attempts might be more transparently pursued, if at all, by the deployment or development of alternative doctrines, rather than the process of contract interpretation. Section V draws some conclusions.

II. Unexpected Events: Plain Meaning Interpretation and Bad Bargains

One option if a dispute arises over the effect of unexpected events on the contract is to enforce the contract terms as written. A court could examine the contract, conclude that the original risk allocation is preserved and the losses lie where they fall, even if this is entirely on the shoulders of only one of the parties. The court may be sympathetic, but nevertheless the parties will be held to the terms of their original agreement: *pacta sunt servanda*. There are good reasons why contract law

[2] PS Davies, 'Bad Bargains' (2019) 72 *Current Legal Problems* 253, 258.

should enforce the contract regardless, even where unexpected circumstances give rise to the bad bargain outcome for a party. One of the central functions of contracts and contract law is to create present certainty over future uncertainty, forestalling the possibility of the losing party reneging when events conspire to turn the agreement into a bad deal. Commercial parties in particular will be aware that performance will still be required even if conditions have changed. Notwithstanding the variety and severity of unexpected events (unpredicted global crises or wars; natural disasters; sudden market shifts; changes in the law), if an issue is generally foreseeable in a market, the parties would be expected to anticipate it (at least in broad terms) and allocate its associated risks in the contract. In addition, contracts are generally open to renegotiation and amendment by the parties to reflect a new reality. Sophisticated commercial parties would be expected to realise that contracts should be kept under review and processes for variation can be included in the contract terms. Courts may also have an expectation that the parties will have insurance against some risks. In light of these considerations, courts generally take a strict line with commercial contract enforcement, resisting the temptation to reinterpret the contract or employ judicial fixes in the wake of unexpected circumstances (the doctrine of frustration aside). The contract is an ex ante allocation of risks which should not be reallocated in line with ex post events, unless the contract specifically permits this.

The inclination to enforce the existing contract, come what may, is reflected in principles of contract interpretation that tend to treat contract meaning (and contract risk allocation) as fixed at the point of formation: unexpected events are of no consequence. In this way, like a statute, the original contract may still be applied, or still speak,[3] notwithstanding that the circumstances around performance turn out to be very different to those anticipated when the contract was created. Bounded rationality and finite resources may prevent the creation of a comprehensive contract that accurately forecasts all eventualities, yet this does not alter the legal perception that the agreement has a stable meaning – and a stable risk allocation – over time. Many of the legal rules around contract interpretation, such as the exclusion of evidence of prior negotiations or subsequent conduct, reflect a conception of contract meaning as static from the outset. Courts have consistently stressed that a contract's meaning is determined in the light of knowledge available to the parties at the time the contract was made.[4] A contract does not mean 'one thing the day it was signed, but by reason of subsequent

[3] 'A further feature of the modern contextual and purposive approach to statutory interpretation that has been focused on in a number of recent cases is the "always speaking" idea': Lord Burrows, *Statutory Interpretation in the Courts Today* (Sir Christopher Staughton Memorial Lecture 2022), University of Hertfordshire, 24 March 2022, at www.supremecourt.uk/uploads/sir_christopher_staughton_memorial_lecture_2022_3428298067.pdf, 6.

[4] 'Commercial common sense is only relevant to the extent of how matters would or could have been perceived by the parties, or by reasonable people in the position of the parties, as at the date that the contract was made' *Arnold v Britton* [2015] UKSC 36, [2016] AC 1619 [19] Lord Neuberger; '[E]vents and the actions of the parties after the conclusion of the contract are not relevant to its interpretation. The court has regard to the facts and circumstances which existed at the time the contract was made

events … something different a month or a year later'.[5] Thus contracts are expected to still speak in future circumstances, while simultaneously remaining impervious to future events.

The common law pivot back to plain meaning contract interpretation methods since the 2015 Supreme Court decision in *Arnold v Britton* exhibits a degree of tolerance towards the bad bargain outcome. In *Arnold*, long lease contracts for chalets in a holiday park contained a provision for service charge increases of around 10 per cent per year compounded. The service charge clause anticipated that the sustained period of high inflation experienced in the UK from the 1970s to the early 1990s (when the contracts were made) would continue. Instead, an extended phase of low inflation from the 1990s onwards led to rapidly increasing service charges that bore little relation to the lessor's actual costs in maintaining the site. Lord Neuberger confirmed that this interpretation of the effect of the clause was correct, despite the disproportionate financial liability inflicted on the lessees as a result. He re-emphasised the 'importance of the language of the provision'[6] and defended the bad bargain outcome:

> [A] court should be very slow to reject the natural meaning of a provision as correct simply because it appears to be a very imprudent term for one of the parties to have agreed, even ignoring the benefit of wisdom of hindsight. The purpose of interpretation is to identify what the parties have agreed, not what the court thinks that they should have agreed … Accordingly, when interpreting a contract a judge should avoid re-writing it in an attempt to assist an unwise party or to penalise an astute party.[7]

In the bad bargain approach, if the contract wording appears clear, then the fact that the contract is predicated on a particular set of expectations and assumptions, which turn out to be wholly incorrect, is neither here nor there. The losing party has simply bet the wrong way on the outcomes from future events or market movements.

Much of the contract case law arising out of the COVID-19 pandemic adopted this strict approach to contract interpretation and enforcement. Many of the disputes reaching trial concerned equipment leasing contracts and commercial tenancies of premises that could not legally operate during the various lockdowns.[8] The measures taken to curb the spread of a highly infectious disease

and which were known or reasonably available to both parties' *National Commercial Bank Jamaica Ltd v NCB Staff Association* [2024] UKPC 2 [32] Lord Hodge.

[5] *Whitworth Street Estates (Manchester) Ltd v James Miller and Partners Ltd* [1970] AC 583, 603 Lord Reid.

[6] *Arnold v Britton* (n 4) [17]. See also Lord Hodge in *National Commercial Bank Jamaica Ltd* (n 4), stating that 'the court's task is to ascertain the objective meaning of the language which the parties have chosen to express their agreement, having regard to the contract as a whole … the court does not depart from an interpretation of the natural language of words just because the contractual arrangement has proven to be a bad bargain for one of the parties' [32].

[7] *Arnold v Britton* (n 4) [20].

[8] See generally J Morgan, 'Frustration and the Pandemic' (2021) 137 *LQR* 563. Other common law jurisdictions have taken a strict line to the interpretation of contracts affected by the pandemic. In Canada see *Cineplex Inc v Cineworld Group plc* 2021 ONSC 8016; in Australia see *Laundy Hotels (Quarry) Pty Ltd v Dyco Hotels Pty Ltd* [2023] HCA 6.

may have been unprecedented and unpredictable, but contractual obligations – notably those involving payments of rent – were enforced unabated. Pleas that leases were frustrated or that rent payments were suspended during the pandemic, either because of a failure of basis or the operation of an implied term, were mostly rejected by courts. In one case, an airline that could not operate flights because of the various travel restrictions imposed by governments remained liable for payments under the aircraft leasing agreement. The contract was 'drafted to make it clear that [the lessee's] obligation to pay rent continued in almost any conceivable circumstances'.[9] Similarly, in cases involving entertainment venues, it was held that tenants bore the risks of closure and loss of revenue resulting from the COVID lockdowns.[10] This followed from a plain meaning interpretation of the contract, including its rent cesser clauses.[11] These clauses were interpreted as applying in the case of physical damage to the property or destruction by an insured risk which, on the wording of the clause, did not include pandemics.[12] There was no gap in the contract to be filled by an implied term or the principles of unjust enrichment (of the landlord), as this would subvert the contract allocation of risk.[13] Thus, the existing terms were interpreted to place the risk (whether foreseen or not) that the premises could not be used for their intended purposes on the tenant.

A strict approach towards the enforcement of leases affected by unanticipated circumstances is nothing new.[14] In *Canary Wharf (BP4) T1 Ltd v European Medicines Agency*, it was held that a lease for premises to house the EMA, an agency of the EU, was not frustrated by Brexit. The EMA had 'the capacity, post the withdrawal of the United Kingdom from the European Union, to continue to use and/or dispose of the Premises and that it continues to have the capacity to pay rent (and perform its other continuing obligations) under the Lease'.[15] One might question whether the strict enforcement of lease obligations following an unexpected event involves an *interpretation* of the contract. If one takes the view that interpretation is only required when the language of the contract is problematic because it is vague, ambiguous or mistaken,[16] then upholding and enforcing the contract's 'ordinary meaning' is arguably not an instance of contract interpretation at all; the courts are not exercising judgement over contract meaning, but simply doing what the contract tells them to do.

[9] *Salam Air SAOC v Latam Airlines Group SA* [2020] EWHC 2414 (Comm) [51].

[10] *Bank of New York Mellon (International) Ltd v Cine-UK Ltd; London Trocadero (2015) llp v Picturehouse Cinemas Ltd and others* [2022] EWCA Civ 1021 (CA) [138].

[11] *London Trocadero* (n 10) [126].

[12] ibid [126].

[13] ibid [147]. A majority of the Supreme Court recently affirmed that unjust enrichment cannot be used to undermine the contractual allocation of risk: *Barton v Morris* [2023] UKSC 3, [2023] AC 684.

[14] *Paradine v Jane* (1647) Aleyn 26: a lessee was still liable for rent even though he was forcibly evicted from the land for three years during the English civil war 'because he might have provided against it by his contract'.

[15] *Canary Wharf (BP4) T1 Ltd & Ors v European Medicines Agency* [2019] EWHC 335 (Ch) [166].

[16] N MacCormick, *Rhetoric and the Rule of Law* (Oxford, OUP, 2005) 121–22; D Patterson, 'Interpretation in Law' (2005) 42 *San Diego Law Review* 685, 686 and 688–90.

The idea that upholding the contract's plain meaning is 'anti-interpretative' is attractive but misguided. A judge's decision to apply the contract terms and enforce a bad bargain still reflects interpretative choices operating at a more general and abstract level than the specific, detailed contract in issue. The strict approach to the enforcement of leases reflects the legal conception and interpretation of commercial tenancies as fundamentally competitive. Commercial leases involve adversarial relationships where landlords and tenants approach the lease 'from their own commercial standpoint … the [l]ease represents the outcome not of a common purpose but of rival negotiations driven by *different* objectives'.[17] The lease agreement is interpreted as a discrete and arm's length transaction where the legal obligations are entirely separate and isolated from other aspects of the business relationship.[18] The lease *is* the relationship, and its constituent commitments are comprehensively set out in the terms. Context is irrelevant because leases have no context, they are 'just leases'.[19]

The characterisation of the lease contract as discrete and lacking any wider material context informs a key interpretative finding in the COVID cases: the contracts in dispute are complete; there are no gaps and there is no reason to depart from the risk allocation specified, even if the precise loss-causing event is unforeseen. The bad bargain outcome is likely influenced by other background factors: the assumption that the parties are advised by competent professionals, that they are sophisticated businesspeople, and that the terms are intended to be detailed, definitive and conclusive, with no space for uncertainties. The silence of the contract in relation to the event that has occurred may be immaterial. In a contract that does not specify what is to happen in a particular eventuality, then the outcome may be that nothing happens, and what *is* stated in the contract, however attenuated, governs the outcome.[20] The contract makes its intentions clear by the *absence* of any provision dealing with the unexpected circumstances.[21]

The contract absolutism evident in the covid lease cases is not a universal response to contracts affected by the unexpected. There is judicial dicta to the effect that parties must make it clear that their contract is intended to apply to unexpected or unforeseen events; otherwise, the contract's provisions will *not* apply. In *Bank of Credit and Commerce International SA (in liquidation) v Ali* Lord Clyde stated, 'Generally people will say what they mean. Generally if they intend their agreement to cover the unknown or the unforeseeable, they will make it clear that

[17] *Canary Wharf* (n 15) [218] emphasis in original.

[18] IR Macneil, *The Relational Theory of Contract: Selected Works of Ian Macneil*, D Campbell (ed) (London, Sweet & Maxwell, 2001) 154.

[19] *London Trocadero* (n 10) [90], [150].

[20] This was the thrust of Lord Hoffmann's reasoning on implied terms in *Attorney General of Belize v Belize Telecom Ltd* [2009] UKPC 10, [2009] 1 WLR 1988 [17]–[18].

[21] For an example, see *Barton v Morris* [2023] UKSC 3, [2023] AC 684, concerning an oral agreement whereby a commission of £1.2 million was payable to the claimant if they introduced a purchaser who paid £6.5 million for a property. When the property sold for £6 million (the agreement was silent on this) no commission was payable.

their intention is to extend the agreement to cover such cases.'[22] A silent contract may be insufficient to indicate this intention to cover the unknown. As we see below, in *BCCI v Ali* the supposed absence of a clear intention that the agreement applied in unforeseen circumstances, together with various elements of context and principle, led the House of Lords to depart from the contract terms agreed by the parties. This was notwithstanding that the terms had a clear meaning that, on the surface at least, encompassed the change in conditions. In some contexts then, a seemingly complete contract will be interpreted as containing a gap in relation to the unexpected event. When this happens, courts will often refer to a wider range of factors beyond the text to fill the gap and rescue a contracting party from the consequences of the unexpected event. We examine this in the next section.

III. Unexpected Events: Contextual Interpretation and Rescue

It is inevitable that courts may have to interpret and apply the contract terms to unforeseen circumstances. We have noted that bounded rationality militates against the formulation of a complete contract that anticipates every conceivable contingency. In *Bromarin AB v IMD Investments Ltd*, Chadwick LJ noted that a contract that only anticipates event A may nevertheless be interpreted as applying in the case of event B, even when B is not expected.[23] He recognised the artificiality of the exercise, but observed that

> [i]t is an exercise which requires the court to look at the whole agreement which the parties made, the words which they used and the circumstances in which they used them; and to ask what should reasonable parties be taken to have intended by the use of those words in that agreement, made in those circumstances, in relation to this event which they did not in fact foresee.[24]

There are various interpretative techniques a court can draw upon to identify party intention in relation to unexpected events. Perhaps the most usual practice is to refer to the rest of the contract. In relation to this, Lord Neuberger in *Arnold v Britton* stated

> in some cases, an event subsequently occurs which was plainly not intended or contemplated by the parties, judging from the language of their contract. In such a case, if it is clear what the parties would have intended, the court will give effect to that intention.[25]

[22] *Bank of Credit and Commerce International SA (in liquidation) v Ali* [2001] UKHL 8, [2002] 1 AC 251 [79] Lord Clyde.

[23] 'The task of the court is to decide, in the light of the agreement that the parties made, what they must have been taken to have intended in relation to the event, event "B", which they did not contemplate' *Bromarin AB v IMD Investments Ltd* [1999] STC 301, 310 Chadwick LJ.

[24] ibid 310 Chadwick LJ.

[25] *Arnold v Britton* (n 4) [22] Lord Neuberger.

It is not easy to establish the parties' intentions regarding an event that is not anticipated by their contract. Sometimes this interpretative task is problematic even if the contract appears to provide the answer, usually because elements of the context (or judicial conscience) suggest that the contract answer is not appropriate. Consideration of the broader context may lead a court to reallocate the risk away from where a strict interpretation of the terms suggests it falls, essentially rescuing a party from the effects of an unexpected event and a bad bargain.

Needless to say, the arguments for departing from the bad bargain outcome in favour of a rescue can be very finely balanced. In *Bank of Credit and Commerce International SA (in liquidation) v Ali*, an employee of a bank, Mr Naeem, was made redundant following a reorganisation of the bank's business. In addition to the various redundancy payments to which he was entitled, he received an extra payment in return for signing a release form. The form stated that, 'the Applicant agrees to accept the terms set out in the documents attached in full and final settlement of all or any claims … of whatsoever nature that exists *or may exist*'.[26] Unexpectedly (at least from Mr Naeem's point of view) and very publicly, BCCI later collapsed amidst scandal when the bank's involvement in money laundering and other financial crimes was exposed. Blameless employees who were unaware of the bank's criminal activities were nevertheless tainted by association and found it difficult to find alternative employment in the banking sector. A further element of surprise, given the long-standing authority of *Addis v Gramophone Co Ltd*,[27] was that the House of Lords had recognised in another decision that, in principle, innocent ex-employees who faced difficulties in the labour market because of their connection to the corrupt bank would have a claim for 'stigma damages'.[28] The issue in *BCCI v Ali* was whether Mr Naeem, and others in a like position, were precluded from pursuing a stigma claim by signing the release, the claim being undeveloped and unpredicted at the time of their redundancy.

In plain language terms, the wording of the release appears unambiguous, and Mr Naeem has no claim. One might speculate that the precise purpose of the clause was to circumvent liability both for: (i) unknown employment-related claims that might be created in the future; and (ii) known employment claims that Mr Naeem was either unaware that he had or was unqualified to pursue at the time of the release. Even if the release is interpreted contextually – the context being redundancy and the end of the employment relationship – the stigma claim seems to be excluded (as opposed to claims unrelated to employment, such as a personal injury claim against the bank, or a claim brought in the capacity as a depositor). Other elements of the background also suggested the clause meant exactly what it said.

[26] *BCCI v Ali* (n 22) [3] emphasis added.

[27] *Addis v Gramophone Co Ltd* [1909] UKHL 1, [1909] AC 488.

[28] *Malik and Mahmud v Bank of Credit and Commerce International SA (in liquidation)* [1997] UKHL 23, [1997] 3 All ER 1.

The purpose of release clauses is to achieve finality and certainty for both parties. It underlines that the relationship is over and there are no further responsibilities or liabilities arising. As in this case, some benefit, such as an enhanced compensation payment, is usually given in return for the release. The employee has not been made to shoulder additional risk without receiving something in return. These considerations supported the ordinary meaning of the term, with the effect that Mr Naeem was prevented from pursuing the novel claim for stigma damages. Mr Naeem had simply made an agreement that he later had cause to regret – a bad bargain.

Despite all these considerations, and using what was described as a contextual interpretation of the release, by a 4:1 majority (Lord Hoffmann dissenting) the House of Lords concluded that the release did not prevent a claim for stigma damages. Lord Clyde suggested that a literal reading would imply that the release sought to exclude liability for all claims of whatever nature, whether employment-related or not. Since that cannot have been the intention of the parties, the literal meaning of the release was rejected.[29] The court was then able to reach an alternative interpretation based on the operation of more general policy matters,[30] including that courts should be slow to infer that a party intended to surrender rights of which they were unaware without clear language (note that silence was insufficient here),[31] the appropriate balance between the right given up and the payment given in return,[32] and who, in the circumstances, bore the risk of a change in the law (on the wording of the release, this appeared to be Mr Naeem).[33] Lord Hoffmann in his dissent also considered the wider background and concluded that the parties intended the release to 'mean what it says' in relation to any claims arising out of the employment relationship.[34] In his view, the majority had erred in confusing the question of what the release meant with the question of whether, in the light of their conduct, BCCI (in reality, the bank's liquidators) should be able to rely on the release in order to resist the stigma claim.[35] Lord Hoffmann expressed here the limits on contract interpretation as a rescue device. We return to this point in section IV below.

The decision in *BCCI v Ali* might be regarded as an outlier. The shocking circumstances surrounding the bank's collapse, the dire implications for the future employment prospects of innocent ex-employees, and the perceived justice of the

[29] *BCCI v Ali* (n 22) [80] Lord Clyde.

[30] Lord Nicholls was perhaps more open about the role of policy in the case at [35]. In an interview given later, Lord Hoffmann criticised the decision of the majority, regarding it as an example of 'equitable construction' motivated by a desire to achieve a fair outcome: K Gibbons, 'A Conversation with Lord Hoffmann' (2010) 4 *Law and Financial Markets Review* 242, 244–45.

[31] *BCCI v Ali* (n 22) [10] Lord Bingham.

[32] ibid [34]–[35] Lord Nicholls.

[33] ibid [35] Lord Nicholls.

[34] *BCCI v Ali* (n 22) [65] Lord Hoffmann. See also J Wightman, 'Beyond Custom: Contract, Contexts, and the Recognition of Implicit Understandings' in D Campbell, H Collins and J Wightman (eds), *Implicit Dimensions of Contract* (Oxford, Hart Publishing, 2003) 143, 158.

[35] *BCCI v Ali* (n 22) [37], [49] Lord Hoffmann.

case combined to make rescue appear the appropriate choice. But *BCCI v Ali* is not an isolated incident of rescue pursued through contextual contract interpretation. In *Aberdeen City Council v Stewart Milne Group Ltd*,[36] the interpretation problem concerned the meaning to be given to the phrase 'gross sale proceeds' when calculating an uplift payment due to the council following the sale of council land to the defendant developer. The Supreme Court looked to the internal context of the agreement, notably how an uplift payment to the council was calculated in events other than outright sale of the land, to conclude that the phrase 'gross sale proceeds' meant the proceeds from a sale conducted at arm's length in the open market, and not the actual proceeds realised from the unanticipated (from the council's point of view) sale of the land at substantial undervalue to an associate company of the defendant. In failing to follow a plain meaning interpretative approach and leaving the council to their bad bargain, the decision was condemned in some quarters as rescuing a party from the consequences of their own folly by a spurious reference to commercial sense,[37] giving the feckless contractor the benefit of a deal they did not make.[38]

As with *BCCI v Ali*, the *Aberdeen City Council* decision is defensible within a contextual contract interpretation regime but less defensible in a plain meaning one. A contextual approach takes enquiries about the parties' intentions outside the contract language and into a wider background (including elements of commercial sense), allowing the Supreme Court to conclude that although the contract did not state expressly that 'gross sale proceeds' assumed an arm's length sale at market value, this was what the contract meant. One might speculate that an essential element of context in the case was that the contractor is a cash-strapped local council, not a commercial contractor acting solely for profit. But if this distinction between contractor-types is material, or if the rescue is motivated by a desire to avoid injustice, or to address the bad faith of the defendant in seizing upon the literal meaning of a poorly drafted contract to capture an unintended advantage, this does not appear on the face of the judgment or as part of its core reasoning. Hence, the attempt to interpret an existing contract contextually to deal with unexpected circumstances can be criticised as lacking transparency, particularly where the plain meaning of the contract is overridden in the process.

A more defendable strategy in circumventing the effects of contract wording after an unexpected event is to rely on the principle that contracts should be interpreted in the light of knowledge available to the parties at the time the contract was made. This principle may allow a court to evade the bad bargain outcome. *Lloyds TSB Foundation for Scotland v Lloyds Banking Group plc*[39] concerned the

[36] *Aberdeen City Council v Stewart Milne Group Ltd* [2011] UKSC 56, 2012 SCLR 114.

[37] M Hogg, 'Fundamental Issues for Reform of the Law of Contractual Interpretation' (2011) 15 *Edinburgh Law Review* 406, 419.

[38] ibid 420.

[39] *Lloyds TSB Foundation for Scotland v Lloyds Banking Group plc* [2013] UKSC 3, [2013] 1 WLR 366.

interpretation to be placed on a deed created in 1997. The financial consequences of the deed were radically altered five years later when an 'unthinkable',[40] 'unforeseen and unforeseeable' change was made to accounting rules.[41] The effect of the change was to transform what was a £10 billion loss from the ordinary trading activities of Lloyds Banking Group into a £1 billion gain following the group's acquisition of a struggling competitor during the global financial crisis of 2008–09. Since the gain was included in the deed's formula for calculating the annual payment due from Lloyds Bank to Lloyds Foundation (a charity), the Foundation claimed that the plain meaning of the deed was that Lloyds Bank owed them some £3.5 million on the 2009 accounts. By contrast, under the accounting rules in place in 1997 when the contract was created, the 2009 payment due from Lloyds Bank to the charity amounted to around £39,000.

Resolving this problem through contract interpretation was not straightforward. Lord Clarke conceded that the natural meaning of the deed suggested that the Foundation's interpretation was correct.[42] But plain meaning was not the appropriate interpretative method to adopt in the case. Lord Mance stated that the deed should be placed in the legal and accounting context at the time it was made, and the law at that time was that profit and loss accounts reflected a firm's ordinary activities before taxation.[43] On this basis, the deed was to be interpreted as if the gain on acquisition was left out of the accounts.[44] It might be argued that the fact that accounting rules had changed previously meant it was not completely 'unthinkable' that they would change again, and in a manner detrimental to one of the parties. Lord Clarke alluded to the fact that, in a long-term contract such as this, changes to accounting standards were likely.[45] Nevertheless, the Foundation's case for the obvious meaning of the term was criticised as a 'mechanical application' of the relevant clauses of the deed, when a contextual and purposive interpretation method was called for.[46] In adopting a contextual approach, therefore, Lloyds Bank was rescued from the consequences of the strict operation of the contract wording, and a bad bargain outcome averted.

IV. Questions Surrounding an Interpretative Approach to Unexpected Events

The different interpretative responses to unexpected events outlined above demonstrate that context matters. The range of interpretative methods at a court's

[40] ibid [1].
[41] ibid [16].
[42] ibid [48].
[43] ibid [7] and Companies Act 1985 Sch 4, para 3(6).
[44] ibid [23]; see also [34] Lord Hope.
[45] ibid [48] Lord Clarke.
[46] ibid [21] and [31] Lord Mance, who criticised the lower court for interpreting the clause literally.

disposal means it is possible to justify either the bad bargain or the rescue outcome depending on the contract background. Contract interpretation is appealing as a technique for resolving problems of unexpected events precisely because of this malleability. As Lord Hodge observed in *Wood v Capita Insurance Services Ltd*:

> The extent to which [textualism or contextualism] will assist the court in its task will vary according to the circumstances of the particular agreement or agreements. Some agreements may be successfully interpreted principally by textual analysis … The correct interpretation of other contracts may be achieved by a greater emphasis on the factual matrix.[47]

Reliance on contextual interpretation to get around problems generated by unexpected events also reflects the lack of options available to a judge between the extremes of the frustration doctrine and the bad bargain outcome. That said, given the recent re-emphasis in the senior courts on the importance of enforcing the language of the contract, we can speculate that it may now be more difficult to achieve rescue outcomes through contract interpretation when the unexpected strikes. If so, what alternatives to interpretation might be available? In *Lloyds TSB Foundation*, Lord Hope discussed (obiter) the possibility of equitable adjustment of the contract to resolve the case, rather than interpretation. Counsel for the bank argued that, had the Foundation's interpretation been correct, there was the possibility of equitable adjustment

> where the alteration in the circumstances in which the contract came to be performed was affected in a material way by supervening events for which neither party was responsible. There had to be a supervening event which was not foreseen and was not foreseeable when the contract was made, and that event must affect the substance of the contract.[48]

On counsel's argument, the doctrine of equitable adjustment followed by degrees from the doctrine of frustration and the principles of unjust enrichment (that is, in cases where the contract has been affected by unexpected events causing loss to one party or a windfall to the other, but the contract was 'not quite' frustrated). Lord Hope doubted that such a doctrine existed in Scots law (and it is even less likely that it exists in English law[49]), and in any case the doctrine was superfluous when contract interpretation is contextual.[50] This suggests that if contract interpretation now proceeds by prioritising the natural meaning of the contract language (rather than context), then alternative legal doctrines may be necessary

[47] *Wood v Capita Insurance Services Ltd* [2017] UKSC 24, [2017] AC 1173 [13].

[48] *Lloyds TSB Foundation* (n 39) [39].

[49] For contracts governed by English law, where the contract is frustrated, the provisions of the Law Reform (Frustrated Contracts) Act 1943 permit a court to order a financial adjustment between the parties which may reverse any unjust enrichment arising from the discharge of the contract.

[50] *Lloyds TSB Foundation* (n 39) [47], see also [37], [38] Lord Hope. For an argument that the doctrine of equitable adjustment may exist in Scots contract law, see H MacQueen '"Coronavirus Contract Law" in Scotland' in E Hondius, M Santos Silva, A Nicolussi, P Salvador Coderch, C Wendehorst and F Zoll (eds), *Coronavirus and the Law in Europe* (Cambridge, Intersentia, 2021) 491, 504ff.

to deal with unexpected circumstances. As well as equitable adjustment, options here might include implied terms, partial or temporary frustration,[51] or other doctrines yet to be developed.

Certainly, there are doubts about whether the problems arising in cases like *BCCI v Ali, Aberdeen* and *Lloyds* should be resolved through contract interpretation or through the operation of some other rule-set. Judicial reservations concerning the limits on interpretation in contract are expressed throughout the case law. In *Aberdeen City Council*, Lord Clarke thought that linguistically the council should probably not succeed. He preferred to formulate an implied term in favour of the council, though he conceded the outcome was the same.[52] Similarly, a majority of the Court of Appeal in *BCCI v Ali* took the view that the material issue was not the interpretation of the release clause (which was relatively straightforward) but whether the bank (liquidators) should be permitted to rely on the release given the circumstances of the bank's collapse. In light of the bank's behaviour (at the time of the redundancy, senior bank officers knew of the financial crimes committed by the bank, though Mr Naeem was unaware), the Court of Appeal decided that equity would intervene, rendering it unconscionable to allow the bank to rely on the release.[53] In distinguishing the issue of contract meaning from the issue of whether that meaning should prevent Mr Naeem's claim, the Court of Appeal accepted that contract interpretation could only go so far. It was necessary to rely on an alternative doctrine to resolve the difficulties presented by the facts.

The question of the limits on what can be achieved through contract interpretation was raised, albeit obliquely, in *Financial Conduct Authority v Arch Insurance (UK) Ltd.*[54] One aspect of this complex litigation concerned the interpretation of disease clauses in business interruption insurance policies taken out by firms that were later forced to close during the COVID pandemic. In the main, policies did not specifically refer to the COVID outbreak or lockdowns. Precise policy wording varied between insurance companies, eight of whom were represented in the litigation, but policies typically stated that cover was provided for business interruption 'following any occurrence of a notifiable disease within the vicinity [or a specified radius, for example, 25 miles] of the premises'. Insurers initially resisted claims under the policies, arguing that the disease clauses limited cover to instances where there was a causal connection between the localised (that is, within 25 miles) outbreak of the notifiable disease

[51] There is no doctrine of partial or temporary frustration in English law, although in *James B Fraser & Co Ltd v Denny Mott & Dickson Ltd* [1944] UKHL 3, 1944 SC (HL) 35, Viscount Simon opined (obiter) 'it may be that the supervening impossibility of fulfilling some minute provision may not be regarded as going to the length of preventing substantial performance of the contract as a whole', 40. See also MacQueen, ibid 500–501.

[52] *Aberdeen City Council* [31]–[33] Lord Clarke.

[53] *Bank of Credit and Commerce International SA (in liquidation) v Ali* [2001] EWCA Civ 1438, [2000] ICR 1410 (CA) [33] Sir Richard Scott VC and [81] Chadwick LJ.

[54] *Financial Conduct Authority v Arch Insurance (UK) Ltd and others* [2021] UKSC 1, [2021] AC 649. For the first instance decision see [2020] EWHC 2448 (Comm), [2020] Lloyd's Rep IR 527 (Butcher J and Flaux LJ).

(COVID-19) and the business closure that resulted in loss. To put this another way, the individual case of COVID within the radius had to be a proximate cause of the loss. Since many of the businesses had closed because of the nationwide lockdown, rather than 'following [an] occurrence' of the disease within the specified radius, there could be no cover. The loss would have occurred irrespective of the local position as a result of the lockdowns which were triggered by COVID cases both within and outside the radius. Thus, the 'but for' test of causation was not satisfied.[55] The Financial Conduct Authority brought a test case against several insurers to determine whether this interpretation was correct.

The case pitted the reasonable expectations of the insured about cover against the strict operation of the wording of the clause. Clearly both the High Court and Supreme Court wanted to avoid the conclusion that the businesses were not covered, particularly if that resulted from what would be perceived as a mechanistic application of the contract language.[56] Though all the courts hearing the case wanted to circumvent the bad bargain outcome for policy-holders, they differed on whether this could be achieved solely through interpretation of the disease clauses in the policies. The majority of the Supreme Court (Lord Hamblen, Lord Leggatt and Lord Reed) took a two-stage approach to the question of insurer liability. The first stage was interpretation of the disease clause. Here, the plain language of the clause indicated that the general COVID outbreak was not part of the insured peril,[57] and there was no ambiguity about this: 'As a matter of plain language, the clause covers only cases of illness resulting from COVID-19 that occur within the 25-mile radius specified in the clause.'[58] This shifted the reasoning on insurer liability away from the interpretation of the disease clause to the second stage: the 'crucial' causation question.[59] The Supreme Court considered that the clause could cover losses resulting from the localised occurrence in combination with the wider pandemic, even if the localised occurrence on its own could not be shown to cause the business losses. In taking this line, the majority of the Supreme Court watered down the 'proximate cause' requirement established in insurance law.[60] For the majority, the question of insurer liability could not be resolved through interpretation of the disease clause (if anything, interpretation tended to support the insurers' case). Instead, attention to the rules around causation was required.

[55] See *FCA v Arch* (SC) (n 54) at [197] for the rejection of this argument.

[56] This is not to say that it is permissible for a court to depart from the contract language when interpreting business interruption clauses in the light of the COVID outbreak: see *Carbis Bay Hotel Ltd v American International Group Ltd* [2025] EWHC 1041 (Comm) where a disease clause that set out the specific infectious diseases covered by the insurance policy (which included SARS but not COVID-19) meant business interruption losses resulting from COVID were not covered. A material factor in this interpretation was that COVID-19 was unheard of when the policy began [39].

[57] *FCA v Arch* (SC) (n 54) [64].

[58] ibid [71].

[59] ibid [161].

[60] *Orient-Express Hotels Ltd v Assicurazioni Generali SpA (trading as Generali Global Risk)* [2010] EWHC 1186 (Comm), [2010] Lloyd's Rep IR 531.

The minority in the Supreme Court (Lord Briggs and Lord Hodge), and the High Court before it, adopted a more purposive interpretative method to reach the same conclusion that the businesses were covered. Lord Briggs and Lord Hodge emphasised the pandemic context rather than the linguistic meaning of the clause. The context incorporated matters such as the unprecedented effect of the COVID outbreak, the response of the authorities to it, and the expectations of policy-holders. Lord Briggs remarked

> construction requires the court to put itself into the mind of the reasonably informed reader of the contract in issue, so as to understand what that hypothetical person (rather than an insurance lawyer) would think that the parties meant by the words which they have used, in the relevant context. To my mind, that person would ask: do clauses with the radius limitations provide cover for the adverse business consequences of a national reaction to a national pandemic disease?[61]

Lord Briggs and Lord Hodge regarded this as a more straightforward route to the finding that the businesses were covered (subject to the wording of the individual policies). The minority noted that

> the reasoning adopted by the majority might be regarded by the hypothetical reader as somewhat circuitous. Its end product is, as already noted, that cover is effectively provided for business interruption caused by a national reaction to a national pandemic, provided that it extends within the radius. If so, the reader might ask, why not interpret it as doing so directly?[62]

The minority's interpretation also accorded with the 'spirit and intent' of the relevant policies, whereas the insurers' more formalistic approach to the wording of the clause tended to render cover largely illusory in the circumstances when it was most needed.[63]

Though one might criticise the minority judgments for using interpretation as a conduit through which to channel considerations surrounding the substantive justice of the policy-holders' case, the minority's purposive-contextual interpretative approach in *FCA v Arch* does offer advantages. It is perhaps least disruptive to the existing rules of contract law and insurance law. Disturbing previously well-established principles (such as those around causation) may cause uncertainty in the market and trigger further litigation. Deploying contract interpretation to resolve problems of extraordinary circumstances makes the outcome highly fact-sensitive (which the judgment in *Arch* almost certainly is) and thus more readily distinguishable from other cases. A result that follows from an interpretation of the contract is more easily contained within the law precisely because it is the most direct way of reaching a decision on the facts. The minority's reasoning also reflects the likely expectations of a 'reasonable person' or 'reasonable/ordinary

[61] ibid [322] Lord Briggs.
[62] ibid [324] Lord Briggs.
[63] ibid [316] Lord Briggs.

policy-holder' that cover was in place, rather than the expectations of an insurance lawyer drilling down into the precise syntactical meaning of the clause in order to deny liability under the policy. The contract may not speak overtly to the exact circumstances of the COVID outbreak and lockdowns, but by interpreting it contextually and purposively, the agreement has not 'run out'.

The majority's plain meaning approach to interpretation also has benefits. Though less flexible, it is consistent with the current direction of travel of the English law on contract interpretation. In refusing to treat the issue of insurer liability as wholly a matter of the interpretation of the disease clause, the majority of the Supreme Court in *Arch* was perhaps keen to preserve the plain meaning interpretative method as the relevant default, notwithstanding the extraordinary circumstances around the pandemic and what must have been a strong inclination to adopt more results-oriented reasoning. The majority's more restrictive approach to interpretation is also appropriate in the context of insurance, where the wording of clauses is critical to establishing the level of cover provided and the extent of the insurer's liability under the policy. A more flexible, contextual interpretative method may be censured as retrospectively altering the allocation of risk presented by the contract on the grounds of some ill-defined notion of justice or fairness. This concern was expressed by Lord Sumption in a minority judgment in *Zurich Insurance PLC UK Branch v International Energy Group Ltd*[64] concerning insurers' liability for mesothelioma cases and the scope of the principle derived from *Fairchild v Glenhaven Funeral Services Ltd*.[65] Lord Sumption felt the majority were allowing the contractual allocation of risk in insurance policies to be overridden by a general policy of ensuring adequate compensation for victims.[66]

The majority's plain meaning approach to the interpretation of disease clauses in *Arch* also keeps contract interpretation in its place. It may be that, pragmatically, the process of contract interpretation in law should be limited to determining the linguistic meaning of the text, as well as resolving instances of genuine ambiguity. Determining the linguistic meaning of the contract terms may not dispose of the case, however. A second step – sometimes called construction – may be necessary to determine the legal effect of the linguistic meaning as applied to the particular facts. This two-stage approach differentiates between two issues: (i) what the contract ordinarily means; and (ii) what should be done about what the contract means. In other words, the issue of interpretation involves an 'is' question (what *is* the meaning of the text?), but construction involves a 'should' question (*should* that meaning apply here?)[67] Finding the answer to the 'is' question does

[64] *Zurich Insurance PLC UK Branch v International Energy Group Ltd (Rev 2)* [2015] UKSC 33, [2016] AC 509.

[65] *Fairchild v Glenhaven Funeral Services Ltd* [2002] UKHL 22, [2003] AC 32.

[66] 'The liabilities of an insurer are wholly contractual. The answer to the questions now before the court necessarily depend on the construction of the contract and on nothing else' *Zurich Insurance* [113] Lord Sumption; see also [155].

[67] See F Schauer, 'Constructing Interpretation' (2021) 101 *Boston University Law Review* 103, 112–13.

not necessarily imply the 'should' question has also been answered, since they involve separate enquiries which proceed under different criteria.[68] Once plain meaning is fixed upon after interpretation, the second stage concerns whether the ordinary or linguistic meaning is allowed to dictate the outcome, or whether that outcome should be avoided based on other considerations outside the text.[69] Of course, for contextualists it is artificial to divide interpretation into stages in this manner: context or other external considerations are part of what it means 'to interpret' the text at any stage. There is no such thing as a plain meaning that is not also a contextual meaning. For textualists, on the other hand, the enquiry about what a judge should do is generally over after the first stage of determining ordinary meaning, unless some other legal rule is applicable.

The validity of this distinction between interpretation and construction will not be considered in any detail here. We note only that the distinction is consistent with the modern tendency of English courts to stress the limits on interpretation and, in particular, to distinguish between interpreting the contract text (resolving textual ambiguity) and rectifying it (correcting mistakes in the text) or implying terms (supplementing the text).[70] However artificial it may be in theory to confine interpretation to a limited textual enquiry, doing so may serve various practical purposes in contract law – it upholds doctrinal boundaries, maintains doctrinal integrity, prevents every contentious issue being reduced to a matter of contract interpretation (raising the risk of judicial interference), and dispenses with the fiction that (reasonable) contracting parties could have any particular intentions over circumstances that they could not possibly have foreseen.

While there are benefits in artificially limiting the scope of contract interpretation, there are also drawbacks. If courts wish to deter the use of contract interpretation to rescue parties from the consequences of unexpected events, then it may be necessary to develop alternative doctrinal solutions operating on a spectrum between enforcement of the bad bargain at one extreme and the application of frustration at the other. The non-interpretative justifications for decisions in *Aberdeen City Council* (implied terms) or *BCCI v Ali* (unconscionability) may take on renewed significance. It might be necessary for courts to engage in openly policy-based reasoning concerning how unanticipated risks should be allocated. A principle of good faith could be developed, or a judicial power to vary, to prevent a party from exploiting a plain meaning interpretation of the contract in changed circumstances in order to secure an unintended advantage or fortuitous windfall (as in *Lloyds TSB Foundation*). The problem is that doctrinal development along these lines seems highly unlikely. In the commercial sphere, the pressure for legal reform tends to emanate from the bottom up (from commercial contractors themselves) rather than from the top down (judicial innovation in the common law). One need only look at the COVID episode to see this. The COVID outbreak

[68] ibid 118.

[69] ibid 120.

[70] *Marks and Spencer plc v BNP Paribas Securities Services Trust Company (Jersey) Ltd* [2015] UKSC 72, [2016] AC 742 [26]–[27] Lord Neuberger.

presented a rare opportunity for judges to consider whether current contract law is fit for purpose in its response to a global disaster that suddenly and unexpectedly rendered many contracts impossible, illegal, prohibitively costly, or potentially harmful to perform. That opportunity has not, so far, been taken. The burden of responding to unexpected events remains primarily with the contracting parties and those who draft their contracts.[71]

V. Conclusion: The Future of the Interpretative Approach to Unexpected Events

Contract case law in the recent past demonstrates that courts have used both contextual and plain meaning interpretative strategies when dealing with the effects of unexpected events on a contract. A more formal, linguistic method of interpretation tends to uphold the existing risk allocation in the contract, despite the changed circumstances, on the basis that one of the parties has made a bad bargain. Enforcing a bad bargain may be the correct outcome in many commercial contract contexts. Contextual interpretation, on the other hand, presents an alternative for dealing with unexpected events outside of the 'all or nothing' outcomes offered by the doctrine of frustration or the enforcement of the original agreement. Resolving problems through interpretation maintains the general stability of the surrounding legal rules, since the outcomes from interpretation are generally fact-dependent one-offs and thus unlikely to cause mischief in other cases. As for which interpretative approach (plain meaning or contextual) is appropriate in a case, this depends on the circumstances, including such matters as the foreseeability of the event, the sophistication of the parties, the complexity of the contract, amongst other things.

In many ways, contract interpretation is a superior strategy for dealing with unexpected events since, on the surface at least, it eschews the kind of overtly policy-based reasoning or doctrinal innovation that is discouraged in contract law, particularly in the commercial sphere.[72] We might speculate that interpreting the contract to resolve problems of unexpected events is preferable to alternatives, such as frustration, 'equitable adjustment',[73] implied terms or the operation of a principle of good faith, which appear as undesirable judicial interventions that remake (or in the case of frustration, extinguish) the bargain.[74] Where alternative doctrines (whether derived from equity or common law) are of uncertain scope,

[71] See further C Mitchell, 'What Does Covid-19 Teach Us About English Contract Law?' (2024) 44 *Legal Studies* 313.

[72] *Philipp v Barclays Bank UK plc* [2023] UKSC 25, [2024] AC 346, [6] and [22]–[24] Lord Burrows.

[73] See MacQueen (n 50).

[74] For warnings about judicial overreach, see the classic dissenting judgment of Lord Wilberforce in *L Schuler AG v Wickman Machine Tools Ltd* [1973] UKHL 2, [1974] AC 235, 263, rejecting the idea that judges were entitled to impose standards of 'easygoing tolerance' on the parties when the contract wording indicated 'aggressive, insistent punctuality and efficiency'.

or of doubtful existence, the exercise of relatively well-established principles of interpretation to resolve unforeseen problems is understandable.

The advantages of using interpretation to deal with unexpected events particularly pertain when interpretation is contextual. Lord Hoffmann in *BCCI v Ali* conceded that equitable interventions in contracts might historically have been necessary to remedy the injustices generated by the operation of rigid interpretation methods.[75] Evidently, more flexible interpretation methods render equitable (or other) interventions into the contract redundant; interpretation can achieve broadly the same outcomes through a technique that draws its answers from a contextual reading of the contract text, rather than the application of an external legal doctrine. Where interpretation proceeds according to a more rigid method, however, some of these advantages evaporate. In a plain-meaning interpretative default, the idea that the *original* contract can be interpreted to resolve problems generated by an unanticipated radical change to the contract environment appears absurd. Bounded rationality entails that there are some circumstances that are entirely unforeseen, and in no sense can the parties (or their objectively reasonable counterparts) be said to have intentions about them. It may be a matter of debate how far contract disputes arising from unanticipated and unforeseeable changes in the contracting environment in long-term agreements, or the onerous, uncommercial or otherwise unfortunate consequences of a contract's plain meaning, can be settled definitively through interpretation of the contract language.[76] Contract context may provide further clues concerning what the parties intended in relation to unexpected events, but drawing inferences concerning the intentions of the parties from 'background', 'context' or 'commercial reasonableness', has become more limited since *Arnold v Britton.* Modern courts see no injustice in holding commercial parties to the terms they have agreed, even if the parties may not have predicted all the consequences of the bargain. The expansive view of what can be achieved through contextual contract interpretation (the correction of errors in the paperwork, for example) has given way to the reassertion of doctrinal borderlines between what were assumed until recently to be facets of interpretation.[77] Evident here is the desire to ensure contract interpretation is kept under control.

Doubts therefore arise about the future of contextual interpretation as a mechanism to deal with unanticipated events in contract. In reasserting the importance of a linguistic approach to interpretation, the Supreme Court in *Arnold v Britton* may have removed one option for dealing with the unforeseen in contract. The neutering of interpretation would not be problematic if contract law had other

[75] *BCCI v Ali* (n 22) [60] Lord Hoffmann.

[76] See the difference of opinion between the Supreme Court (rescue) and the Court of Appeal (bad bargain) in *Rainy Sky SA v Kookmin Bank* [2011] UKSC 50, [2011] 1 WLR 2900 (SC); [2010] EWCA Civ 582, [2011] 1 Lloyd's Rep 233 (CA) [51]. Both courts claimed to be interpreting the contract.

[77] See, eg, *SATA Internaçional-Azores Airline SA v Hi Fly Ltd and anor* [2024] EWHC 2762 (Comm) on interpretation and rectification [131]. See also *Bellini NE Ltd v Brit UW Ltd* [2024] EWCA Civ 435 on correcting errors through interpretation and the limitations on this [14].

doctrines available to respond to the problem of unexpected events. The difficulty here is that there are few doctrinal alternatives. It is very doubtful that courts will develop a common law power to vary, or principles around equitable adjustment, or a doctrine of good faith, to deal with the unexpected. The reliance on contextual contract interpretation to mount a rescue precisely reflects the paucity of doctrines directed to remedying the effects of unforeseen circumstances on a contract. If we are now in a plain meaning interpretative environment, it seems likely that the bad bargain outcome will become the standard response to unexpected events in commercial contracts.

6

Purposive Interpretation of Longer-term Charters

MIRIAM GOLDBY

I. Introduction

The unexpected is an inherent feature of the business of transporting cargoes across the world by sea. Aside from natural perils and geopolitical events that can affect shipping, events affecting the global supply of and demand for goods have significant knock-on impact on ship-chartering markets, which, for the last two decades, have been highly volatile. Stakeholders in this sector therefore operate in a very unpredictable environment. A major benefit of a longer-term chartering arrangement is that it introduces an element of predictability into the inherently unpredictable. For shipowners, these contracts provide an assurance of a stable income from the operation of their vessels over the contractual period (which may be required by their financiers). For charterers, they provide an assurance of stable chartering costs, regardless of market movements.

This chapter analyses the nature of longer-term chartering contracts, considering the implications of interpreting them purposively. Taking as case studies disputes involving such contracts decided by the English courts since the early 2000s, it considers the extent to which the notion of mutual recognition as conceived by David Campbell can aid the courts in deciding such disputes. Campbell conceives of contracting as 'exchange conscious of mutual recognition', ie, exchange that, while driven by self-interest, requires recognition by each contracting party of the other's interest. This recognition creates a relationship that the law of contract requires each party to prioritise over their own subjective self-interest.[1]

I argue that acknowledging the existence of a bargain which is distinct from the self-interested motivations of either party assists in understanding the purpose of longer-term chartering contracts, which in turn enables purposive interpretation of their terms whenever the meaning of such terms is in dispute. London

[1] D Campbell, *Contractual Relations: A Contribution to the Critique of the Classical Law of Contract* (Oxford, OUP, 2022) 67.

Maritime Arbitration tends to be the selected mode of dispute resolution for these contracts, and disputes on the merits that reach the courts tend to do so via the process set out in the English Arbitration Act 1996, section 69, which makes available to arbitrating parties, in very limited circumstances, a right of appeal to the courts on a point of law. The points of law in question tend to revolve around how (standard) contractual terms ought to be construed and whether the behaviour of one of the parties constituted a (repudiatory) breach of the contract in the specific circumstances.

The issues that needed to be decided in the cases that are discussed in this chapter were challenging ones on which different judges had conflicting views. In this chapter I argue that adopting Campbell's approach in articulating the purpose of the exchange and interpreting the contractual terms in accordance with such purpose provides a more rigorous and consistent way of deciding these disputes than asking which outcome provides more certainty to future contracting parties.

II. Mutual Recognition and Purposive Interpretation

David Campbell's notion of mutual recognition by contracting parties of each other's interests is key to understanding the commercial purpose of a contract, which is distinct from the self-interest which drove each contracting party to enter into it. In turn, understanding the contractual purpose will inform processes of contractual construction should disputes arise. This section outlines the elements of mutual recognition and purposive interpretation.

A. Mutual Recognition

i. *The 'Functional Reason' for a Contract*

For Campbell, 'a relationship of mutual recognition of each other's interests is, as it always has been, necessary to make a market economy based on general voluntary exchange actual'.[2] He views 'economic action through contracting' as being 'intrinsically moral'[3] and views contract as 'a social system of *mutual* advantage'[4] designed to realise Pareto optimality, which therefore imposes a duty on each party to recognise the other's interests. According to Campbell, of necessity, this requires parties to act in good faith towards each other.[5]

[2] Campbell (n 1) 6–7. He notes that 'an exchange cannot take place because one economic actor believes it will benefit from the exchange. It can take place only when a pair of actors both believe they will benefit, and for this reason voluntarily enter into the exchange.' ibid 24.

[3] ibid 7.

[4] ibid 27. Emphasis in original.

[5] ibid 27.

Campbell's approach thus requires contractual parties to act in mutual recognition of each other's interests in all cases, ensuring that each gets precisely what they bargained for.[6] Campbell argues that 'the functional reason parties enter into a contract'[7] is what Wolfgang Friedmann called the provision of 'insurance against calculated economic risks'.[8] Because this driver for the formation of an agreement is common to both parties, unlike appropriation, exchange cannot be understood as merely a solipsistic exercise of self-interest. Rather, it 'has the moral, other-regarding component of mutual recognition as an analytically essential feature'.[9] In other words, an agreement cannot be formed unless it has a purpose that brings together the interests of both parties. After the bargain has been struck, acting in mutual recognition of each other's interests can be understood as performing the contract in accordance with this common purpose.

However, the parties will rarely expressly articulate this common purpose in the terms of their agreement.[10] Thus, to establish what 'economic risks' the parties sought to 'insure against' by entering into the contract, the agreement must be viewed within the market context in which it was formed, where parties meet and exchange

> … replete with a host of normative expectations, social and moral presuppositions, prior experiences and vaticinations. Some of these are expressly written into the contract but most are implicit and are not inscribed or agreed but are rather the accepted and known hypotheses underlying any economic action that it would be both purposeless and untimely to include in the contract itself.[11]

Once it has been established, in interpreting the contract, one should give 'maximum effect to the mutually recognised, overriding purpose of the venture ….'[12]

ii. Contracts as 'relational'

On Campbell's view, mutual recognition makes every contract relational, entailing, it has been argued, that it should be performed in good faith, ie, without

[6] P Goodrich, 'Against the Spirit of the Age: The Rationale of Relational Contracts' (2023) 43 (4) *OJLS* 848, 849: 'Campbell's view entails giving rigorous effect to the theory that the expectations freely negotiated and objectively created by agreements must be honoured in law.'

[7] Campbell (n 1) 57.

[8] W Friedmann, *Law in a Changing Society*, 2nd edn (London, Penguin, 1972), 119.

[9] Campbell (n 1) 67.

[10] This is in line with comments of Leggatt J as he then was in Mr Justice Leggatt, 'Contractual duties of good faith', Lecture to the Commercial Bar Association, 18 October 2016, at www.judiciary.uk/wp-content/uploads/2016/10/mr-justice-leggatt-lecture-contractual-duties-of-faith.pdf, as cited in V Selvaratnam KC, 'Good faith: is English law swimming against the international tide?' [2020] *Lloyd's Maritime and Commercial Law Quarterly* 232, 245, where he said: 'If contract law is to perform that function effectively, it is necessary to recognise that not all the shared understandings and expectations which contracting parties have and which are necessary to realise their joint aims are ever spelt out, or are capable of being spelt out, in their contractual document.'

[11] Goodrich (n 6) 851, citing D Campbell, H Collins and J Wightman (eds), *Implicit Dimensions of Contract* (Oxford, Hart Publishing, 2013) ch 2.

[12] Goodrich (n 6) 860.

engaging in opportunism.[13] By contrast, under English law, a duty to act in good faith in performing a contract is one that is recognised as applying not to the generality of contracts, but only to a specific type of contract that can be classified as 'relational'.[14] In *Yam Seng Pte Ltd v International Trade Corporation Ltd*,[15] relational contracts were defined as contracts that involve a 'longer term relationship between the parties [where] they make a substantial commitment', and that 'may require a high degree of communication, cooperation, and predictable performance based on mutual trust and confidence'.[16] Another important feature of such contracts, highlighted in *Bates*, is that '[t]he spirits and objectives of [the parties'] venture may not be capable of being expressed exhaustively in a written contract'[17] with the consequence that market context can be key to understanding the contract's purpose.[18] The rejection of good faith as a duty of general application in English law has been attributed to excessive party-centricity in the approach to contract performance, an approach that emphasises individual interests rather than the parties' shared interests.[19]

It is at least arguable that, even on the English law view that only specific types of contract are relational, longer-term chartering contracts could fall into that category: they are long-term arrangements, requiring open communication to be performed, and they are performed in a high-risk, extremely unpredictable, physical, political and legal/regulatory environment which cannot be exhaustively provided for in the contract. So even if one were to reject Campbell's contention that every contract is relational, there are grounds for arguing that longer-term charters display features that would enable them to be classified as relational under English law, entailing a duty on the parties to perform their obligations towards each other in good faith. This view is, however, contested[20] and not one that the courts have (at least so far) embraced. Undeniably, parties to such contracts would be wary of an approach that contractually requires them to act in good faith because of the impact this approach would have on certainty: they would never know for sure whether they have complied with this requirement when determining whether they are legally entitled to withhold performance in any given situation. On the other hand, parties are unlikely to take kindly to being on the receiving end of opportunistic behaviour that deprives them of the benefit

[13] ibid 857.

[14] *Bates v Post Office (No 3)* [2019] EWHC 606 (QB). See indicia of such contracts identified by the court at [725].

[15] *Yam Seng Pte Ltd v International Trade Corporation Ltd* [2013] EWHC 111 (QB).

[16] ibid [142]. See also *Sheikh Al Nehayan v Kent* [2018] EWHC 333 (Comm), [152].

[17] *Bates* (n 14) [725].

[18] As noted by Goodrich (n 6) 859. Citing Campbell (n 1) 67.

[19] D Christie, S Saintier and J Viven-Wilksch, 'Industry-Led Standards, Relational Contracts and Good Faith: Are the UK and Australia Setting the Pace in (Construction) Contract Law?' (2022) 43 *Liverpool Law Review*, 287, 289.

[20] Sir D Foxton, 'Why Shipping Law Still Matters' [2021] *Lloyd's Maritime and Commercial Law Quarterly* 440, 447: 'the defining approach of English shipping law has been to approach those contracts on the assumption that they are not so much relational, as risk-allocational'.

of their bargain in a situation where adopting an alternative interpretation of the contract would have kept the right to demand performance (or compensation in its absence) alive. As aptly noted by Selvaratnam, 'good faith is not altruism and does not require a party to subordinate its own commercial interests to those of the other party to the contract. Good faith simply requires loyalty to the agreement – to the bargain'.[21]

I argue that it is not necessary to classify longer-term charters as relational contracts to conclude that opportunism and bad-faith behaviour are inimical to their purpose[22] and that interpreting longer-term charters in a purposive manner requires an approach that discourages opportunism and bad-faith behaviour in the face of the unexpected.

B. Purposive Interpretation

A purposive approach to the interpretation of contracts entails understanding and enforcing the contract in accordance with its purpose. A theory of purposive interpretation was advanced by Aharon Barak in an impressive treatise numbering several volumes, published in the 1990s and translated into English in the early 2000s. According to Barak:

> the purpose of a contract … is the interests, goals, values, aims, policies and function that the contract is designed to accomplish …. Subjective purpose reflects the actual intent of the parties: the interests, values, aims, policies, and function that the parties (subjectively) sought to accomplish. Objective purpose is the interests, values, aims, policies, and function that a contract of that type is (objectively) designed to accomplish. It reflects hypothetical not actual intent.[23]

Barak argues that purposive interpretation 'openly seeks and achieves subjective purpose when possible and efficacious …. Otherwise it openly adopts the rhetoric and practice of objective purpose …'.[24] By subjective purpose, Barak means the parties' joint intent, determined by a legal investigation into facts.[25] He explains

[21] Selvaratnam (n 10) 245.

[22] M Warren, 'Good Faith: Where Are We At' (2010) 34 *Melbourne University Law Review* 344, 347 notes that 'the courts have three mechanisms at their disposal in which to approach a good faith problem – implication by law, implication in fact, or purposive interpretation', and, in regard to the last of these, that the commercial purpose test should be a fundamental consideration in all contractual dealings. The test was articulated in the Australian case *International Air Transport Association v Ansett Australia Holdings Ltd ('JATA')* (2008) 234 CLR 151, 160, where it was held that '[a]n appreciation of the commercial purpose of a contract calls for an understanding of the genesis of the transaction, the background, and the market.' See also discussion in M Raczynska, 'Good Faiths and Contract Terms' ch 5 in PS Davies and M Raczynska (eds), *Contents of Commercial Contracts: Terms Affecting Freedoms* (Oxford, Hart Publishing, 2020) 65, 84 and in PS Davies and P Sales, 'Controlling Contract Discretions: Wednesbury reasonableness, Good Faith And Proper Purposes' (2024) 140 *LQR* 106.

[23] A Barak, *Purposive Interpretation in Law* (Princeton, Princeton University Press, 2005) 325–26.

[24] ibid 321.

[25] ibid 320.

that in seeking to give effect to the parties' subjective purpose, purposive interpretation 'seeks the purpose of the contract, not the meaning that the parties attach to its language.'[26]

He explains how objective purpose should be used as follows:

> Objective purpose constitutes the background for understanding subjective purpose. It may resolve contradictions among conflicting subjective purposes. Most importantly, objective purpose applies to situations in which there is no subjective purpose that can resolve the judge's interpretive problem. It is then that objective purpose is decisive.[27]

The determination of the objective purpose can be done at various levels of abstraction ranging from the lowest level (the purpose that the parties would have envisioned had they thought about the matter),[28] an intermediate level (the purpose that the parties would have had had they behaved as reasonable people),[29] a higher level (the purpose typical of the type of contract in question),[30] and the highest level (the purpose determined by the fundamental values of the system, eg, human rights).[31] Barak considers it preferable to start with the lower levels of abstraction, only resorting to the higher levels if the lower levels fail to assist in resolving the problem.

Barak thus holds that the estimated joint intent of parties is to be deduced, not only from the language of the contract, but also from all the circumstances in which the contract was formed. It is not his view that resort should only be had to the latter if the former fails.[32] Thus, in order to achieve the 'true purpose' of the contract, a judge may 'alter the language'[33] where it 'misses the true purpose on which the contract is based'[34] in order to avoid the contract's purpose being frustrated. The gap in the contract that remains where the language is thus disregarded may, according to Barak, be filled 'in accordance with the principle of good faith.'[35]

This aspect of Barak's theory has been criticised on the basis that it runs counter to the principle of contractual freedom, undermining the parties' reasonable expectations.[36] Karanikić Mirić questions the inquiry proposed by Barak into the actual joint intent of the parties at the time of their entering into the contract, noting that another person's past or present intentions 'cannot be learned as a physical reality, but only as

[26] ibid 327.
[27] ibid 321.
[28] ibid 332.
[29] ibid 333.
[30] ibid 333.
[31] ibid 333–34. See also ibid 164.
[32] ibid 330–32. As aptly put by G Shalev, 'Interpretation in Law: Chief Justice Barak's Theory' (2002) 36 *Israel Law Review* 123, 136: 'The analysis is to swing, in a pendulum-like movement, from the language to the circumstances and back, with each source shedding light on the other, recognizing that neither is able to produce a valid subjective purpose on its own.'
[33] *The State of Israel v Aprofim Housing and Enterprise* (1991) Ltd. 49(2) PD. 265, per Justice Barak in the Supreme Court of Israel, as cited by Shalev (n 32) 143.
[34] ibid.
[35] ibid.
[36] Shalev (n 32) 138–39.

a socially constructed fact',[37] and that it is only the expression of an intent that can be interpreted and not the intent itself.[38] The same author notes that there appears to be a merging between Barak's subjective purpose of contract with his objective purposes of contract at the lower levels of abstraction.[39]

The notion of the subjective joint intent of the parties is rejected in English law and by English commentators on the basis that:

> The greater clarity provided by a focus on objective meaning has advantages for the processes of both interpretation and implication. It makes clear the irrelevance in all or almost all cases of the actual intentions of the parties, and the irrelevance of the fact that, on the issue in question, the parties may very well have not formed a common intention. A focus on objective meaning also highlights the irrelevance of the parties' personal characteristics and preferences. … it makes it clear that contractual purposes can only be inferred from the instrument and its context, and cannot be derived from speculation about the parties' individual goals or interests, or speculation about what the parties were or were not 'concerned with.[40]

Thus, under English law, the purpose of the contract is more likely to be determined objectively than subjectively, although it is not unheard of for the parties' stated intentions to be taken into account in disputes about how contractual terms should be interpreted.[41] The notion of 'purposive construction' of commercial contracts has on occasion been rejected by judges who preferred the notion of 'business common sense',[42] but it has been argued that 'purposive construction is best understood, not as an alternative to business commonsense, but as a distinctive interpretive technique within that broader category'.[43] It seems clear from Lord Clarke's judgment in *Rainy Sky*,[44] that reference to the agreement's commercial

[37] MK Mirić, 'A Critical Look at the Subjective and Objective Purposes of Contract in Aharon Barak's Theory of Interpretation' (2016) 9 (2) *Baltic Journal of Law & Politics*, 1, 11.

[38] ibid 6, 12. See also ibid 13: 'It is not only that a meeting of the minds is not possible if the intents are not communicated; it is that the difference between the true intents and the expressed intents cannot be discovered or proven as a physical fact.'

[39] ibid 14, 17–18. See esp. ibid 14: '[Barak] does not propose a method, a technique of accessing this 'true' intent of another from the outside – apart from saying that the judge needs to look into the language of the contract as a whole, and into some circumstances external to the contract, such as the circumstances surrounding its formation.'

[40] A Robertson, 'Purposive Contractual Interpretation' (2019) 39 *Legal Studies* 230, 233.

[41] See *The Karen Oltmann* [1976] 2 Lloyd's Rep 708: '[S]ince the word 'after' in cl.26 was capable of bearing two meanings, the Court was entitled to examine the pre-contractual exchanges to see whether they (the exchanges) supported the owners' contention that the parties were in agreement as to the meaning of the word …. The telex message exchanges clearly showed that the words 'after 12 months trading' was used in the agreed sense of 'on the expiry of' and not 'at any time after the expiry of' ….' But note that this approach was criticised in the House of Lords in *Chartbrook v Persimmon Homes* [2009] UKHL 38 [43]–[47], per Lord Hoffmann. His Lordship (ibid at [47]) noted that the approach in the *Karen Oltmann* was subsequently superseded by estoppel by convention, developed since *Amalgamated Investment & Property Co Ltd v Texas Commerce International Bank Ltd* [1982] QB 84.

[42] *Antaios Compania SA v Salen AB (The Antaios)* [1985] AC 191, 201, per Lord Diplock; *Mannai Investment Ltd v Eagle Star Assurance Co Ltd* [1997] AC 749, 770, per Lord Steyn.

[43] Robertson (n 40) 235 see also discussion ibid 241 et seq.

[44] *Rainy Sky SA v Kookmin Bank* [2011] UKSC 50, [2011] 1 WLR 2900, [25].

purpose is the appropriate way to choose between or among available contractual constructions.[45] Robertson also argues that

> Inconsistency between the meaning of the language and an apparent contractual purpose may be said to create an ambiguity or constructional choice. Since it is clearly incorrect as a matter of law to read a particular contractual provision in isolation from the remainder of the agreement, a contractual provision cannot properly be said to be unambiguous or to bear a plain meaning if it is inconsistent with a contractual purpose manifested by the agreement.[46]

He notes, however, that there will be cases where a contractual provision will be construed in accordance with the meaning it would convey to a reasonable person, even if this meaning is not in line with its commercial purpose,[47] especially if the provision has been drafted with some care and with the benefit of legal advice and if the construction does not undermine the contract's purpose but only goes further than this purpose requires.[48]

Contextual interpretation of the contract's language is particularly important for longer-term chartering arrangements. Negotiation of these contracts has been described as 'messy and haphazard',[49] and, while legal expertise may be involved in formulating model forms and standalone 'rider clauses' which can be incorporated into contracts, the negotiations of individual fixtures do not tend to involve legal expertise,[50] so parties will not have deliberately discussed between themselves the meaning of the incorporated standard or model clauses that become part of the contract.

C. What would an Approach to Deciding Disputes Based on Mutual Recognition and Purposive Interpretation Entail?

Based on the theories outlined above, when a dispute arises regarding whether or not, on the contract's terms, a party was entitled to withhold performance of

[45] See also comments on 'teleological construction' in *Phillips v Rafiq* [2007] EWCA Civ 74, [22], per Ward LJ.

[46] Robertson (n 40) 237. See also *Glynn v Margetson & Co* [1893] AC 351, 357.

[47] ibid 239–41 citing *Wood v Capita Insurance Services Ltd* [2017] UKSC 24, *Cherry v Steele-Park* [2017] NSWCA 295.

[48] ibid 241.

[49] J Hjalmarsson 'Trip Charterparties and their Binary Endgames' [2018] *Lloyd's Maritime and Commercial Law Quarterly* 376, 379: 'The negotiation of a charterparty may be a messy and haphazard affair: the negotiating phase is characterised by shorthand contract-making following speedy negotiations, only rarely involving legal advice. This results only in a recap rather than a well-presented contract ….'

[50] For a sense of the lack of formality that characterises charterparty negotiations and contract formation see, eg, *Golden Ocean Group Ltd v Salgaocar Mining Industries* [2012] EWCA Civ 265; *Hellenic Petroleum Cyprus v Premier Maritime* [2015] EWHC 1894 (Comm), [3]; *The Golden Endurance* [2014] EWHC 3917 (Comm), [13]; *Toptip Holding v Mercuria Energy Trading* [2017] SGCA 64; *Americas Bulk Transport v Cosco Bulk Carrier The Grand Fortune* [2020] EWHC 147 (Comm).

their contractual obligations, establishing the contract's purpose can be central to understanding those terms and deciding the dispute.

Establishing the contract's purpose requires an acknowledgement that the contract has its basis not in solipsistic self-interest but in recognised mutual benefits, the pursuance of which is the reason for entering into and performing the contract. An examination of the context within which the contract is negotiated is key to identifying these mutual benefits and the contract's purpose, which are rarely expressly articulated in the contract itself.

Where performance must be undertaken in an unpredictable environment, changes in which may affect the extent to which the self-interest of one or other of the parties continues to be served by the contract, enforcing the contract in accordance with its purpose may require it to be interpreted in a way that prevents opportunistic (or bad faith) withholding of performance.

III. Longer-term Vessel Charters

In this chapter I use 'longer-term vessel charters' to refer to two types of contract. The first type is contracts of affreightment (CoAs), whereby the shipowner agrees to undertake a series of voyages for the charterer over a certain period, the price payable to the shipowner, called 'freight', being a flat rate per voyage. The second type is Time Charters, whereby the shipowner places the vessel at the charterer's disposal for a defined period, the consideration being a daily rate called 'hire'.

In each of these two types of contract, the contract's *function* is to give the charterer the use of the shipowner's vessel while the contract is in effect. But what is the contract's *purpose*? A ship can be chartered for a single voyage, for a series of voyages or for a period of time. Chartering a ship for a single voyage is done over what is called the 'spot' market, where the cost of the charter will depend on the current market conditions. Longer-term vessel charters have the effect of hedging against market movements and providing some predictability for both shipowner and charterer as to the terms on which their business will be undertaken for the period of the charter: ie, they shield both against market volatility.[51] From an objective perspective, this is a major raison d'être for longer-term charters, providing the parties with 'insurance against calculated economic risks'.[52] As shall be seen below, the relevant markets are volatile, a feature likely to affect the relationship between the parties during the period of the contract. Market movements during the contractual period will always be in favour of one party and against

[51] See *SA Maritime et Commerciale of Geneva v Anglo-Iranian Oil Co Ltd* [1953] 1 WLR 1379, 1382, where Devlin J held that the object of a particular charterparty was 'to provide for a ship that will, *at the agreed rate*, perform the voyages which the charterers want performed.' Emphasis added.

[52] Friedmann (n 8), Campbell (n 1) 57.

the other, so the purpose of the contract will not be achieved if it is construed in a way that enables parties to act in an opportunistic and self-interested manner. Thus, such constructions should not be adopted in the absence of clear and unambiguous language.

A. Market Movements

The Baltic Dry Index shows rates secured for chartered vessels in the dry bulk sector and was first published in January 1985. As can be seen from figure 1 below, the market for freight did go up and down between 1985 and 2001 but started to experience a period of extreme volatility from about 2002. This coincided with China joining the World Trade Organisation on 11 December 2001. Volatility was exacerbated by the global financial crisis of 2008–09, and another, albeit less marked, spike and then dip in freight rates was experienced during the SARS – CoV-2 pandemic in 2020–22.

Figure 1 Baltic Dry Index – Historical Data[53]

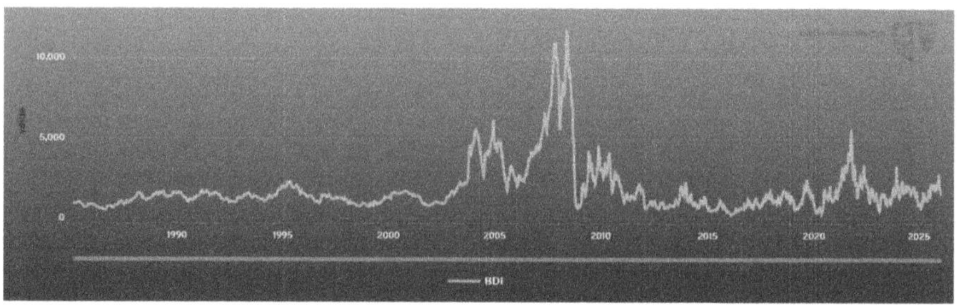

The increased market volatility starting from the early 2000s means that longer-term charters can be an attractive option for shipowners and charterers seeking greater predictability of costs and earnings. It is submitted that this is an important factor to consider in understanding the purpose of these contracts.

IV. Opportunistic Suspension or Termination of Contractual Obligations

One way of addressing the risks of market volatility is to enter into a longer-term chartering arrangement that gives the charterer use of a ship for a period of months or years at a pre-negotiated rate of freight (in the case of a CoA) or hire

[53] © The Baltic Exchange, published with the kind permission of the Baltic Exchange.

(in the case of a Time Charter) that applies no matter what the market is doing during the given period. The contract thus allocates the risk of market movements and promotes stability in business operations. Hence Foxton J, writing extra-judicially, termed charterparties contracts of risk allocation rather than relational contracts.[54]

However, if the market makes unexpected sharp movements in one direction or the other during the period of charter, this may affect the willingness of one of the parties to continue with performance and may give rise to one or the other of two types of contractual dispute. First, an incentive is created for the contracting party in whose favour the market is moving (the shipowner if it is going up, the charterer if it is going down) to cease performing the now disadvantageous contract in order to benefit from the favourable market. For this reason, this party may seek to argue that any breach of contract by the other party, no matter how slight or inconsequential, is repudiatory. They may also seek to argue that frustration of contract or force majeure excuses them from performance.

Second, it may be the party in whose favour the market is moving who breaches the contract. The most common instance of this is when the market starts to go down and the charterer refuses to pay in full and/or on time. The shipowner will then be in the awkward situation of having to decide whether the charterer's breach is repudiatory, enabling them to terminate and claim damages. Should they walk away despite the breach not being repudiatory, they will lose their entitlement to the agreed rate of payment. Should they decide to carry on with the contract, they would need to ensure that continuing with performance does not constitute acceptance of varied contractual terms.

Where these disputes go to court, judges will be asked to decide on whether the alleged breach is actually repudiatory, which may involve the question of whether a term should be classified as a condition,[55] or how a force majeure clause should be construed,[56] or what constitutes a frustrating delay under the specific contract that was entered into.[57] These decisions are often not clear-cut, and dissenting judgments or reversals of decisions of lower courts on appeal are not uncommon. As shall be seen in the discussion below, the choice of a particular contractual construction allowing a party to walk away from the contract may be justified by the stated need to promote certainty for contracting parties, but this approach can also encourage opportunism and enable a party who wants to take advantage of market movements that have occurred since the contract was entered into to escape what has turned out to be a bad bargain. If the purpose of the contract was to hedge against market movements and stabilise costs for the charterer and

[54] Foxton (n 20) 447.

[55] *The Astra* [2013] EWHC 865 (Comm); *Spar Shipping AS v Grand China Logistics Holding* [2016] EWCA Civ 982.

[56] *MUR Shipping BV v RTI Ltd* [2024] UKSC 18.

[57] *The Evia (No. 2)* [1982] 2 Lloyd's Rep 307 (HL); *The Lucille* [1983] 1 Lloyd's Rep. 387 (CA).

income for the shipowner, allowing a party to resile from their contractual obligations in the absence of a genuine repudiation, frustration or inability to perform due to force majeure flouts the contract's purpose.

Over the years, the traditional approach to interpreting and enforcing contracts has caused the courts difficulties due to the tension between upholding the notion that, within the confines of what was agreed, parties are entitled to act in a purely self-interested manner and the frequent need to determine precisely what was agreed. The latter exercise is rendered challenging by the fact that the right to withhold performance often rests on the meaning of standard contractual terms which have not been specifically discussed in the negotiations.

This chapter argues that replacing solipsistic self-interest with Campbell's notion of mutual recognition enables a more authentic conceptualisation of the purpose of these contracts and, therefore, a purposive interpretation of these terms. The next section analyses some cases that were decided since market volatility increased in the early 2000s that illustrate the tension experienced by the courts between the wish to adhere to traditional contract law approaches and the instinctive understanding of what would constitute a just and fair outcome in the circumstances. It will be shown that the decisions justified by the desire to promote certainty for the contracting parties (who, it is argued, benefit from knowing when they are entitled to withhold performance) also promote opportunistic behaviour that does not sit well with a recognition of the contract's mutuality and its purpose in shielding against adverse market fluctuations.

V. Construction of Charterparty Contracts

A. Classification of a Term as a Condition

A large volume and variety of risks may disrupt maritime ventures and lead to contractual breaches. Depending on the circumstances, the consequences of a given breach may be trivial or serious, and indeed the concept of innominate terms appears to have been developed by the courts precisely to increase flexibility in dealing with breaches of charterparty contracts.[58]

The difficulties the courts have faced in establishing precisely how a term is to be classified can be amply illustrated by examining the facts of two cases involving

[58] The first reference to the concept was in *Universal Cargo Carriers Corporation v Citati* [1957] 2 QB 401, 431, per Devlin J, a case involving anticipatory breach of a voyage charterparty. While the reference here was to a contract being brought to an end 'by breach of warranty', it was clear that the court meant 'a term that is not a condition'. The first discussion of the implications for the purposes of classification of contract terms occurred in *Hong Kong Fir Shipping Co Ltd v Kawasaki Kisen Kaisha Ltd* [1962] 2 QB 26, 70 per Lord Diplock, where his Lordship spoke of terms 'which cannot be categorised as being 'conditions' or 'warranties'....' This case involved a Time Charter.

a falling market and a reluctant charterer. In both *The Astra*[59] and *Spar Shipping*[60] cases, the shipowners eventually decided to accept the charterer's breach as repudiatory, terminate the contract and claim damages for the breach. The first two circles in Figure 2 show, respectively, the date that *The Astra* charter was entered into and the date at which the charterer's repudiation was accepted by the shipowner. The last two circles show the date on which the *Spar Shipping* charters were entered into and the date when the charterers' repudiation was accepted by the shipowner.

Figure 2 The Astra and Spar Shipping

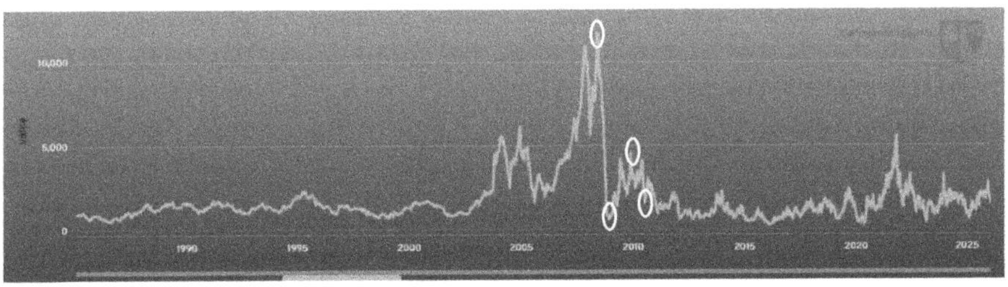

Both these cases involved a widely used standard charterparty form, the New York Produce Exchange (NYPE). Clause 5 of *The Astra* charter (on the 1946 version of the NYPE form) and Clause 11(a) of the *Spar Shipping* charters (on the 1993 version of the NYPE form) provided as follows: '... failing the punctual and regular payment of the hire ... the Owners shall be at liberty to withdraw the vessel from the service of the Charterers ....' This clause is designed to give the shipowner the right to withdraw the vessel on the charterer's late payment so that the shipowner does not have to wait for the charterer's breach to become repudiatory before taking advantage of a rising market. It is accompanied by an anti-technicality clause (clause 31 in *The Astra* charter and clause 11(b) in the *Spar Shipping* charter) which provides for a grace period, designed to ensure that the right to withdraw does not arise if the breach is due to 'oversight, negligence, errors or omissions on the part of the Charterers or their bankers' and if the breach is rectified within the notice period indicated in the contract.

In both *The Astra* and *Spar Shipping*, the charterers argued that in withdrawing their vessel, the owners were exercising a contractual right, thus discharging the contract by agreement rather than terminating it for breach. Consequently, a right to damages, they argued, did not arise. The courts thus had to determine whether the charterers' breach was repudiatory and whether in withdrawing the vessel the shipowners had been terminating for breach rather than merely exercising a contractual right.

[59] *Kuwait Rocks Co v AMN Bulkcarriers Inc (The Astra)* [2013] EWHC 865 (Comm).
[60] *Spar* (n 55) affirming *Spar Shipping AS v Grand China Logistics* [2015] EWHC 718 (Comm).

Both cases were decided in favour of the shipowners on the basis of anticipatory breach,[61] and there was thus no need to classify the contractual term in order to reach a conclusion, but the courts engaged in the exercise regardless. Classifying the term proved challenging. On the one hand, if punctual payment were a condition of the contract, what need would there be to include an express contractual right to withdraw the vessel upon its breach? On the other hand, if it were not a condition, why would the parties consider withdrawal to be justified?

Flaux J in *The Astra*, after careful analysis, concluded that the term was a condition. He justified this conclusion by alluding to the certainty such a classification would give to the shipowner on whether they could walk away from the contract if the charterers failed to pay punctually.[62] In *Spar Shipping*, Popplewell J in the High Court classified it as an innominate term. His decision was affirmed by the Court of Appeal, where it was held that where the consequences of breaching a term could range from trivial to very serious, the term is more in the nature of an innominate term than a condition.[63] Gross LJ held that: 'greater certainty would be achieved by categorising cl. 11 as a condition but at a cost of disproportionate consequences flowing from trivial breaches – in my view, an unsatisfactory balance'.[64]

On the classification point, taking into account the commercial purpose of longer-term charterparties, the conclusion reached by the Court in *Spar Shipping* that it is not a condition is correct. In a falling market situation, against which they have taken the precaution of protecting themselves by negotiating longer-term rates, shipowners are going to be reluctant to walk away from the contract. They are unlikely to avail themselves of the right to withdraw unless the consequences to them of the charterers' behaviour are serious. The express right to withdraw the vessel set out in the provision is clearly intended to provide the shipowner with certainty that they have the right to walk away in a rising market without having to wait for the breach to become sufficiently serious and is not intended to classify the term as a condition.[65] Purposive interpretation that takes into account reasons why the longer-term arrangement was entered into in the first place therefore points to the term requiring punctual payment not being a condition.

[61] *The Astra* (n 55) [28]; *Spar Shipping* (n 55) [103].
[62] *The Astra* (n 55) [77], [80]–[86], and [115]–[116].
[63] *Spar Shipping* (n 55) [65].
[64] ibid.
[65] This is in line with two prior decisions in both of which one of the disputants argued that particular terms had been expressly classified as conditions in the contract, namely *Rice (t/a Garden Guardian) v Great Yarmouth BC* [2000] 6 WLUK 829 (Court of Appeal Civil Division) and *L Schuler AG v Wickman Machine Tool Sales Ltd* [1974] AC 235 (House of Lords). In the former the court held that the right to terminate did not arise unless the breaches were repudiatory, despite the fact that the contract provided that one of the parties would have the right to terminate the contract should the other commit 'a breach of any of its obligations under the Contract'. In the latter it was held that where a breach of term was remediable per the contract, breach of the term did not automatically give rise to the right to terminate even though the term had been expressly called a 'condition': here adopting a 'common sense' approach to construction led to the conclusion that as used in the particular term 'condition' could not have been intended as a term of art. See esp. ibid 251 per Lord Reid.

Following the High Court's decision in *The Astra* but prior to the decisions in *Spar Shipping*, the Baltic and International Maritime Council (BIMCO) amended the standard NYPE form, issuing a 2015 version, which includes a revised clause 11, paragraph (c)(ii) of which now provides that upon the expiry of the grace period for payment, the owners are not just entitled to withdraw the vessel, but also 'to damages, if they withdraw the vessel, for the loss of the remainder of the Charter Party'. This addition has the effect of making the clause more similar to a condition and demonstrates that certainty can be served by appropriate contractual drafting, although there is little evidence that the market has started to favour the 2015 version of the NYPE form over earlier versions.[66] Regardless, it is unlikely that shipowners will avail themselves of the right to walk away lightly in a falling market. This can be seen from the case of *The Aquafaith*.[67]

In *The Aquafaith*, under a charterparty on the NYPE form dated 19 September 2006, the vessel was chartered by the shipowners to the charterers for a duration of 59–61 months, expiring at the earliest on 10 November 2011. On 6 July 2011, in an admitted anticipatory breach of the charter, the charterers stated that they would re-deliver the vessel on dropping the last outward sea pilot after discharge in China under the then current voyage. The owners refused to accept repudiation and affirmed the contract. The two circles in Figure 3 below show the market position at the time the charter was entered into in 2006 and the time that the charterer attempted to repudiate the contract. The latter occurred in a situation where the market was falling, and it would have been extremely challenging for the owner to find alternative employment for the vessel and maintain an income stream while waiting to recover damages.

Figure 3 The Aquafaith

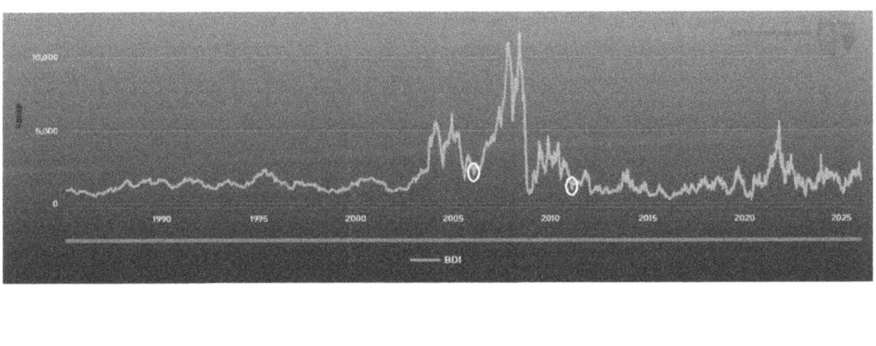

[66] A case search of both Westlaw and Lexis databases using the search term 'NYPE 2015' yielded no results apart from a mention in the *Spar Shipping* case where the Court of Appeal commented on the new form, contrasting it with the 1993 form in dispute before it (*Spar Shipping AS v Grand China Logistics Holding* [2016] EWCA Civ 982, [55]). A search was also conducted of LMAA awards published in the Lloyd's Maritime Law Newsletter, which also yielded no results. See also P Todd 'NYPE 2015: Wholesale Reform or an Invitation to Cherry-pick?' [2016] *Lloyd's Maritime and Commercial Law Quarterly* 306–19.

[67] *The Aquafaith* [2012] EWHC 1077 (Comm).

The court found that the shipowners were entitled to elect to affirm, with both the tests set out in *White and Carter (Councils) Ltd v McGregor*[68] having been met in this case. In particular, with regard to the legitimate interest test, the court held as follows:

> With only 94 days left of a 5 year time charter in a difficult market where a substitute time charter was impossible, and trading on the spot market very difficult, it would be impossible to characterise the owners' stance in wishing to maintain the charter and a right to hire as unreasonable, let alone beyond all reason, wholly unreasonable or perverse.[69]

It is hard to argue, therefore, that not classifying the term as a condition causes the contracting parties uncertainty. Where the market is moving in the shipowner's favour, they can exercise the right to withdraw if the punctual payment term is breached, without suffering any loss and without having to sue for damages. Where the market is moving against the shipowner, it is unlikely that they will want to walk away from the contract unless the breach is sufficiently serious.

Another type of standard contractual clause to which resort may be had to suspend or terminate performance is the force majeure clause, to which we turn next.

B. Force Majeure Clauses

Historically, longer-term charters did not tend to include force majeure (FM) clauses[70] and indeed many of the frustration cases that went to court tended to be cases involving disruption of such contracts by supervening unforeseen events.[71] BIMCO did not introduce a standard FM clause until 2022,[72] and even then, preceded it with a 'user warning' noting that

> *This is a model clause and the parties should adapt it to fit the nature of their agreement. It should not be included in any agreement without careful consideration. Caution is urged when including the clause in a period time charter party with a broad trading area.*[73]

The suggestion that the clause may need to be adapted to time charters with broad trading areas is apt, because where the trading area is broad, disruptive events

[68] *White and Carter (Councils) Ltd v McGregor* [1962] AC 413. The two tests are as follows: the performance of the affirming party is not dependent upon the co-operation of the party in breach; the election to affirm must pass the 'legitimate interest test'.

[69] *The Aquafaith* (n 67) [54].

[70] See N Austin and L Hyne, 'Expecting the Unexpected – BIMCO Releases Force Majeure Clause', 4 February 2022, at www.shiplawlog.com/2022/02/04/expecting-the-unexpected-bimco-releases-force-majeure-clause/: 'Force majeure clauses in carriage contracts are traditionally quite rare, with English law preferring to treat the issue as one of risk allocation.'

[71] See, by way of example, *The Eugenia* [1964] 2 QB 226; *The Mihalis Angelos* [1971] 1 QB 164; *The Nema* [1982] AC 724; *The Super Servant Two* [1990] 1 Lloyd's Rep. 1; *The Safeer* [1994] 1 Lloyd's Rep. 637; *The Florida* [2007] 1 Lloyd's Rep. 1; *The Sea Angel* [2007] 2 Lloyd's Rep. 517; *The Andra* [2012] 2 Lloyd's Rep. 587.

[72] Austin and Hyne (n 70).

[73] BIMCO, 'Force Majeure Clause 2022' at www.bimco.org/contractual-affairs/bimco-clauses/current-clauses/force-majeure-clause-2022/. Emphasis in original.

affecting one region may be avoided by employing the ship elsewhere. More recently, FM or exclusion clauses have started to appear in longer-term chartering contracts,[74] particularly CoAs, as these contracts tend to provide for a series of voyages between specified ports and do not tend to have a broad geographical scope, meaning that it is more likely that performance will be impeded if disruptions occur in the specific trading area.

BIMCO's FM clause has some similarities to but also important differences from a clause which was recently interpreted by the Supreme Court in *MUR Shipping BV v RTI Ltd*.[75] The facts were as follows: on 6 April 2018 the charterer's parent company was placed on the Specially Designated Nationals List by the US Office of Foreign Assets Control, which meant that the charterer faced difficulty paying freight in United States Dollars (USD), as it was contractually required to do. Paragraphs 1–3 of cl.36 of the CoA provided:

> 36.1. Subject to the terms of this Clause 36, neither Owners nor Charterers shall be liable to the other for loss, damage, delay or failure in performance caused by a Force Majeure Event as hereinafter defined. While such Force Majeure Event is in operation the obligation of each Party to perform this Charter Party (other than an accrued obligation to pay monies in respect of a previous voyage) shall be suspended.
>
> 36.2. Following the end of the Force Majeure Event, the Parties shall consult in good faith to make such adjustments as may be appropriate to the shipment schedule under this Charter Party.
>
> 36.3. A Force Majeure Event is an event or state of affairs which meets all of the following criteria:
>
> (a) It is outside the immediate control of the Party giving the Force Majeure Notice;
>
> (b) It prevents or delays the loading of the cargo at the loading port and/or the discharge of the cargo at the discharging port;
>
> (c) It is caused by one or more of acts of God, extreme weather conditions, war, lockout, strikes or other labour disturbances, explosions, fire, invasion, insurrection, blockade, embargo, riot, flood, earthquake, including all accidents to piers, shiploaders, and/or mills, factories, barges, or machinery, railway and canal stoppage by ice or frost, any rules or regulations of governments or any interference or acts or directions of governments, the restraint of princes, restrictions on monetary transfers and exchanges;
>
> (d) It cannot be overcome by reasonable endeavors from the Party affected.[76]

On 10 April the shipowner gave notice of FM, noting that 'it would be in breach of sanctions for Owners to continue with the COA' and that 'the sanctions will prevent dollar payments which are required under the COA'. The charterer rejected

[74] See *Classic Maritime Inc v Limbungan Makmur Sdn Bhd* [2019] EWCA Civ 1102 and *MUR* (n 56).

[75] *MUR* (n 56). See comment in M Goldby, 'Force Majeure in the Supreme Court: *MUR Shipping BV v RTI Ltd* [2024] UKSC 18' (2024) 44(4) *Legal Studies* 748–52.

[76] *MUR* (n 56) [4].

the notice. The shipowner reverted, pointing to 'restrictions on monetary transfers' as being a FM event and claiming that 'if monetary transfers from Charterers to Owners are restricted Owners cannot be expected to load and discharge the cargo without receiving payment in accordance with the COA'. The charterer proposed that it should make payment in euros which could be converted into US dollars (USD) as soon as they were received by the shipowner's bank and agreed to bear any additional costs or exchange rate losses in converting the euros into USD. The shipowner initially rejected this proposal and refused to make nominations under the COA, only resuming on 25 April. The question to be decided was whether a shipowner was entitled to rely on the FM clause as suspending its obligation to load seven cargoes of bauxite under the CoA between 6 April and 25 April 2018. The London Maritime Arbitrators' Association arbitrators said it was not; Jacobs J in the High Court, on an Arbitration Act 1996, section 69 appeal, said it was.[77] The majority in the Court of Appeal[78] reversed the High Court decision, and the Supreme Court in turn unanimously reversed the Court of Appeal majority decision.

Because the case came to the courts on a section 69 appeal under the Arbitration Act 1996, the Court was restricted to deciding the narrow point of law which was put to it, namely whether the shipowner's obligation to exercise reasonable endeavours to overcome the Force Majeure Event under clause 36.3(d) required them to accept payment in euros, with the Supreme Court deciding that such reasonable endeavours clauses did not entail an obligation to accept non-contractual performance. There was no discussion of the purpose of FM clauses generally or the specific purpose such a clause can be understood to have in this particular kind of contract. This is unfortunate, as in this case it was not the shipowner's performance that was prevented,[79] it was the charterer's, and yet it was the shipowner who invoked FM. The reason why can be surmised from Figure 4 below, which shows, circled, the state of the market at the time that the contract was entered into and its state at the time the shipowner suspended performance.

Figure 4 MUR Shipping

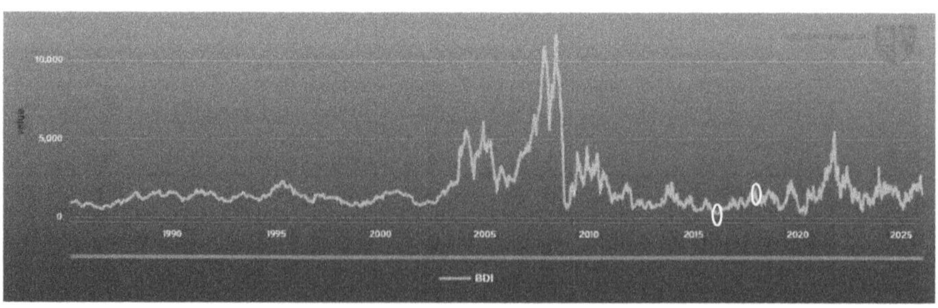

[77] *MUR Shipping BV v RTI Ltd* [2022] EWHC 467 (Comm).
[78] *MUR Shipping BV v RTI Ltd* [2022] EWCA Civ 1406.
[79] See discussion in Goldby (n 75) 751.

Indeed, there were suggestions in the Court of Appeal decision that the shipowners were acting opportunistically in suspending performance.[80] This flies in the face of the purpose of FM clauses, which is to allocate the risk of unexpected events that are such as to prevent performance. While FM clauses may operate in a broader set of circumstances than the doctrine of frustration, precisely because they operate to relieve the parties from binding contractual obligations, it would be contrary to the contractual purpose to interpret them other than strictly, and as has been held by the House of Lords with respect to frustration, it is submitted they are 'not lightly to be invoked to relieve contracting parties of the normal consequences of imprudent commercial bargains'.[81]

The Court justified its decision in favour of the shipowner partly by reference to the importance of ensuring certainty in commercial relations,[82] noting that if an obligation to exercise reasonable endeavours to overcome the obstacles to performance entailed the obligation to accept non-contractual performance, this would create too much uncertainty for the contractual parties. This approach focused too closely on the reasonable endeavours proviso taken in isolation and insufficiently on the FM clause as a whole, which was being invoked by a party whose performance was manifestly not impeded and who had no need to invoke it other than to escape what had turned out to be a bad bargain. This may have been due, at least partly, to the narrowness of the point of law that the Court was asked to decide, but it is also problematic that the Court decided the question on the basis of 'principle' rather than through construing the contract and the clause purposively.[83]

The BIMCO Force Majeure Clause 2022 emphasises that parties should perform unless they are genuinely prevented from doing so. The clause makes it explicit that notice of FM must come from the party whose performance is affected by the FM event,[84] and that

> The parties shall cooperate to minimise the effects of the Force Majeure on performance of the contract and *shall discuss in good faith alternative ways in which the contract can be performed* and/or the effect of the Force Majeure can be minimised.[85]

It is clear from this provision that the intent of the clause is to ensure that parties do not remain liable to perform in a situation when performance is genuinely prevented by events out of their control. The obligation to cooperate in good faith points to the desirability of preserving the contractual relationship despite disruption by the unexpected. It is to be hoped that, were a case similar to *MUR Shipping* to turn on a clause with the BIMCO wording, the outcome would be different and the courts would not countenance opportunistic suspension of performance.

[80] *MUR* (n 78) [60]. See also *MUR* (n 77) at [25], citing an email sent by MUR's CEO.

[81] *BTP Tioxide Ltd v Pioneer Shipping Ltd and Armada Marine SA (the 'Nema')* [1981] 2 Lloyd's Rep 239 (HL), at 253 per Lord Roskill.

[82] See *MUR* (n 56) [47]–[59].

[83] *MUR* (n 56) [25].

[84] BIMCO Force Majeure Clause 2022 (n 73) paras (a) and (c).

[85] BIMCO Force Majeure Clause 2022 (n 73) para (d). Emphasis added.

A final aspect of the impact of 'the unexpected' on longer-term chartering contracts which is worthy of discussion comes in the law relating to the payment of damages.

C. Contractual Purpose and the Right to Damages

Time charterparties invariably include a duration clause which sets out when and where the shipowner is entitled to their ship back. These clauses are often expressed with some flexibility to allow for any developments that might take place in the course of the charter,[86] and thus have often required interpretation where a dispute has arisen as to whether the charterer redelivered late in breach of contract. A common question to be addressed in such disputes is whether the final voyage that the charterer ordered the vessel to undertake was 'legitimate' or otherwise. As was aptly explained in *The Peonia*[87] by Bingham LJ in the Court of Appeal:

> … in [ordering the vessel to perform an illegitimate last voyage] the charterer commits a breach of contract (perhaps a repudiatory breach but that we need not decide). The owner need not comply with such an order, because he has never agreed to do so. Alternatively, he may comply with the order although not bound to do so: if he does comply, he is entitled to payment of hire at the charter-party rate until redelivery of the vessel and (provided he does not waive the charterer's breach) to damages (being the difference between the charter rate and the market rate if the market rate is higher than the charter rate) for the period between the final terminal date and redelivery. In the further alternative, if (which we do not decide) the charterer's breach is repudiatory, the owner may accept the repudiation, treat the charter as at an end and claim damages.[88]

The issue, of course, is that market movements may make it crucial for the shipowner to regain the vessel in time to perform a follow-on charter that is more lucrative, especially if such a follow-on charter is negotiated at a time of high market volatility. When the market is relatively stable or going up steadily, as appears to have been the case in 1987–88 when the facts of *The Peonia* occurred, the dispute is likely to be concerned merely with how much the charterer should pay in damages for the period of overrun, but if the market is moving up and down erratically, as it was when the facts of *The Achilleas*[89] unfolded, the question of whether damages are payable for any losses suffered consequently to the breach beyond the period of overrun becomes a crucial one.

[86] The following are some examples: '6 months, 20 days more or less in charterer's option' (*The Dione* [1975] 1 Lloyd's Rep. 115); 'minimum 11/ maximum 13 months' (*The Johnny* [1977] 2 Lloyd's Rep. 1); 'about minimum 10 months maximum 12 months' (*The Peonia* [1991] 1 Lloyd's Rep. 100).
[87] *The Peonia* [1991] 1 Lloyd's Rep. 100.
[88] ibid 107–108, per Bingham LJ.
[89] *The Achilleas* [2008] UKHL 48.

The Achilleas involved a time charter on the NYPE form entered into on 22 January 2003 for a period of 'about five to seven months' at a daily hire rate of US$13,500. The duration was extended for a further period of 'about five to seven months' at a daily hire rate of US$16,750, with the maximum duration of the extended period expiring on 2 May 2004. The market had more than doubled by late April 2004, so on 21 April 2004, just after the charterers had given notice of redelivery between 30 April and 2 May, the owners fixed a follow-on time charter of 'about four to six months' at a rate of US$39,500 per day. The follow-on charterer had the right to cancel if the ship was not delivered to it by 8 May 2004. There was no indication that the final voyage on which the charterer ordered the ship was illegitimate, however, the vessel was delayed after she had discharged her final cargo and was not in fact redelivered until 11 May. It had become clear by 5 May that the shipowner would not be able to deliver her to the follow-on charterer by the cancelling date, so they were forced to renegotiate a lower rate for the follow-on charter of US$31,500, losing US$8,000 for each of the 191.46 days of the follow-on charter, and they claimed this amount in damages.

Each of the five Law Lords wrote their own judgment in *The Achilleas*, and no two adopted identical reasoning. Broadly, one can identify two separate lines of reasoning. The first line of reasoning, which can be identified in the judgments of Lord Hoffmann and Lord Hope of Craighead, was based on the importance of 'market understanding' for determining the type or kind of loss for which a contractual party undertook responsibility. This line of reasoning, therefore, approached the question by undertaking a contextual interpretation of the contract. Lord Hoffmann, in effect, implied a limitation of liability term into the charterparty reflective of what he considered to be the market understanding as articulated by the dissenting arbitrator, noting that he was doing so in the process of interpreting the contract.[90]

The second line of reasoning, identified in the judgments of Lord Rodger of Earlsferry and Baroness Hale of Richmond, contended that, in line with the ratio of *Victoria Laundry*,[91] the owners' loss of profits in excess of the difference between the charter rate and any higher market rate during the period of overrun had been caused by volatile market conditions which amounted to an unusual occurrence outside the parties' contemplation. The judgment of Lord Walker of Gestingthorpe contained elements of both lines of reasoning.

As can be seen from Figure 5, this kind of market volatility was unprecedented prior to this particular period of time: it had never risen so sharply only to dive so quickly since the BDI had started to be published. Since then, high volatility appears to have become the norm.

[90] ibid [26]. See also discussion in M Goldby, 'Enforceability of Spontaneous Law in England: Some Evidence from Recent Shipping Cases' in M Goldby and L Mistelis (eds), *The Role of Arbitration in Shipping Law* (Oxford, OUP, 2016) 37–62, esp. paras 3.38–3.45.

[91] *Victoria Laundry v Newman Industries* [1949] 2 KB 528.

Figure 5 The Achilleas

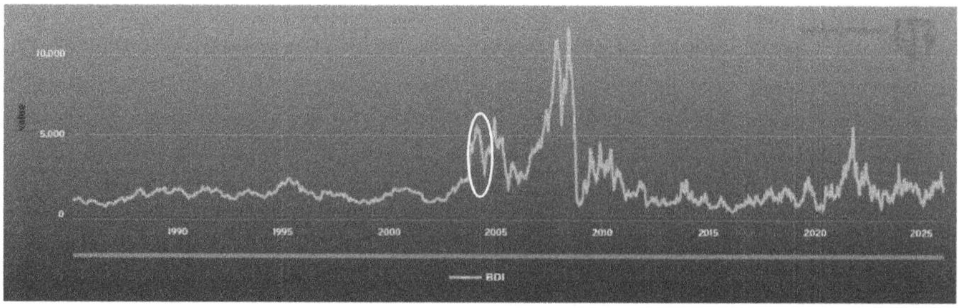

The second line of reasoning is in any case problematic. It is true that the market's volatility was unprecedented and would not have been within the parties' contemplation at the time they entered into the contract: why would the shipowner have fixed their vessel at a rate of US$16,750 for six months had they predicted the steady (and as it turned out dramatic) rise in the market? By fixing the vessel for six months, the shipowner was hedging against a possible downturn, and the charterer was hedging against a possible upturn. If the contract's function and raison d'être were to insure against adverse market movements, why should the risk of loss due to market movements be borne by the shipowner rather than the charterer, given it was the charterer who breached the contract by redelivering late? It should have been foreseeable to the parties at the time the contract was entered into that once notice of redelivery had been given, the shipowner would enter into a follow-on charter at a rate reflective of the market current at the time of the notice.[92] Additionally, there was nothing extraordinary about the length of the follow-on charter: it was for a similar period to that of the previous charters.

What of the first line of reasoning? Lord Hoffmann said that 'market understanding' was crucial to establishing the limits of the responsibility that the charterers had assumed. He indicated that this understanding could be gleaned from the minority arbitrator's dissenting award:

> The general understanding in the shipping market was that liability was restricted to the difference between the market rate and the charter rate for the overrun period and 'any departure from this rule [is] likely to give rise to a real risk of serious commercial uncertainty which the industry as a whole would regard as undesirable.[93]

It appears from the majority award as quoted by Lord Hoffmann, however, that this 'market understanding' was actually a lawyer's understanding and that:

> A broker 'in a commercial situation' would have said that the 'not unlikely' results arising from late delivery would include missing dates for a subsequent fixture, a dry-docking or the sale of the vessel.[94]

[92] This was acknowledged by Lord Hoffmann. See *The Achilleas* (n 89) [5].
[93] ibid [6].
[94] ibid [8].

Indeed, the 'market understanding' as articulated by the dissenting arbitrator would seem to reflect closely the pronouncement of the Court of Appeal in *The Peonia*, quoted above, a case where the issue of loss of a follow-on charter did not arise. Lord Hoffmann himself noted that '[t]here is no case in which the question now in issue has been raised.'[95] However, he went on to say

> … that in itself may be significant. This cannot have been the first time that freight rates have been volatile. There must have been previous cases in which late redelivery caused the loss of a profitable following fixture. But there is no reported case in which such a claim has been made. Instead, there has been a uniform series of dicta over many years in which judges have said or assumed that the damages for late delivery are the difference between the charter rate and the market rate.[96]

As already noted, and as can clearly be seen from Figure 5, this type of market volatility was wholly unprecedented at the time, and Lord Hoffmann may have been wrong to assume that this could not have been the first time that a dispute arose due to a lucrative follow-on fixture being lost as a consequence of late redelivery.

It is notable that the dissenting arbitrator's appeal to the need to avoid serious commercial uncertainty was alluded to by four out of the five judges in the House of Lords.[97] It may have swayed the Court sufficiently to depart from orthodox rules on damages, which, I argue, would have been more faithful to the general purpose of this type of contract, namely insuring against adverse market movements. Contractual interpretation should not have the goal of promoting commercial certainty but that of achieving the contract's purpose. Despite Lord Hoffmann's observations, the best way to safeguard commercial certainty is to include an express provision in the contract, which it would not have been difficult for the charterers to do, given the existence of standard clauses to that effect.[98]

VI. Conclusion

Contractual construction should not be dictated by a need to promote certainty: parties are in a position to do this at the time they enter into the contract by explicitly classifying terms or setting out the consequences, should any term be breached. Rather, contractual construction should be purposive. Longer-term chartering arrangements provide both parties with predictability, assuring them of a specific financial outcome regardless of market movements, which are highly likely to occur through the duration of the contractual period, and which will be

[95] ibid [10].
[96] ibid [10].
[97] ibid Lord Hoffmann at [6], Lord Hope of Craighead at [29], Lord Rodger of Earlsferry at [65], Baroness Hale of Richmond at [90] and [93].
[98] This was argued by the shipowners in this case; ibid [26].

in favour of one of the parties' self-interest and against the other's. When in light of market movements, it becomes advantageous for one of the parties to withhold performance, mutual recognition of each other's interests by the parties to such contracts requires the parties to act so as to achieve the purpose of the contract (insurance against the risk of adverse market movements), and therefore continued performance of the contract in the absence of genuine repudiation by the other party or genuine inability to overcome external obstacles to performance.

Purposive interpretation can limit opportunistic behaviour without specifically requiring the implication of an obligation to act in good faith into the contract. Because it entails reading the contract in line with business common sense, it both accords with the principles of interpretation embraced by English law and provides a principled basis for deciding these disputes, one that is not driven by a quest for certainty that the parties can provide for themselves by means of advance agreement, but by fidelity to the bargain and its purpose.

7

Hardship

EWAN McKENDRICK

I. Introduction

Unexpected events that occur after the time of entry into a contract can be the cause of significant hardship for contracting parties. For example, the cost of performance may increase exponentially as a result of the occurrence of an event or series of events that are beyond the control of the parties. Alternatively, the financial return from performance may be drastically reduced as a result of the occurrence of such an event. In these instances, the hardship to which reference is being made is hardship that is measured in financial terms. In other words, the concern is not with the case where further performance has become impossible, either physically or legally. Rather, the focus is on the case where it is possible for the parties to carry out their contractual obligations in the changed circumstances, but the cost of doing so has increased significantly or the return which it was expected would be obtained has reduced substantially in value. It is also important to note that the events that are the subject of this chapter are events that are beyond the control of the contracting parties and were not within their reasonable contemplation at the time of entry into the contract.[1] In such a situation what impact, if any, does or should hardship have on the obligations of the parties to perform their contractual obligations in accordance with the terms of their contract?

The answer to this question is not straightforward. Indeed, it has been a subject of considerable controversy. There is, perhaps, no better example of this controversy than the debates which surrounded the introduction of Article 1195 of the new French Civil Code.[2] For many years, French law, at least in the context of contracts which were not administrative in nature, declined to recognise a doctrine

[1] Difficulties can, of course, arise in determining when an event is beyond the control of the contracting parties and in deciding whether or not a particular event was within the reasonable contemplation of the parties at the time of entry into the contract, but these difficulties are not the subject of the present chapter.

[2] A brief summary of which can be found in S Rowan, *The New French Law of Contract* (Oxford, OUP, 2021) 182–83 which outlines the competing proposals that were put forward and the attempt by the Senate to remove Art 1195 from the new Code.

of change of circumstances and instead insisted that a contract which remained possible of performance be performed in accordance with its terms.[3] Article 1195 effected a fundamental change to French law by conferring on a contracting party the right to request the renegotiation of a contract where an unforeseeable change of circumstances has rendered performance excessively onerous for a party who had not accepted the risk of such a change. In the event that the renegotiations fail to produce an agreed outcome, the parties may terminate the contract or request the court to revise or terminate the contract. Article 1195 has thus brought French law into line with a trend that is emerging in European and international restatements of contract law[4] and in a number of legal systems around the world.[5]

English law, by contrast, has seen no equivalent build-up of pressure for the introduction of a doctrine of hardship or change of circumstances. While the financial crash of 2008 and the COVID-19 pandemic caused significant hardship for many contracting parties whose contracts were governed by English law, these events did not lead to widespread demands for the introduction of a change to English law of the type that was made in France in Article 1195. Given the lack of a doctrine of hardship or change of circumstances, what are the options open to contracting parties in the situation where an unforeseen change of circumstances has caused significant hardship to one or other of the contracting parties?

The aim of this chapter is to explore the principal options open to contracting parties in such a situation. In many ways the most obvious solution is for contracting parties to insert a hardship clause into their contract. However, it may be no easy task to persuade a contracting party to agree to such a term, and even where it is willing to negotiate such a term, difficulties are likely to arise in relation to the definition of hardship and the remedial response to the occurrence of an event of hardship. As we shall see, it is not particularly difficult to draft a term which gives to a contracting party the right to walk away from a contract on the occurrence of an event of hardship, but it is much more difficult to draft a contract in such a way as to ensure that there is effective renegotiation of the terms of the contract. In the absence of a route to effective renegotiation via an express contract term, is there any other option available to the parties as a matter of English contract law? While there are some options, they are of limited utility, and, insofar as they offer some relief from possible hardship, they do not lead to the renegotiation of the contract unless the parties are willing to embark upon such a renegotiation following the decision of the court. While a court may hold that a contract has been terminated or resolve a dispute between the parties as to the express or implied terms of the

[3] The example that is commonly cited in this context is the *Canal de Craponne* case civ 6 March 1876, 1876.1.193, an English translation of which can be found in H Beale, B Fauvarque-Cosson, J Rutgers and S Vogenauer, *Cases, Materials and Text on Contract Law*, 3rd edn (Oxford, Hart Publishing, 2019) 1213–14.

[4] See further section VI below.

[5] A recent example is Belgium. Art 5.74 of the Belgian Civil Code, which entered into force on 1 January 2023, provides '*Chaque partie doit exécuter ses obligations quand bien même l'exécution en serait plus onéreuse, soit que le côut de l'exécution ait augmenté, soit que la valuer de la contre-prestation ait diminué.*'

contract on the occurrence of an event which causes hardship to a contracting party, it will not itself engage in the renegotiation of the contract. Any such renegotiation is entirely a matter for the parties themselves.

Having thus outlined the scope of the chapter, we now turn to the options available to contracting parties.

II. Express Provision

The first option, and in many ways the most obvious one, is for the contracting parties to agree how to deal with the impact of hardship or to agree a mechanism that may prevent hardship from arising. Where the parties reach such an agreement after the event itself has occurred, then English law will give effect to the agreement provided that the requirements for a binding contract have been satisfied. This option does not give rise to any particular difficulty, and so nothing further need be said about it.

Slightly more difficult is the case where the parties seek to reach agreement in advance as to how to deal with the impact of a possible change of circumstances. The drafting of such a clause may not be a straightforward matter. First, it is necessary to secure agreement on the need for such a clause. A contracting party may not see the need for it, perhaps being of the view that the short-term nature of the contract renders it unlikely that such a clause will be required or out of a concern that the clause may be used as a vehicle to get out of what is no more than a bad bargain created by an unexpected movement in market prices. However, there are situations, typically involving contracts which require performance over a long-time horizon, where the need for some provision to be made is more evident and more likely to be agreed by the parties themselves (or their lawyers).

Second, there are a number of options open to contracting parties who wish to make provision, either directly or indirectly, for the impact of hardship or potential hardship on their contractual obligations. If, for example, the concern is a specific one, such as the likelihood that prices will rise over the lifetime of the contract, then that concern can be met, in part or in whole, by inserting a price escalation clause or an index-linking clause into the contract.[6] On the other hand, if the

[6] See, eg, *Multiservice Bookbinding Ltd v Marden* [1979] Ch 84. While such clauses may be effective in addressing the problem they may not solve all of the difficulties which may arise. For example, the method of indexation chosen may turn out, with the benefit of hindsight, to be inappropriate (as would appear to have been the case in *Arnold v Britton* [2015] UKSC 36, [2015] AC 1619) or the index agreed upon by the parties may subsequently cease to exist and the parties disagree as to how the terms of the contract relating to the choice of an alternative index are to operate in the circumstances which have occurred (on which see *Contact Energy v Attorney General* [2005] UKPC 13 and *Buckinghamshire v Barnardo's* [2018] UKSC 55, [2019] ICR 495). Further, in the case where the term is to be found in a contract between a trader and a consumer it may be found to be an unfair contract term and so not enforceable: see H Beale (ed), *Chitty on Contracts*, 36th edn (London, Sweet & Maxwell, 2025) paras 41-376–41-379.

concern is a more general one, a different type of contract term may be required. Here the parties have a range of options open to them, and the choice between them will depend not only on the bargaining power and skill of the parties but also on the outcome which they wish to achieve.

For example, in some circumstances it may suffice to give to the contracting parties an entitlement to walk away from the contract on the occurrence of a sufficiently serious change of circumstances. If this is, indeed, the aim of the parties, then the solution may lie in drafting a termination clause which permits termination of the contract for convenience or on the giving of an appropriate period of notice.[7] However, the continued existence of the contract may be a matter of considerable value to the contracting parties, and, in such a case, a widely drafted termination clause may not be the most appropriate way to deal with the challenge.[8] In such a situation there are other options available to contracting parties, and these include a force majeure clause, a material adverse change clause, a clause making provision for the variation of the contract or a hardship clause.

Of these four clauses, the least likely to be invoked may be the force majeure clause. While examples can be found of force majeure clauses of considerable sophistication which make provision for a variety of possible outcomes (from suspension to termination and including the possibility of adaptation), the more traditional form of force majeure clause is drafted with physical impediments to performance in mind, as evidenced by the fact that many such clauses require that the event said to constitute force majeure must render a party 'unable' to perform its contractual obligations or 'prevent' or 'hinder' contractual performance.[9] Wording of this nature has been held not to encompass the case where performance remains physically possible but has simply become more expensive for one of the contracting parties.[10] It is, of course, possible to address this challenge by re-wording the force majeure clause so that it is triggered whenever an event occurs which will seriously and adversely affect a party's ability to carry out its obligations under the contract.[11] However, it may be no easy task to persuade a contracting party

[7] eg, *Looney v Trafigura Beheer BV* [2011] EWHC 125 (Ch) where the contract conferred on a contracting party the right to terminate the contract on the giving of notice and on payment of a termination fee of £1 million. The submission that the entitlement to terminate was confined to situations where there were 'proper and reasonable grounds' to terminate the contract was rejected in light of the width of the clause as drafted. See further Goldby ch 6 in this volume.

[8] Although, once the contract has been brought to an end, it is always open to the parties to enter into negotiations for the conclusion of a new contract, albeit this does depend upon the willingness of both parties to enter into negotiations of this type.

[9] eg, *Tennants (Lancashire) Ltd v CS Wilson & Co Ltd* [1917] AC 495 where Earl Loreburn (at [510]) and Lord Finlay LC (at [509], albeit the latter was a dissenting judgment) held that even a very great rise in price would not 'prevent' or 'hinder' delivery within the meaning of the force majeure clause.

[10] eg, *Thames Valley Power Ltd v Total Gas & Power Ltd* [2005] EWHC 2208 (Comm), [2006] 1 Lloyd's Rep 441 where the clause specified that the force majeure event must render a party 'unable wholly or in part to carry out any of its obligations under this agreement'. The fact that it was considerably more expensive for a party to supply the contracted for gas did not render it 'unable' to carry out its obligations with the consequence that it was held not to be entitled to rely upon the force majeure clause (see [50]).

[11] For such a drafting suggestion see A Berg 'The Detailed Drafting of a Force Majeure Clause' in E McKendrick (ed), *Force Majeure and Frustration of Contract*, 2nd edn (London, Lloyd's of London Press, 1995) 63 at 96–97.

to agree to such a widely drafted force majeure clause, particularly where it is the party least likely in practice to wish to rely upon such a clause.[12] A further limitation of many force majeure clauses is that they are drafted with a view to shielding a party from a liability in damages in respect of any non-performance or with the aim of suspending the obligation to perform for the duration of the force majeure event. These are important functions but in the case where the parties wish their contract to continue, albeit under adjusted terms, force majeure clauses are not generally drafted in such a way as to achieve that objective (although there is no legal impediment to force majeure clauses being drafted in this way).

Another option is to include a material adverse change clause or a material adverse effect clause in the contract. There has been surprisingly little litigation on the effect of such clauses as a matter of English law, to the extent that the English courts have resorted to reliance upon Delaware case law in order to assist them when seeking to interpret such clauses.[13] Material adverse change clauses are most likely to be encountered in contracts for the acquisition of a business or in lending commitments made by banks.[14] In the case of share purchase agreements, they are often drafted with the aim of giving to the purchaser a right to withdraw from the transaction before closure[15] or to provide the buyer with a warranty that there has been no material adverse change in the financial position or prospects of the company, the breach of which will give to the buyer a right to recover damages.[16] Within these limits material adverse change clauses perform a useful commercial function, but their use tends to be confined to particular types of transaction and with particular consequences in mind. So, for example, they do not appear to be used as a means by which parties can be required to renegotiate the terms of their deal.

A third option is to confer on a contracting party a broad right to vary the terms of the contract. Clauses of this nature are often to be found in construction contracts where the employer is given a right to require changes to be made to the specifications of the project as it is developed, subject to the contractor having a right to refuse to accept unreasonable changes and to charge the employer for the extra cost which is attributable to the change instruction given by the employer.[17] The triggering factor for the exercise of such a right is not typically the occurrence of an event of hardship,

[12] Where the obligation of a party under a contract is to pay a sum of money, it is unlikely to wish, or be able to rely on a force majeure clause which is more likely to be invoked by a party who is under an obligation to deliver goods or provide a service of some kind.

[13] eg, *Travelport Ltd v WEX Inc* [2020] EWHC 2670 (Comm), [175]–[190]; *BM Brazil I Fundo De Investimento Em Participações Multistrategia v Sibanye BM Brazil (Pty) Ltd* [2024] EWHC 2566 (Comm), [198]–[204].

[14] See further R Hooley, 'Material Adverse Change Clauses After 9/11' in S Worthington (ed), *Commercial Law & Commercial Practice* (Oxford, Hart Publishing, 2003) 305.

[15] As was the case in *Travelport Ltd v WEX Inc* [2020] EWHC 2670 (Comm) and *BM Brazil I Fundo De Investimento Em Participações Multistrategia v Sibanye BM Brazil (Pty) Ltd* [2024] EWHC 2566 (Comm). See also *Finsbury Food Group plc v Axis Corporate Capital UK Ltd* [2023] EWHC 1559 (Comm).

[16] As was the case in *Decision Inc Holdings Pty Ltd v Garbett* [2023] EWCA Civ 1284.

[17] A particularly striking example of such flexibility is to be found in the 'golden contract' which was the subject of litigation in *R (on the application of Cobalt Data Centre 2 LLP) v Commissioners for His Majesty's Revenue and Customs* [2024] UKSC 40, [2024] 1 WLR 5213. See further ch 9 in this volume.

but it is not impossible that a broadly worded right to vary the terms of the contract[18] could prove to be useful to a party who wishes to alter the terms of a contract in order to mitigate the effects of the hardship which it is experiencing.

The fourth option, and the one most directly relevant to the present discussion, is a hardship clause.[19] While hardship clauses do differ in their wording,[20] the core of a hardship clause consists of the identification of the circumstances in which 'hardship' is agreed to occur and the procedure that is to be adopted on the occurrence of such circumstances. In broad terms, the occurrence of the event will create an obligation for the parties to meet with a view to renegotiating the terms of the contract in an attempt to alleviate the hardship which has arisen.[21] In this respect a hardship clause could be said to be a party-agreed equivalent of Article 1195 of the French Civil Code.

Hardship clauses are most likely to be found in long-term contracts given the perceived need to be able to adapt the terms of the contract to deal with the impact of events which occur over the lifetime of the contract. The drafting of a hardship clause is not, however, free from difficulty. Three particular difficulties can be identified as a matter of English law.

The first is whether English law recognises and gives effect to a contract term which requires parties to renegotiate the terms of their contract. English law has not, historically, been receptive to the existence of a contractual obligation to negotiate,[22] nor has it been willing to recognise the existence of an obligation to act in good faith in the negotiation of a contract. The case which most obviously creates difficulty in this context is the decision of the House of Lords in *Walford v Miles*.[23] However, *Walford* was not a case which concerned an express term of the contract that required the parties to re-negotiate the terms of their contract in good faith, and, to that extent, it can be said to be distinguishable. While English law remains reluctant to imply a good faith duty into a contract,[24] it has generally been willing to recognise and give effect to an express term of the contract which requires the parties to act in good faith, at least in the performance of the

[18] Note that it is possible that a broadly worded right may be subject to the *Braganza* implied term (*Braganza v BP Shipping Ltd* [2015] UKSC 17, [2015] 1 WLR 1661).

[19] On which see generally CM Schmitthoff, 'Hardship and Intervener Clauses' [1980] *Journal of Business Law* 82.

[20] The ICC has sought to provide guidance which may ensure a degree of standardisation through its Model Hardship Clause, the current version of which is dated March 2020 (see www.iccwbo.org/wp-content/uploads/sites/3/2020/03/icc-forcemajeure-hardship-clauses-march2020.pdf).

[21] eg, *Superior Overseas Development Corporation v British Gas Corporation* [1982] 1 Lloyd's Rep 262; *Associated British Ports v Tata Steel UK Ltd* [2017] EWHC 694 (Ch).

[22] *Courtney & Fairbairn Ltd v Tolaini Bros (Hotels) Ltd* [1975] 1 WLR 297, 301.

[23] *Walford v Miles* [1992] 2 AC 128.

[24] While it is possible that such a term could be implied (*Yam Seng Pte Ltd v International Trade Corporation Ltd* [2013] EWHC 111 (QB), [2013] 1 All ER (Comm) 1321), such cases are the exception rather than the rule (see *Greenclose Ltd v National Westminster Bank plc* [2014] EWHC 1156 (Ch), [2014] 2 Lloyd's Rep 169, *Hamsard 3147 Ltd v Boots UK Ltd* [2013] EWHC 3251 (Pat) and *Portsmouth City Council v Ensign Highways Ltd* [2015] EWHC 1969 (TCC), [2015] BLR 675).

contract.[25] It is perhaps more questionable whether this willingness to give effect to an express term of the contract will extend to an express obligation to act in good faith in the negotiation or the re-negotiation of the terms of the contract, although, even here, more recent authority can be cited in support of the proposition that English law should not refuse to give effect to an express term of the contract which requires the parties to renegotiate its terms in good faith.[26] In this still rather uncertain state of affairs, hardship clauses remain vulnerable to challenge on the ground that they are too uncertain to be enforceable and so must be drafted with great care if they are to survive judicial scrutiny.[27]

The second difficulty lies in defining what is to constitute hardship for the purposes of the clause.[28] Hardship clauses tend not to seek to define what is to constitute hardship with any degree of precision, preferring to rely on broad terms such as 'substantial economic hardship'[29] or 'any major physical or financial change in circumstances'.[30] The difficulty here is the obvious one, namely, deciding what 'substantial' or 'major' means in this context. These are questions of degree which do not admit of an easy answer that will hold good for all circumstances and all types of contracts. Although it is possible to inject a greater degree of precision into the definition of hardship (by, for example, specifying the percentage increase in prices or cost that will suffice to trigger the operation of the clause), greater certainty would come at the price of a degree of arbitrariness in terms of the exact percentage increase that is to trigger the operation of the clause. Given the difficulty of defining in advance the precise circumstances in which the clause

[25] eg, *Re Compound Photonics Group Ltd* [2022] EWCA Civ 1371.

[26] eg, *Petromec v Petroleo Brasileiro SA Petrobas* [2005] EWCA Civ 891, [2006] 1 Lloyd's Rep 121, [115]–[121]); *Knatchbull-Hugessen v SISU Capital Ltd* [2014] EWHC 1194 (QB), [23]; *The Football Association Premier League Ltd v PPLive Sports International Ltd* [2022] EWHC 38 (Comm), [86]. See also *RTI Ltd v MUR Shipping BV* [2024] UKSC 18, [2025] AC 675 where Lord Hamblen and Lord Burrows (at [46]) did not appear to see any difficulty in giving effect to a term of the contract which required the parties to 'consult in good faith to make such adjustments as may be appropriate' to the shipping schedule following the ending of a Force Majeure Event.

[27] An example of a clause which did pass judicial scrutiny is to be found in *Associated British Ports v Tata Steel UK Ltd* [2017] EWHC 694 (Ch) where the hardship clause was held to be sufficiently certain to create a binding obligation to refer the dispute between the parties to arbitration.

[28] eg, is the hardship to be measured by the impact of the change of circumstances on the solvency of the contracting parties or is it to be measured by reference to the impact on the cost or benefit of contractual performance? It is possible to envisage a circumstance in which the change of circumstances could be said to create a situation of hardship when viewing the individual contract in isolation, but it may not have such a significant effect on the business of a contracting party taken as a whole.

[29] The phrase used in *Superior Overseas Development Corporation v British Gas Corporation* [1982] 1 Lloyd's Rep 262.

[30] The phrase used in *Associated British Ports v Tata Steel UK Ltd* [2017] EWHC 694 (Ch). The validity of the clause was challenged on the ground that it was too uncertain to be given effect. Rose J rejected that challenge and held that it was possible to identify some changes which would clearly amount to a 'major physical or financial change in circumstances' and some changes which would fall outside of its scope. On this basis the clause was sufficiently certain to be enforceable even though it may be difficult in the abstract to draw a precise dividing line between changes falling either side of the line.

is to operate, parties may prefer to accept a degree of uncertainty and rely on more general wording of the type noted above.

The third and more substantial difficulty concerns the remedial consequences of any failure on the part of the parties to reach agreement on the re-negotiation of the contract. What remedial response does English law provide where one of the parties refuses to meet or the parties do meet but fail to reach agreement? An initial difficulty is likely to lie in proving that the failure to reach agreement was caused by a breach of contract by one of the contracting parties. The fact that the parties have failed to reach agreement does not of itself demonstrate that there has been a breach of contract. Contracting parties who agree to renegotiate their contract in good faith do not thereby agree to give up the pursuit of self-interest in the renegotiation process (although such an obligation may qualify or limit the pursuit of self-interest), and so it is entirely possible that the renegotiations may not produce any agreed adjustment to the original contract. The situation in which it is more likely to be possible to establish the existence of a breach of contract is one where a party absolutely refuses to enter into any renegotiations without providing any basis for its refusal to do so. However, even if the hurdle of establishing a breach of contract is overcome, this leads on to the next difficulty, namely identifying an appropriate remedy in respect of the breach.

An English court would not issue a specific performance order which required the parties to enter into, or to continue, negotiations, nor would an English court adapt the terms of the contract for the parties.[31] This leaves the remedy of damages, but the challenge here will lie in proving the expectation loss that has been suffered as a result of the breach, given that the outcome of a renegotiation conducted in accordance with the terms of the hardship clause cannot be known with any certainty. Further, a remedy in damages confined to the wasted expenses incurred in any abortive renegotiations is unlikely to be of much value. This being the case, the absence of an efficacious remedy risks leaving the hardship clause as an aspirational statement which has a signalling value but is otherwise largely devoid of effect.

However, this may be to overstate the case. There is a way of giving content to the clause by conferring jurisdiction on a third party to resolve any impasse in the renegotiation process. Thus, while the courts will not themselves adapt the terms of the contract for the parties, they will not prevent a third party, such as an arbitrator,[32] from doing so where the parties have expressly conferred such a jurisdiction on the third party. In this way effect can be given to a hardship clause should the parties agree to draft the clause in this form.

[31] While there is no authority directly in point, there is no authority of which I am aware which would support the existence of a jurisdiction to adapt a contract when the parties themselves have failed to reach agreement on any such adaptation.

[32] eg, *Associated British Ports v Tata Steel UK Ltd* [2017] EWHC 694 (Ch) where the clause provided that, if the parties failed to reach agreement within six months, the matter was to be referred to an arbitrator whose decision was agreed to be binding on the parties.

III. Frustration

But what is to be done in the situation where the parties have not made express provision for an event of hardship in their contract? What are the default powers of the court in such a situation? It is to this matter that we now turn. The first legal doctrine to consider is the doctrine of frustration. However, as is well known, the doctrine operates within very narrow limits, and there is 'a well-established proposition of English law that an increase in expense, however great, will not of itself frustrate a contract'.[33] Some of the leading cases on the doctrine of frustration in English law have been cases in which the cost of performance for one contracting party has increased significantly, but the change in economic circumstances was held not to be sufficient to frustrate the contract.[34] The law in this respect was classically expressed by Viscount Simon LC in *British Movietonews Ltd v London & District Cinemas Ltd*[35] when he stated:

> The parties to an executory contract are often faced, in the course of carrying it out, with a turn of events which they did not at all anticipate – a wholly abnormal rise or fall in prices, a sudden depreciation of currency, an unexpected obstacle to execution, or the like. Yet this does not in itself affect the bargains they have made.[36]

Two features of these statements should, however, be noted. The first is the use of the words 'of itself' or 'in itself', which indicate that a change in economic circumstances, in combination with some other factor, may suffice to frustrate a contract. The second is that there has been some academic challenge to the apparently absolute nature of the proposition that an increase in price can never, of itself, frustrate a contract.[37] There is no authority which states in unequivocal terms that a change in economic circumstances can *never* constitute a frustrating event and some judges have been careful to leave the door open to such a possibility.[38] But, to the extent that the judges may be said to have left the door open to such a possibility, it is likely that the door will only be opened in extreme circumstances such as hyperinflation of a type which the UK has never seen but which Germany witnessed in the aftermath of the First World War. A jurisdiction to intervene only in such extreme circumstances is unlikely to be of much practical utility.

[33] J Beatson 'Increased Expense and Frustration' in FD Rose (ed), *Consensus Ad Idem: Essays on the Law of Contract in Honour of Guenter Treitel* (London, Sweet & Maxwell, 1996) 121.

[34] eg, *Davis Contractors v Fareham Urban District Council* [1956] AC 696; *Tsakiroglou & Co Ltd v Noblee Thorn GmbH* [1962] AC 93.

[35] *British Movietonews Ltd v London & District Cinemas Ltd* [1952] AC 166.

[36] ibid 185. See also the statement of Lord Loreburn in *Tennants v C.S. Wilson & Co Ltd* [1917] AC 495, 510.

[37] eg, J Beatson (n 33) (where reliance was placed in part on a line of cases concerned with the abandonment of a voyage) and A Forte 'Economic Frustration of Commercial Contracts: A Comparative Analysis With Particular Reference to the United Kingdom' [1986] *Juridical Review* 1.

[38] eg, the judgment of Lord Reid in *Tsakiroglou & Co Ltd v Noblee Thorn GmbH* [1962] AC 93, 118 when he stated that he did not have to 'consider what the result might be if the increase had reached an astronomical figure'.

A further difficulty with the doctrine of frustration is to be found in the consequences that follow from its application. Frustration operates to bring about the automatic prospective discharge of the contract between the parties,[39] subject to the limited financial relief which the courts can provide under the Law Reform (Frustrated Contracts) Act 1943.[40] In particular, the courts do not have a jurisdiction to adapt the terms of a contract which has been frustrated. This refusal to countenance the possibility of judicial adaptation of the contract in cases of 'economic frustration' has been criticised on the ground that 'it flies in the face of commercial reality to hold that frustration can only terminate contracts'.[41] The limited remedial options currently available in English law would become apparent in the unlikely circumstance that the English courts chose to develop a more liberal doctrine of frustration. Were such a development to occur, it would lead to the discharge of a greater number of contracts, but it is unlikely that this is what the commercial community would wish to occur. Jurisdictions which have a more liberal equivalent of the doctrine of frustration tend to provide the judiciary with greater remedial options, including the adaptation of the contract. However, it is almost impossible to conceive of the English courts developing a more liberal doctrine of frustration given that the doctrine itself has been developed by numerous decisions of the highest courts in the land over more than a century and the ability to develop broader remedial responses is limited by the enactment of the 1943 Act, which the courts cannot 'supplement' by the development of an alternative set of remedial responses.

It is therefore highly unlikely that the doctrine of frustration will be of much utility to a contracting party who is experiencing significant hardship as a result of a change in economic circumstances subsequent to entry into the contract. That this is so is, perhaps, evidenced by the response of the English courts to the 2008 financial crisis and the COVID-19 pandemic, both of which resulted in substantial economic hardship for contracting parties but did not result in the liberalisation of the doctrine of frustration. It is therefore unlikely that the doctrine of frustration will have any significant role to play in cases of hardship caused by a change in economic circumstances.

IV. Interpretation

What role might be played in cases of hardship by the principles applied by the courts to the interpretation of contracts? At first sight, this may seem a surprising question to ask because the principles applied by the courts to the interpretation of contracts are designed to give effect to the meaning of the words chosen by the

[39] *Hilji Mulji v Cheong Yue SS Co* [1926] AC 497.

[40] The effect of which, in broad terms, is to enable a court to reverse an unjust enrichment but it does not enable a court to engage in loss apportionment in the absence of an enrichment.

[41] Forte (n 37) 23.

parties and not to rescue a party from the hardship it is experiencing as a result of a change of circumstances subsequent to the making of the contract. However, it is a feature of some of the leading cases on the interpretation of contracts that an unexpected event has occurred for which the contract has not made clear provision and which has caused, or will in future cause, hardship to one of the contracting parties if a particular interpretation of the contract is adopted. To what extent will the courts take account of the hardship that may be suffered by one of the contracting parties when deciding what is the correct interpretation of the term of the contract that is in dispute between the parties?

A good example of this process is provided by the decision of the Supreme Court in *Arnold v Britton*.[42] The issue before the Court was the interpretation of a clause making provision for the calculation of a service charge in leases with a 99-year term. The construction for which the landlord contended was one which would cause significant hardship to the lessees in that it would result in the service charge increasing at a compound rate of 10 per cent per annum over the lifetime of the lease. The tenants sought to resist this construction on the ground that it would result in such 'an increasingly absurdly high annual service charge' in the later years of the leases that it could not 'be right'.[43] Some idea of the impact of the landlord's construction for the lessees can be gleaned from an example given by Lord Carnwath in his dissenting judgment in which a service charge of £90 per year would increase to a charge of £1,025,004 per year in 2072.[44] This construction was acknowledged by Lord Hodge to be a 'highly unsatisfactory outcome'[45] for the tenants, while Lord Carnwath, stated that the consequences for the tenants were 'potentially catastrophic'[46] and he described such an outcome as 'grotesque'.[47] The tenants sought to avoid this outcome by submitting that the words relied upon by the landlord were not intended to fix the amount that was to be paid by the tenants but rather were to operate as a cap on their liability.

The majority rejected this construction on the basis that it was not consistent with the wording of the clause, which created a fixed charge of £90 with an escalator to deal with future inflation and not, as the tenants contended, a variable service charge which was subject to a cap to which the escalator applied.[48] The majority placed emphasis on the importance of the natural meaning of the words used by the parties and were not willing to read into the lease words which were not there.[49] Thus Lord Neuberger stated that 'the purpose of interpretation is to

[42] *Arnold v Britton & Ors* [2015] UKSC 36, [2015] AC 1619.
[43] ibid [10].
[44] ibid [100]. A different example, with not quite such extreme consequences, was given by Lord Neuberger (at [30]) of a lease entered into in 1980 with a service charge of £90 per year which would rise to £2,500 in 2015 but by 2072 would rise to a 'sum over £550,000'.
[45] ibid [66].
[46] ibid [80].
[47] ibid [104], [138].
[48] ibid [75].
[49] ibid [32].

identify what the parties have agreed, not what the court thinks they should have agreed'[50] and that 'there is no principle of interpretation which entitles a court to re-write a contractual provision simply because the factor which the parties catered for does not seem to be developing in the way in which the parties may well have expected'.[51] The fact that the agreement had 'worked out badly, or even disastrously' for these particular tenants[52] was held not to be 'a reason for departing from the natural language'[53] of the lease.

It is, however, worth noting the potentially extreme nature of the consequences of the majority conclusion for these tenants. They were acknowledged by counsel for the landlord, who stated that his client recognised that the dismissal of the tenants' appeal would result in the 'renegotiation' of the leases 'for pragmatic if not for legal reasons'.[54] Lord Neuberger also noted the landlord's apparent recognition of the need for 'appropriate amendments' to the leases and expressed the hope that 'a fair and just amendment can be agreed'[55] while Lord Hodge stated that 'if the parties cannot agree an amendment of the leases on a fair basis, the lessees will have to seek parliamentary intervention'.[56] The responses of Lord Neuberger and Lord Hodge thus reflect the need for some form of re-negotiation of the leases, but they placed the responsibility for entry into these renegotiations and their outcome on the shoulders of the parties. It was not the task of the Court to re-negotiate the deal for the parties despite the fact that the leases as interpreted by the Supreme Court had such potentially devastating consequences for the tenants, at least in the longer term.

A second case worthy of note is the decision of the Supreme Court, on an appeal from the Inner House of the Court of Session, in *Lloyds TSB Foundation for Scotland v Lloyds Banking Group plc*.[57] The defender banking group covenanted in a deed entered into in 1997 to pay to the pursuers, a charitable foundation, the greater of a fixed share of pre-tax profits or the sum of £38,920. As a result of a change in accounting practice introduced in 2005 in relation to the tax treatment of negative goodwill, the defender's accounts for the relevant year turned what would otherwise have been a loss of over £10 billion into a profit before tax of over £1 billion. The pursuer claimed that it was entitled to the agreed share of

[50] ibid [20].

[51] ibid [41].

[52] It would appear that the landlord had negotiated a poor deal with some of the earlier tenants on the site and so the increased charges payable by the tenants who were parties to the litigation may have been one means by which the landlord sought to recoup her losses on the pre-1980 leases (see [156]). The concern for equity between the tenants was a factor which featured prominently in the judgment of Lord Carnwath (see [118] and [157]).

[53] ibid [19].

[54] ibid [155].

[55] ibid [64].

[56] ibid [79].

[57] *Lloyds TSB Foundation for Scotland v Lloyds Banking Group plc* [2013] UKSC 3, [2013] 1 WLR 366, on which see more generally E McKendrick 'Economic Frustration Revisited' in ARC Simpson, S Crichton Styles, E West and ALM Wilson (eds), *Continuity, Change and Pragmatism in the Law: Essays in Memory of Professor Angelo Forte* (Aberdeen, Aberdeen University Press, 2016) 413.

that profit, which amounted to £3,543,333. The defender declined to pay, and the Supreme Court upheld that decision.

A point of interest for the current discussion is that there were two doctrines in play before the courts in Scotland and the Supreme Court. The first was whether the defender was entitled to an equitable adjustment of the contract. It was held that it was not. There was no suggestion that the 1997 deed had been frustrated[58] and Lord Hope expressly rejected the submission that Scots law conferred on the Court a jurisdiction to engage in the equitable adjustment of a contract on the basis that its performance, while not frustrated, was no longer that which was originally contemplated by the parties.[59]

Given that the deed had not been frustrated and there was no possibility of an equitable adjustment to the deed, the question for the Supreme Court was held to be how the language of the deed 'best operates in the fundamentally changed and entirely unforeseen circumstances in the light of the parties' original intentions and purposes'.[60] It was held that the language of the deed did not confer upon the pursuer an entitlement to recover the sum claimed. One of the principal factors which was relied upon by the Supreme Court in concluding that the pursuer was not entitled to payment was the unexpected change of circumstances in relation to the tax treatment of negative goodwill. Thus Lord Mance held that pre-tax profit for the purpose of the deed was defined as 'group profit before taxation', and this was held to mean 'realised profit or loss before taxation'. This was held to exclude 'a wholly novel element which was included in the income statement by a change which was neither foreseen nor foreseeable and which, had it been foreseen when the deeds were executed, would not have been accepted as part of the computation of profit or loss'.[61] The effect of this purposive approach to the interpretation of the deed was to achieve a result which was very similar to, if not identical with, that which might have been achieved by the application of a principle of change of circumstances or of equitable adjustment.

It could be said that the Lloyd's litigation did not involve hardship because there was no suggestion that the defender banking group would suffer particular hardship if required to make payment to the pursuer. The concern was more to avoid the conferral of an unwarranted windfall on the pursuer. Nevertheless, the case does show that the courts can and do take account of the consequences of their conclusions when choosing between competing meanings of a disputed term. As Lord Reid once observed, 'the more unreasonable the result the more

[58] ibid [23].

[59] ibid [47]. Equitable adjustment does have a role to play in Scotland, but it applies in the case where the contract has been frustrated (see [40]). Here it is important to recall that the Law Reform (Frustrated Contracts) Act 1943 does not apply to Scotland. This being the case, it is for the Scottish courts to develop the applicable rules of law. In any event, the existence of a jurisdiction known as 'equitable adjustment' in the context of the frustration of a contract does not support the existence of such a jurisdiction where the contract has not been frustrated.

[60] *Lloyd's TSB* (n 57) [23].

[61] ibid [25].

unlikely it is that the parties can have intended it, and if they do intend it the more necessary it is that they shall make that intention abundantly clear'.[62]

However, there are two limits upon the power of the courts that must be taken into account in this context. The first is that the court is confined to choosing between the competing meanings of the disputed words. While, occasionally, one can find cases in which the courts have adopted the construction of a contract for which neither party has contended,[63] the courts do not have a jurisdiction to devise a fresh solution of their own choosing as a means by which hardship to a party to a contract can be reduced or eliminated. In this respect it is important to note that the re-negotiation contemplated by the Supreme Court in *Arnold* was a renegotiation conducted by the parties in light of the decision of the Court, and not a re-negotiation by the Court itself. Second, the mere fact that a contract has turned out to be a bad bargain, even an extremely bad bargain, for one of the parties does not necessarily mean that the contract is devoid of commercial sense. It can be explained on the ground that one party has made a very good bargain and the other a very bad one. Cases in which a meaning of a disputed term is held to be devoid of commercial common sense are more often cases where the term appears to produce entirely haphazard outcomes for which there is no rational explanation.[64] Where, however, the outcome is one which consistently favours one party to the contract, then it is capable of rational explanation, namely that one party has made a good bargain and it is not the function of the court to intervene in order to make the contract a fairer one. Finally, while the courts can engage in 'corrective interpretation', they can only do so where both the mistake and the solution are clear. In a case such as *Arnold*, if the assumption is made that the parties can be seen, with the benefit of hindsight, to have chosen the wrong mechanism to index-link the service charge, this does not give the court jurisdiction to then select what it believes to be a more appropriate mechanism to do so. So, while the principles applied by the courts to the interpretation of contracts may, on occasion, be of assistance to a party who is experiencing significant hardship after a change of circumstances, they are unlikely to provide a solution except in a rare case.

V. Implication

A further possibility is for the court to imply a term into the contract in order to mitigate or eliminate the hardship which is being experienced by a contracting party. The difficulty here, however, is the obvious one, namely the limited scope

[62] *L Schuler AG v Wickman Machine Tool Sales Ltd* [1974] AC 235, 251.

[63] An example here is the decision of the Supreme Court in *Sara & Hossain Asset Holdings Ltd v Blacks Outdoor Retail Ltd* [2023] UKSC 1, [2023] 1 WLR 575 at [50].

[64] An example here might be *Chartbrook Ltd v Persimmon Homes Ltd* [2009] UKHL 38, [2009] 1 AC 1101.

within which the courts will imply a term into a contract. There is no general jurisdiction to imply such a term, for example, as a term implied in law into commercial contracts generally, and so any such implied term would have to be implied into a particular contract as a matter of fact. This would require a party to demonstrate that the term is a necessary one in the sense that, without the term, the contract would lack commercial or practical coherence.[65] In particular, it does not suffice to show that the term is reasonable or that it would render the contract fairer or even that the parties would have agreed to it had it been suggested to them.[66]

An example of the difficulties involved in seeking to imply a term into a contract in order to mitigate the effects of hardship caused by an unforeseen event is provided by the decision of the Court of Appeal in *Bank of New York Mellon (International) Ltd v Cine-UK Ltd*[67] where tenants under a 35-year lease for the use of premises as a cinema sought to imply a term into their lease, the effect of which would have been to relieve them of their obligation to pay rent when the premises could not be used as a cinema because of the lockdown measures imposed by government as a response to the COVID-19 pandemic. The Court of Appeal declined to imply any such term, holding that the lease worked 'perfectly well'[68] without the suggested implied term and that the tenants had come 'nowhere near'[69] satisfying the necessity test for the implication of terms into a contract. The tenants were therefore left to bear the cost of paying the entirety of the rent for premises which they could not lawfully use.[70]

However, it does not follow from this that implied terms can have no possible application in cases of hardship. An interesting example,[71] albeit one that is difficult to classify in doctrinal terms, is the decision of the Court of Appeal in *Staffordshire Area Health Authority v South Staffordshire Waterworks Co.*[72] In 1929 the parties entered into a contract under which the defendants contracted to supply water to the claimants 'at all times hereafter' at a fixed price per 1,000 gallons of water supplied. The fixed price, after translation into decimal currency, was 2.9 pence per 1,000 gallons in 1929, whereas by the mid-1970s the 'ordinary rate'[73] for the supply of water was 55 pence per 1,000 gallons. This increase led the defendants on 30 September 1975 to give the claimants six months' notice

[65] *Marks and Spencer plc v BNP Paribas Securities Services Trust Co (Jersey) Ltd* [2015] UKSC 72, [2016] AC 742, [21].

[66] ibid.

[67] *Bank of New York Mellon (International) Ltd v Cine-UK Ltd* [2022] EWCA Civ 1021.

[68] ibid [138].

[69] ibid [141].

[70] Contrast the response of the Dutch courts to cases of this type where in a number of cases rent payments were temporarily discounted by 50% for the period of the lockdown caused by the COVID-19 pandemic: see V Mak 'Covid-19 and Long-Term Contracts' [2022] *European Review of Private Law* 419.

[71] The case may be said to be of heightened interest insofar as the facts bear some resemblance to the famous case of *Canal de Craponne* Cass Civ 6 March 1876, 1876.1.193 where the French courts declined to adjust the terms of the contract between the parties.

[72] *Staffordshire Area Health Authority v South Staffordshire Waterworks Co* [1978] 1 WLR 1387.

[73] ibid 1393.

in order to terminate the contract. In these circumstances the claimants sought a declaration that the defendants were not entitled to terminate the contract without their consent so that the notice issued by the defendants was void and of no effect. The defendants for their part sought declarations that the agreement was terminable on the giving of reasonable notice, that six months' notice was reasonable in all the circumstances and that from the date of termination they were entitled to charge the claimants for the supply of water at the 'normal rate'.[74] The Court of Appeal granted a declaration that the agreement was determinable on the giving of reasonable notice but did not make any declaration in relation to the terms on which water was to be supplied in the future.

Although the Court of Appeal was unanimous in its conclusion, the same cannot be said of the reasoning of the three members of the Court. Goff and Cumming-Bruce LJJ were willing to make an 'inference' of a power to determine on giving reasonable notice.[75] In making this 'inference', the words 'at all times hereafter' were held to be but a 'factor'[76] in reaching this conclusion, which was displaced 'by other circumstances attending the formation of the agreement'.[77] It is not entirely clear whether this inference was made as a matter of interpretation or implication, and it may be that the distinction did not matter to either judge because the overall aim was to give effect to what was believed to be the objective intention of the parties.[78] Similar difficulties arise in classifying the judgment of Lord Denning. He made a number of references to what he termed 'the modern rule of construction'[79] and concluded that the situation had changed 'so radically' since 1929 in light of, amongst other things, 'mountainous inflation',[80] that the words 'at all times hereafter' had ceased to bind.[81] One view of his judgment is that he concluded that the contract had been frustrated[82] but, if it had been frustrated, it should have come to an end automatically and not on the giving of six months' notice by the defendants. The conclusion that the contract was frustrated also does not fit with Lord Denning's view that the defendants remained bound to supply water to the claimants.[83] An alternative explanation is that he implied a

[74] A summary of the terms of the declarations sought can be found at [1978] 1 WLR 1387, 1389 and the text of the third and fourth declarations sought by the defendants is set out by Goff LJ at 1403–1404.

[75] ibid 1403A and 1403G (Goff LJ) and 1406D (Cumming-Bruce LJ).

[76] ibid 1400D (Goff LJ) and 1406D (Cumming Bruce LJ).

[77] ibid 1406D.

[78] In this respect perhaps anticipating the approach of Lord Hoffmann in *Attorney General of Belize v Belize Telecom Ltd* [2009] UKPC 10, [2009] 1 WLR 1988.

[79] *Staffordshire Area Health Authority* (n 72) 1396A, 1397A and 1398F.

[80] ibid1397, 1404E-F.

[81] ibid 1395G and 1398F.

[82] eg, E Peel *Treitel The Law of Contract*, 16th edn (London, Thomson Reuters, 2025) 19–038; M Furmston, *Cheshire, Fifoot and Furmston's Law Of Contract*, 17th edn (Oxford, OUP, 2017) 722. This interpretation gains some support from Lord Denning's reference to his own judgment in *British Movietonews Ltd v London and District Cinemas* [1951] 1 KB 190. However, the difficulty with this reference, as Treitel points out, is that it is based on a passage which was expressly rejected on appeal to the House of Lords: [1952] AC 166, 185.

[83] *Staffordshire Area Health Authority* (n 72) 1398H.

term into the contract, a suggestion which gains some support from the judgment of Cumming-Bruce LJ,[84] but at no point did Lord Denning use the language of implication.

A further point worth noting is that the declaration issued by the Court of Appeal was confined to the determination of the agreement and did not make the declaration requested by the defendants in relation to the price of any future supply of water. Although Lord Denning commended to the parties a solution under which the claimants would pay 70 per cent of the current market rate,[85] the declaration issued by the Court said nothing about payment. The hope was expressed that the parties might be able to reach a compromise.[86] However, it was not the task of the Court to devise that compromise, although both Goff and Cumming-Bruce LJJ acknowledged that, in the event that the parties failed to reach agreement, the matter should be referred back to the first instance judge.[87] Here again, any renegotiation of the terms of supply was a matter for the parties and not for the Court of Appeal.

The *Staffordshire* case is a difficult one. One senses that the Court was straining to find a solution which was fair in the circumstances in which the parties found themselves,[88] but, in the absence of a clearly established legal doctrine which enabled the Court to adapt the terms of the contract in the light of the radically changed circumstances since the parties entered into the agreement in 1929, they had to make use of such doctrinal devices as they could in order to permit the agreement to be brought to an end, while leaving it to the parties to then negotiate, if they could, the new terms on which water was to be supplied by the defendants to the claimants.

VI. Changing the Default Rule

The lack of a general hardship doctrine in English law can be contrasted with developments in international re-statements of contract law and in a growing number of national legal systems. Thus a hardship or change of circumstance provision is to be found in Articles 6.2.2 and 6.2.3 of the UNIDROIT Principles of International Commercial Contracts ('PICC'), Article 6:111 of the Principles of European Contract Law ('PECL') and Book III Article 1:110 of the Draft Common Frame of Reference ('DCFR'). A hardship provision has also recently been introduced

[84] Thus, while acknowledging his respect for Lord Denning, he declined to base his judgment on the existence of an implied term that the agreement should not continue to bind the parties upon the emergence of circumstances which the parties did not then foresee or an implied term that was 'akin to frustration' (ibid 1406F-D).

[85] ibid 1399A which was the same percentage of the market rate that was charged in 1929 (1393A). See also the judgment of Cumming-Bruce LJ at 1407B-D.

[86] ibid 1399A and 1404E-F.

[87] ibid 1404G and 1407D.

[88] SA Smith, *Atiyah's Introduction to the Law of Contract*, 6th edn (Oxford, OUP, 2006) 304.

into the Civil Codes of China,[89] France,[90] Germany[91] and Belgium[92] and is a more established part of a number of civilian legal systems.[93] Within common law systems, a broader doctrine of commercial impracticability can be found in American law, and there is authority, albeit controversial, for the exercise by the courts of more flexible remedial powers than an English court would enjoy.[94] A factor behind some of the more recent expressions of support for the development of a hardship doctrine is the worldwide impact of the COVID-19 pandemic,[95] in particular for those contracting parties who wished to be able to preserve and adapt their contract through changing and challenging times.

However, the fact that other legal systems seem to be moving in a different direction from English law does not mean that English law should follow suit. But it should give us pause for thought. One advantage of changing the default rule is that it reduces the need for contracting parties to make their own provision for hardship, and they can rely on the default rule that is supplied by the governing law. The disadvantage, however, is that it may generate a level of uncertainty with which English law may be uncomfortable, although the doctrine of hardship does not seem to be a cause of undue uncertainty in those jurisdictions which have introduced the doctrine because the general rule remains that a party remains bound to fulfil its contractual obligations even if performance has become more onerous.[96] It would appear to operate more as a safety valve than as a mechanism by which a contracting party can seek to escape from what has proved to be a bad bargain.

That said, the hardship jurisdictions to be found in international re-statements and in national law struggle with very similar issues to those experienced by a lawyer seeking to draft a hardship clause in a contract governed by English law. The first lies in defining 'hardship' or the trigger for the operation of the rule. In the case of PECL, and Article 1195 of the French Civil Code, performance of the contract must have become 'excessively onerous'[97] for the party seeking to invoke the doctrine, whereas in the case of the PICC the event must fundamentally alter the equilibrium of the contract[98] and in the case of the DCFR, performance must

[89] Art 533 of the Chinese Civil Code.

[90] Art 1195 of the French Civil Code.

[91] Art 313 of the BGB, albeit in this instance the Code is making express provision for a doctrine which previously had to find its home in the good faith provision of Art 242.

[92] Art 5.74 of the Belgian Civil Code.

[93] eg, Art 1467 of the Italian Civil Code; Art 6:258 of the Dutch Civil Code; Art 388 of the Greek Civil Code.

[94] The example that is commonly cited in this context is the decision in *Aluminium Company of America v Essex Group Inc* 499 F Supp 53 (1980).

[95] eg, KP Berger and D Behn, 'Force Majeure and Hardship in the Age of Corona: A Historical and Comparative Study' (2019-2020) 6 *McGill Journal of Dispute Resolution* 78.

[96] Thus the starting point for both PICC Art 6.2.1 and PECL Art 6:111 is that a party remains bound to perform its contractual obligations where performance becomes more onerous for that party. Hardship is thus the exception rather than the rule.

[97] PECL Art 6:111(2).

[98] Art 6.2.2.

have become so onerous that it would be manifestly unjust to hold the party to the terms of the contract.[99] It is not clear that this difference in wording is of any particular significance, but the problem lies in identifying how onerous a change must be before it qualifies as excessive or fundamental. No universal answer can be given to this question because much will depend upon the facts of the individual case. As has been noted, the same problem confronts a lawyer responsible for drafting a hardship clause except that in this instance the definition of hardship has to be agreed in advance rather than applied by a court with the benefit of hindsight. However, one potential advantage of a party-agreed clause is that the parties can define for themselves what is to constitute hardship and so need not rely on the one-size-fits-all definition of the type that will be found in a legal rule.

The second relates to the rights of the party seeking to invoke the hardship doctrine. In the case of the PICC[100] and Article 1195 of the French Civil Code, that party is given a right to request the re-negotiation of the contract, and in the case of the PECL, the parties are stated to be 'bound to enter into negotiations with a view to adapting the contract or ending it',[101] but no such right is to be found in the DCFR where, instead, a court asked for relief should only accede where the party seeking relief has attempted, reasonably and in good faith, to achieve by negotiation a reasonable and equitable adjustment of the terms of the contract.[102] PECL goes furthest in creating a right to recover damages in respect of any loss suffered as a result of a party refusing to negotiate or breaking off negotiations contrary to good faith and fair dealing.[103]

The third relates to the role and power of the courts. The power given to the court is typically to bring the contract to an end or to adapt the contract in order to restore the equilibrium of the contract or to distribute between the parties the losses and gains in a just and equitable manner. It is the power to adapt the contract that is likely to be most controversial from the perspective of English law because, as we have seen, the English courts have typically taken the position that any renegotiation of the contract is a matter for the parties and not for the courts. It seems highly unlikely that such a power will be given to English courts, although one effect of the continued focus on the importance of mediation may be to incentivise parties to seek to find a negotiated or mediated solution to their dispute rather than seek to stand on their rights and litigate the matter through to a conclusion.

It is a matter for debate whether English law should develop in the direction of recognising a hardship jurisdiction. The development of such a jurisdiction would appear to be beyond the reach of the courts, given that the narrow scope of the doctrine of frustration is so well established, and it is almost impossible to

[99] Book III, Art 1:110(2).
[100] Art 6.2.3(1).
[101] Art 6:111(2).
[102] Book III Art 1:110 (3)(d).
[103] Art 6:111(3).

conceive of legislation being brought forward, as was the case in France. However, there is one step that the English courts could usefully take, and that is to remove the threat that *Walford v Miles*[104] hangs over the enforceability of hardship clauses. If parties freely accept an obligation to re-negotiate their contract on the occurrence of an event of hardship, why should a court decline to recognise the validity of such an obligation? Freedom of contract and sanctity of contract point clearly in favour of giving effect to such an obligation. A more difficult question is the remedial powers that should be available to the courts in the event that the parties fail to reach agreement in any such renegotiation. For the reasons given, it is unlikely that the courts will themselves adapt the contract, even in the case where the parties expressly agree to confer such a power on the court. This being the case, the better course would appear to be to confer such a power on an arbitrator, mediator or other third-party intervener. This places the onus on the parties to make provision for the occurrence of the event of hardship, rather than being able to rely on a default hardship provision created by a rule of law but placing the onus on the parties to make such provision seems more in keeping with the traditions of English law. But it does require the courts to be willing to give effect to a hardship clause and not strike it down on the ground that it is too uncertain to be enforceable.

[104] *Walford v Miles* [1992] 2 AC 128.

8

'Hell or High Water' Clauses

JORDAN ENGLISH*

I. Introduction

Contracting parties who face uncertainty about the future, in particular their ability to perform their contractual obligations and to obtain the agreed exchange in return, often seek to mitigate their risk by inserting 'force majeure' or 'material adverse change' clauses that provide for a degree of flexibility. But parties may also seek to provide for uncertainty in another way: by affording no flexibility. A 'hell or high water' clause is a clause in which a party promises to perform 'come hell or high water': their obligation is said to be absolute and unconditional, irrespective of any contingency. Such clauses are principally (although not exclusively) found in finance leases.

This chapter considers the operation of hell or high water clauses in circumstances that might ordinarily be said to give rise to a 'frustrating' or 'force majeure' event. The question posed is whether the common law doctrine of frustration has any role to play in relieving parties from the effects of these clauses. The issue has arisen in a number of cases both in England and the US.[1] Parties who had entered into finance leases on hell or high water terms sought to argue that their lease had been frustrated when a supervening event impacted their ability to use the chattel or access the premises. Courts in both jurisdictions have uniformly rejected such arguments but, at least in England, they have not gone so far as to say that the doctrine of frustration can never apply in such circumstances.[2]

* I am grateful to Kabir Suri for his able research assistance and Jonas Atmaz Al-Sibaie, Paul S Davies, Peter MacDonald-Eggers, Magda Raczynska, Robert Stevens, and Michael Sturley for their comments on an earlier draft. I am also grateful to the attendees at the Contract Law and the Unexpected Conference (at which a draft of this chapter was presented) for their perceptive questions.

[1] In England, see *Salam Air SAOC v Latam Airlines Group SA* [2020] EWHC 2414 (Comm), [2021] 1 CLC 795; *Wilmington Trust SP Services (Dublin) Ltd v Spicejet Ltd* [2021] EWHC 1117 (Comm); *Iris Helicopter Leasing Ltd v Elitaliana Srl* [2021] EWHC 2459 (Comm). In the US, see *General Electric Capital Corp v FPL Service Corp*, 986 F Supp 2d 1029 (ND Iowa 2013); *Hugo Boss Retail Inc v AR Retail LLC*, 2021 NY Slip Op 50458(U) (NY Sup Ct 2021) para 10, citing *35 East 75th Street Corporation v Christian Louboutin LLC*, 2020 NY Slip Op 34063(U) (NY Sup Ct 2020), *Victoria's Secret Stores v Herald Sq Owner LLC*, 2021 NY Slip Op 50010(U) (NY Sup Ct 2021), and *Valentino USA Inc v 693 Fifth Owner LLC*, 2021 NY Slip Op 50119(U) (NY Sup Ct 2021).

[2] eg, *Wilmington Trust* (n 1) [61].

The refusal to rule out completely the applicability of frustration in these cases in turn raises a question of what the doctrine of frustration is for. The chapter argues that the doctrine should have no role to play where a hell or high water clause is present. That is because the doctrine of frustration is simply a question of construction: did the party who seeks to be released from their obligation promise to perform conditionally or unconditionally? And self-evidently, the party subject to a hell or high water clause has promised to perform unconditionally. Absent statutory authorisation, courts have no power to rewrite or improve the parties' agreement.

While the chapter argues that the common law doctrine of frustration is irrelevant where a hell or high water clause is concerned, this does not mean that contract law (in the broader sense, including statute law) has no role to play. In particular, hell or high water clauses highlight the importance of statutory protections against unfair terms, particularly for small- to medium-sized businesses that may have no choice but to agree to such clauses. Unfortunately, hell or high water clauses fall within a current gap in protection for non-consumers and are not, for example, caught by the Unfair Contract Terms Act 1977 ('UCTA'). Nonetheless, as the final part of the chapter argues, there may be an indirect mechanism for regulating the use of hell or high water clauses in business-to-business contracts, which ensures that they will be used in a fair and reasonable way.

The chapter proceeds in three parts. Part II ('Hell or high water clauses in practice') explores what hell or high water clauses are, how they are drafted, and where they are used. Part III ('Is there any role for the doctrine of frustration?') considers the cases in England on hell or high water clauses and the doctrine of frustration and considers whether frustration does or ought to have any role. Finally, Part IV ('Statutory protections against unfair terms') identifies the dangers of hell or high water clauses and the ways in which the existing patchwork of statutory protections may be able to regulate their use in England, particularly in non-consumer contracts.

II. Hell or High Water Clauses in Practice

Ordinarily, parties 'do not promise to perform "come what may" but instead make their promises subject to all kinds of express and implied conditions'.[3] Hell or high water clauses are the exception to that rule.[4] By such clauses, one party promises to perform absolutely and unconditionally, irrespective of any contingency. Their promise is therefore not subject to either an express or implied condition.

[3] J English, *Discharge of Contractual Obligations* (Oxford, OUP, 2025) para 10.2.
[4] ibid paras 6.73, 7.73–7.74.

A. Typical Drafting of Hell or High Water Clauses

A typical hell or high water clause will state that one party's obligation (often a lessee's obligation to pay rent) is absolute and unconditional, irrespective of any contingency whatever, including (but not limited to):

(a) any right (set-off, counterclaim, or recoupment, etc) that either party may have against each other;
(b) the unavailability of the leased item for any reason, any prohibition on its use, or any interruption of, interference with, or restriction of the lessee's use, operation, or possession of the leased item;
(c) any lack or invalidity of title, including ineligibility for registration or use in any trade or profession, or any other defect in title arising from the condition, design, operation, satisfactory quality, or fitness for use or purpose of the leased item;
(d) any total loss or damage to the leased item;
(e) any insolvency or similar proceeding by or against either party;
(f) any lack of authorisation or defect in the agreement.[5]

The precise wording of these clauses takes various forms, but when drafted in these broad terms their effect is the same – the party subject to it has promised to perform come what may. It is, of course, possible that a clause which resembles a hell or high water clause might be drafted more narrowly, or in such a way that the court concludes that it does not actually impose an unconditional or absolute obligation. To some extent, whether a clause is truly a hell or high water clause will depend on the precise wording of that clause. But in this chapter, a hell or high water clause will only be used to refer to these broadly drafted clauses that do impose absolute and unconditional obligations.

It is also important to note that while often hell or high water clauses will be standalone provisions, sometimes they are drafted as exceptions to force majeure provisions.[6] Thus, in a number of recent cases in the United States, the hell or high water clauses in issue were drafted so as to provide, for example, that 'force majeure "shall in no wise" forgive payment of rent'[7] or that 'nothing contained in this Section shall operate to excuse Tenant from the prompt payment of Rent or any other payments or charges required by the terms of this Lease'.[8]

[5] For examples of the drafting of such hell or high water clauses in the English context, see *Bitumen Invest AS v Richmond Mercantile Ltd FZC* [2016] EWHC 2957 (Comm), [2017] 1 Lloyd's Rep 219 [12]; *ACG Acquisition XX LLC v Olympic Airlines SA (in liq)* [2012] EWHC 1070 (Comm), [2012] 2 CLC 48 [110]; *Salam Air* (n 1) [12]; *Wilmington Trust* (n 2) [6]; *Iris Helicopter* (n 1) [33]. See also M Harvey, 'Leasing and Hire' in D Rosenberg (ed), *Practical Commercial Precedents* (London, Thomson Reuters, 2025) vol 1, para N3-016.

[6] eg, *Hugo Boss* (n 1) para 10, citing *35 East 75th Street* (NY Sup Ct 2020); *CW A&P Mamaroneck LLC v PFM WC-1 LLC* 74 Misc 3d 1222(A) (NY Sup Ct 2022).

[7] *Hugo Boss* (n 1) para 10, citing *Victoria's Secret Stores* (NY Sup Ct 2021).

[8] ibid, citing *Valentino USA Inc v 693 Fifth Owner LLC* (NY Sup Ct 2021).

B. Hell or High Water Clauses in Finance Leases

The type of hell or high water clause that is the focus of this chapter is the kind commonly found in finance leases. In England, hell or high water clauses are used across a wide range of industries. They can be found in aircraft leases,[9] demise or bareboat charters,[10] leases of railway rolling stock,[11] and equipment leases generally.[12] In the US context, so ubiquitous are these clauses that s 2A-407 of the Uniform Commercial Code 'extends the benefits of the classic "hell or high water" clause to a finance lease that is not a consumer lease'[13] (at least once the goods have been accepted by the lessee) by making the lessee's obligations absolute and unconditional. That section provides that '[i]n the case of a finance lease that is not a consumer lease, the lessee's promises under the lease contract become irrevocable and independent upon the lessee's acceptance of the goods.'[14] Moreover, at the international level, the UNIDROIT Convention on International Financial Leases[15] (albeit with only 11 contracting states)[16] and the UNIDROIT Model Law on Leasing[17] are premised, in part, upon the common use of hell or high water clauses in such contracts.[18]

The rationale for hell or high water clauses in this context is that finance leases are in substance a form of credit.[19] The justifying idea is that just as a borrower of cash could not complain to their lender that the goods they purchased with

[9] *ACG Acquisition* (n 5) [110]; *Salam Air* (n 1) [12]; *Wilmington Trust* (n 1) [6]; *Iris Helicopter* (n 1) [33]. See also in the US context, *Peyton Holdings LLC v Clover Aviation Company* No 18-CIV-3165, 2020 WL 4273981 (SDNY 2020); *Paulicopter Cia v Bank of America* 182 AD3d 458 (2020).

[10] *Bitumen Invest AS v Richmond Mercantile Ltd FZC* [2017] 1 Lloyd's Rep 219 [8], [12]–[13]; *OCM Maritime Nile LLC & Anor v Courage Shipping Co & Ors* [2024] EWHC 1226 (Comm) [4]).

[11] A Gonzalez, 'Labour's railway renationalisation should be directed at ROSCOs' (*Leasing Life*, 18 July 2024) www.leasinglife.com/comment/labours-railway-renationalisation-should-be-directed-at-roscos/?cf-view ('These companies have benefited from "hell or high water" clauses in their contracts, ensuring lease payments continue despite falling passenger revenues.'). See also G Topham, 'Profits of UK's private train-leasing firms treble in a year' (*The Guardian*, 18 February 2024) at www.theguardian.com/business/2024/feb/18/profits-of-uks-private-train-leasing-firms-treble-in-a-year ('"Hell and high water" clauses protect lease contracts on rolling stock despite passenger revenue virtually disappearing in 2020 during the pandemic').

[12] Harvey (n 5) para N3-016.

[13] R Lord, *Williston on Contracts*, 4th edn (London, Thomson Reuters, 2024) Vol 19, ch 53 §22.

[14] Uniform Commercial Code, s 2A-407(1).

[15] UNIDROIT Convention on International Financial Leases, Art 10.

[16] At present, Belarus, France, Hungary, Italy, Latvia, Nigeria, Panama, Russia, Ukraine, Uzbekistan: see UNIDROIT, 'Status – UNIDROIT Convention On International Financial Leasing (Ottawa, 1988)' (*UNIDROIT.org*) www.unidroit.org/instruments/leasing/convention/status/.

[17] UNIDROIT Model Law on Leasing, Art 7.

[18] See the discussion in Roy Goode, 'Creativity and Transnational Commercial Law: From Carchemish to Cape Town' (2021) 70 *ICLQ* 1, 12–13.

[19] Lord (n 13); *Wells Fargo Financial Leasing, Inc v Mountain Rentals of Gatlinburg, Inc* No E2007-00480-COA-R3-CV (Tenn App 2008); *Trans Leasing International v Schmer* 194 III App 3d 70 (1990); *Colonial Pacific Leasing Corp. v McNatt* 486 SE2d 804 (Ga, 1997). This characterisation is supported by the fact that in jurisdictions such as Australia, finance leases are characterised as security interests under personal property securities legislation: Personal Property Securities Act 2009 (Cth), s 12(3)(c).

the money were defective or subsequently destroyed, a lessee under a finance lease cannot rely upon the same arguments to avoid making lease payments. As the Court of Appeals of Tennessee put it in *Wells Fargo Financial Leasing, Inc v Mountain Rentals of Gatlinburg, Inc*:

> A finance lease is a method to finance the acquisition of goods. Normally, a lender who enables a buyer to acquire the goods is not subject to a refusal by the buyer to repay the loan if the goods are not what the buyer expected. Similarly, a finance lessee cannot refuse to pay a lessor an agreed payment. … The parties entered into a financial transaction in which the lessor is lending money and dealing largely in paper, not goods.[20]

Another justification sometimes given for the use of hell or high water clauses is that the lessor will often not have dealt with the supplier of the goods, and therefore it is appropriate that the risk of any defects should be borne by the lessee, who will have dealt with the supplier and had the chance to inspect the goods.[21] The lessor simply 'expects to be paid, even though the [equipment] might prove to be defective or totally unsuitable for the [lessee/business's] particular business'.[22]

Both these arguments, it will be noted, depend to some extent upon the lessee actually having the ability to sue the supplier of the goods in damages for any defects.[23] So while the argument that these transactions are 'functionally the equivalent of an extension of credit',[24] might support throwing the risk of frustrating events onto the lessee, the risk of defects is different. Ordinarily, a person who borrows cash to purchase goods is able to sue the seller for any defects in the goods. If the lessee is left without any remedy in damages whatsoever, either against the supplier (with whom they will often not have contracted) or the lessor, and must nonetheless pay the rent pursuant to the hell or high water clause, then they are in a materially worse position than what they would have been had they purchased the goods directly.

Similarly, as for the argument that the lessee will be the one to have dealt with the supplier, ordinarily a person dealing with a supplier of goods would have a contract with them and be able to sue under that contract for any defects. But in the finance lease context, the lessee (as opposed to the lessor) will not have contracted with the supplier, giving rise to a privity of contract problem. And to make matters worse, usually the lessor (with whom the lessee did contract) will have excluded any implied or statutory warranties in respect of defects.[25] In the

[20] *Wells Fargo* (n 19) [5]. See also *Colonial Pacific* (n 19).

[21] Lord (n 13); P Breslauer, 'Finance Lease, Hell or High Water Clause, and Third Party Beneficiary Theory in Article 2A of the Uniform Commercial Code' (1992) 77 *Cornell Law Review* 318, 326; *Colonial Pacific* (n 19) 807, quoting E Huddleson, 'Old Wine in New Bottles: UCC Article 2A – Leases' (1988) 39 *Alabama Law Review* 615, 660.

[22] *Colonial Pacific* (n 19) 807.

[23] *Wells Fargo* (n 19); *Colonial Pacific* (n 19). In the US, s 2A-209 of UCC makes provision for this. See too Art 10 of the UNIDROIT Convention on International Financial Leases and Art 7 of the UNIDROIT Model Law on Leasing.

[24] *Colonial Pacific* (n 19) 807 quoting Huddleson (n 21) 660.

[25] E McKendrick, 'Bailment' in H Beale (ed), *Chitty on Contracts*, 35th edn (London, Sweet & Maxwell 2023) 111, 157 fn 463.

US, under s 2A-209 of the Uniform Commercial Code, the benefits of any promise made by a supplier to a lessor under a supply contract are extended to the lessee to overcome these problems. No such provision exists in England.[26]

C. Hell or High Water Clauses as a Way of Managing Antitrust Risk

There is one further context in which hell or high water clauses are said to be used – that is, to manage antitrust or competition-law risks in acquisition contracts.[27] In the UK, the Competition and Markets Authority can, in certain cases, review a pending transaction and impose requirements designed to address any substantial lessening of competition that has or will result from the proposed deal.[28] The subsequent intervention of competition-law authorities therefore at least has the potential to be a force majeure event. To address this risk, as Professor Ugo Draetta has explained:

> [T]he seller tries, often successfully, to transfer the antitrust risk upon the buyer, through a '*hell or high water clause*'. These clauses are now very common also because the antitrust authorities, rather than blocking a deal, often prefer to subject the approval to certain obligations on the part of the buyer to dispose of critical pieces of the acquired company – prior to the acquisition or within a short delay. As a consequence of such clauses the buyer undertakes the obligation to buy the company in any case and to resell it entirely – in case of total rejection by the antitrust authorities – or to comply with the dispositions imposed by such authorities as a condition for the approval.[29]

But the extent to which these 'hell or high water' clauses are the same as those which have been considered above is debatable. First, in the mergers and acquisitions context, often such clauses are confined to taking steps to obtain regulatory approval and so are confined in scope. The deal may still be conditional in other respects, including being conditional on actually obtaining (as opposed to taking steps to obtain) regulatory approval. For example, in *Re Anthem-Cigna Merger Litigation*[30] – litigation concerning a proposed merger, which would have resulted

[26] See further discussion in Part IV below.

[27] U Draetta, 'Hardship and Force Majeure Clauses in International Contracts' [2002] *International Business Law Journal* 347, 355–356; A Maguire, 'Private equity surge spurs faster auctions' (*Financial Times*, 7 February 2017) at www.ft.com/content/b06a8838-ec63-11e6-930f-061b01e23655 ('Private equity groups are making increasing use of so-called hell or high water clauses, meaning that if anything goes wrong after the sale has been agreed – including potential regulatory hurdles – the buyer is expected to make the deal work regardless of extra costs'). See also S Fraidin, J Mitnick and R Steinberg, 'Hell or High Water Provisions in Merger Agreements: A Practical Approach' (*Harvard Law School Forum on Corporate Governance*, 25 May 2022) at www.corpgov.law.harvard.edu/2022/05/25/hell-or-high-water-provisions-in-merger-agreements-a-practical-approach/.

[28] Enterprise Act 2002, ss 41, 82, 84.

[29] Draetta (n 27) 355–356.

[30] *In re Anthem-Cigna Merger Litigation* CA No 2017-0114-JTL, 2020 WL 5106556 (Del Ch 2020).

in the largest healthcare insurance provider in the US – the relevant clause provided that the parties would take 'any and all actions necessary to avoid each and every impediment under the HSR Act, any Healthcare Law, antitrust law, insurance law or other applicable law that may be asserted by or on behalf of any Governmental Entity with respect to this Agreement'.[31] In an action for breach of that clause, the Court of Chancery of Delaware noted that the clause 'did not obligate the parties to use this level of effort to close the Merger by satisfying *all* of the conditions to closing. The [clause] applied only with respect to the "discrete regulatory subject" covered by the provision.'[32]

Secondly, despite sometimes being called hell or high water clauses, the obligations such clauses impose in this context are not always absolute.[33] So again, for example, in *Re Anthem-Cigna Merger Litigation*, the relevant clause was, at least so far as Anthem was concerned, subject to a 'Burdensome Condition Exception', whereby Anthem was not required to take any step that would have a materially adverse effect on the new company created by the transaction.[34] Similarly, in *Vintage Rodeo Parent, LLC v Rent-A-Center, Inc*,[35] a clause that required the parties to use 'commercially reasonabl[e] efforts to promptly undertake any and all action necessary or advisable to avoid, prevent, eliminate or remove the actual or threatened commencement of any action by any Government Entity that would prevent the consummation of the Merger'[36] was expressly described by the court as a hell or high water clause, despite clearly imposing something less than an absolute obligation.

Nonetheless, if the hell or high water clauses in the mergers and acquisitions context are not quite the same as those used in the finance leases context, they are, at least, close cousins. They also demonstrate the potential for hell or high water clauses of some form or another to be used across a wide range of contexts. The remainder of this chapter, however, focuses on hell or high water clauses in finance leases.

III. Is there Any Role for the Doctrine of Frustration?

The question that needs to be considered in this part is whether there is any role for the doctrine of frustration where a party seeks to be relieved of an obligation, which they have committed to by way of a hell or high water clause. In both England

[31] ibid para 93.

[32] ibid. See also *All Data Systems Corp v Blackstone Capital* 963 A2d 746 (Del Ch 2009).

[33] For examples where the clauses appear to have been absolute, see *Akorn v Fresenius* 2018 WL 4719347, 46 (Del Ch 2018); *Hexion Specialty Chems Inc v Huntsman Corp* 965 A2d 716, 756 (Del Ch 2008).

[34] *In re Anthem-Cigna* (n 30) paras 92–95.

[35] CA No 2018-0928-SG (Del Ch 2019)).

[36] Various ellipses in the original quote have been removed.

and the US there have been a number of cases in recent times that have considered this question. The focus in this part, however, is on the cases in England.[37] As will be seen, while the cases have uniformly rejected arguments based upon frustration in this context, courts have occasionally left the door open to the possibility that on different facts, such an argument might succeed. This in turn raises a question of what the doctrine of frustration is for and whether it should ever have a role in this context.

A. The Aircraft-Lease Cases

The cases that have come before English courts on this issue all happen to involve aircraft leases. The issue first arose in *ACG Acquisition XX LLC v Olympic Airlines SA (in liq)*.[38] In that case, an aircraft was leased for five years by ACG Acquisition XX LLC to Olympic Airlines SA. The aircraft was delivered in August 2008 and put into service that month but in September 2008 defects were discovered, resulting in the Greek aviation authority suspending the aircraft's airworthiness certificate. The aircraft was sent to France for repairs in order to enable the airworthiness certificate to be restored but these took longer than expected, with the result that the aircraft did not return to Athens until July 2009. Despite the work undertaken, the aviation authority was not satisfied with the repairs and the aircraft's airworthiness certificate was not restored. Olympic entered into a creditor's special liquidation in October 2009. ACG served termination and redelivery notices, and the aircraft was returned to them in November 2010.

In the litigation that ensued, ACG sought to claim, among other things, unpaid rent and maintenance reserves from Olympic in the amount of US$4.6 million for the period up until November 2010. Olympic, for its part, sought to claim damages for the aircraft being delivered in an unairworthy condition. Mr Justice Teare rejected this latter claim, not because the aircraft was airworthy on delivery (he found it was not)[39] but because Olympic was estopped, due to representations it had made in the certificate of acceptance, from making this argument.[40]

As for ACG's claim in debt, one of the defences put forward by Olympic was that the lease had been frustrated by the withdrawal of the airworthiness certificate and the refusal of the aviation authority to renew it.[41] However, this argument too was rejected. Noting that clause 5.14 of the lease agreement made the lessee's

[37] For the US, see *General Electric* (n 1); *Hugo Boss* (n 1) para 10, citing *35 East 75th Street* (n 1), *Victoria's Secret Stores* (n 1), and *Valentino USA* (n 1).
[38] *ACG Acquisition* (n 5).
[39] ibid [113].
[40] ibid [163].
[41] ibid [173].

obligations – including an obligation to maintain a certificate of airworthiness – absolute (ie, it was a hell or high water clause), Teare J said:

> In circumstances where Olympic is obliged by the lease to maintain a certificate of airworthiness and where Olympic's obligations are described as absolute and unconditional irrespective of any contingency whatever there would appear to be difficulty in saying that the suspension of the airworthiness certificate in September 2008 and the refusal of the HCAA to reinstate it in August 2009 was an event which rendered Olympic's obligations radically different from those which it had undertaken in the lease.[42]

Nonetheless, after referring to the 'guidance given by Rix LJ'[43] in *Edwinton Commercial Corp v Tsavliris Russ (The Sea Angel)*[44] in relation to the doctrine of frustration, Teare J went on to apply the 'multi-factorial approach' set out in that case, under which the factors to be considered in deciding whether a contract has been frustrated include:

(i) 'the terms of the contract itself, its matrix or context, the parties' knowledge, expectations, assumptions and contemplations, in particular as to risk, as at the time of contract, at any rate so far as these can be ascribed mutually and objectively';
(ii) 'the nature of the supervening event, and the parties' reasonable and objectively ascertainable calculations as to the possibilities of future performance in the new circumstances'; and
(iii) whether frustration would 'be in the interests of justice and not against those interests'.[45]

Ultimately, Teare J was not persuaded, on the facts, that the lease had been frustrated.[46]

The issue next arose in *Salam Air SAOC v Latam Airlines Groups SA*,[47] a case arising out of the effects of the COVID-19 pandemic. In this case, Latam Airlines Group SA had, in 2017, leased to SalamAir SAOC three aircraft on hell or high water terms for a period of six years. SalamAir was a company registered in Oman, which had been set up to provide budget flights, initially domestically between Muscat and Salalah, and, eventually, medium-haul internationally. In March 2020, as a consequence of the COVID-19 pandemic, a regulation was passed prohibiting flights to or from Oman airports.[48] In May 2020, Latam Airlines filed for

[42] ibid [175].
[43] ibid [178].
[44] *Edwinton Commercial Corp v Tsavliris Russ (The Sea Angel)* [2007] EWCA Civ 547, [2007] 2 All ER (Comm) 634 [111]–[112].
[45] ibid.
[46] *ACG Acquisition* (n 5) [185].
[47] *Salam Air* (n 1).
[48] Subject to an irrelevant exception, namely, 'cargo flights and flights to and from the Omani exclave of Musandam': ibid [21].

Chapter 11 bankruptcy in the US. Meanwhile, in June 2020, SalamAir physically re-delivered the aircraft, purporting to terminate the leases.

SalamAir sought a without-notice injunction in the Commercial Court to restrain Latam Airlines from making a demand on three standby letters of credit, which had been confirmed by Barclays Bank plc and which were intended to secure payment of the rent under the aircraft leases. SalamAir's argument was that the lease had been frustrated by the prohibition on flights imposed by the authorities in Oman, where both the aircraft and SalamAir were located.[49]

The case primarily dealt with the question of whether the Court should interfere with the operation of the standby letters of credit by granting an injunction. Mr Justice Foxton ultimately held that it should not for reasons unconnected with the substantive merits of the underlying claim.[50] But in obiter comments, he went on to consider whether SalamAir's case on frustration rose to the sufficient level of arguability (which, in these circumstances, he held would have required them to show a strong case of arguability rather than simply an arguable case).[51]

Like Teare J in *Olympic Airlines*, Foxton J quoted with approval the approach of Rix LJ in *The Sea Angel*,[52] and accepted 'that the terms of the contract in issue [were] not necessarily determinative of the issue of frustration'.[53] Nonetheless, Foxton J noted that they were of 'obvious relevance'[54] and he placed great weight on the fact that SalamAir had contracted on hell or high water terms. He said:

> [T]he Aircraft Leases were drafted to make it clear that SalamAir's obligation to pay rent continued in almost any conceivable circumstances (what is sometimes referred to as a "hell or highwater" basis …) … These clauses are, in my opinion, fundamentally inconsistent with any suggestion that regulations in Oman which (for so long as they remained in force) prevent SalamAir from using the Aircraft to earn revenue through passenger flights with an Omani terminus, or any long-term suppression of air travel even after such regulations had ceased to have effect, had the effect of terminating the Aircraft Leases and freeing SalamAir of its obligation to pay rent.[55]

The result was that SalamAir's case was 'too weak' to justify granting the injunction[56] However, Foxton J did note that had the question been whether there was a 'serious issue to be tried' the frustration case would have been sufficiently arguable to satisfy this test.[57]

The third case to deal with this issue was *Wilmington Trust SP Services (Dublin) Ltd v Spicejet Ltd*.[58] This was a claim for summary judgment brought by three

[49] ibid [3].
[50] ibid [23]–[44].
[51] ibid [43]–[44].
[52] ibid [46].
[53] ibid [47].
[54] ibid.
[55] ibid [51].
[56] ibid [56].
[57] ibid [55].
[58] *Wilmington Trust* (n 1).

different lessors against Spicejet Ltd, an Indian airline, in respect of outstanding amounts under three aircraft leases, all of which were for 10 years and on hell or high water terms. Two of those aircraft were Boeing 737-MAX 8 aircraft, which had been grounded by the Indian aviation authority following 'crashes of similar aircraft as a result of design defects'.[59] As Miss Julia Dias QC (sitting as a Deputy Judge of the High Court) noted, similar bans had been imposed worldwide and, at the time of judgment, were likely to continue indefinitely.[60] The effect was that the aircraft could not be operated lawfully in India or elsewhere. The defendant therefore sought to resist summary judgment in respect of these two leases on the basis that it had realistic prospects of establishing that the leases had been frustrated.

Miss Julia Dias QC ultimately rejected the defendant's frustration arguments and granted summary judgment on the rent claims. However, she did not treat the hell or high water clause as determinative. By contrast, she assumed (expressly without deciding the point) that the clause did 'not operate to exclude the possibility of frustration'.[61] While recognising the similarity between the present case and *Olympic Airlines*, the Deputy Judge thought that the fact that the grounding here was 'related to the defective design of the aircraft themselves, not simply to government regulations … or matters of maintenance which can reasonably be expected to be resolved' added potentially 'another dimension to the question which [was] deserving of fuller argument'.[62] Instead, refusing to rule out the possibility that these leases could be frustrated in the future, Miss Julia Dias QC placed emphasis on the short duration of the prohibition compared to the lifetime of the lease. She said:

> I am far from saying that these leases can never be frustrated. It may be (I express no view one way or the other) that if there is still no sign of the ban being lifted in, say, three years' time, that might amount to frustration. But in the context of a ten-year lease, I find it very difficult to say that a suspension of use for roughly 10% of the term of the lease amounts to a change of circumstances which renders performance of the lease "radically different" rather than simply more onerous. I am therefore quite satisfied that, whatever the position may be in the future, the leases have not yet been frustrated as at today's date.[63]

It is worth noting too that, like the two cases above, Miss Julia Dias QC agreed that the approach to be applied was the multifactorial approach of Rix LJ in *The Sea Angel* and quoted it with approval.[64]

The final decision in this quartet of cases is *Iris Helicopter Leasing Ltd v Elitaliana Srl*.[65] Iris Helicopter Leasing Ltd sought summary judgment against

[59] ibid [3].
[60] ibid.
[61] ibid [61].
[62] ibid [63].
[63] ibid [65].
[64] ibid [58].
[65] *Iris Helicopter* (n 1).

Elitaliana Srl and an associated company that had guaranteed Elitaliana's obligations under a six-year lease of a specialist helicopter. The helicopter, which had been leased on hell or high water terms, had been seized by the Italian authorities. The defendants argued that they had realistic prospects of successfully establishing that this seizure was wrongful and therefore had operated to frustrate the lease. Mr Justice Jacobs rejected this argument and granted summary judgment. Noting that what had occurred fell squarely within the hell or high water clause, he said:

> If events occur which are within the hell and high water clause which result in the unavailability of the aircraft because taxes have not been paid then I cannot see any basis on which it can be said that the risk of those events should, via the doctrine of frustration, be reallocated to the Lessor.[66]

However, continuing what is now a familiar theme, Jacobs J refused to rule out the possibility of frustration on different facts. Again applying the approach from 'what might be regarded as the currently leading judgment'[67] of Rix LJ in *The Sea Angel*, he said:

> I have taken into account the fact that the contract terms are not determinative. It may be that in a particular case some set of facts occur which causes the court to say that nevertheless, despite the contract terms, the contract has been frustrated. But that is not the position in this case.[68]

B. What is Frustration For?

In each of these cases concerned with hell or high water clauses, the courts held that the leases were not frustrated on the facts. But in all of them, the courts appear to have proceeded on the basis that with different facts, the doctrine of frustration might have had a role to play. Indeed, in *Salam Air* and *Iris Helicopter Leasing*, both Foxton J and Jacobs J accepted that the terms of the contract were not determinative.[69] And in *Spicejet*, Miss Julia Dias QC, while expressly not deciding whether the hell or high water clause was determinative of the question, was at pains to keep open the possibility of frustration being invoked successfully on different facts.[70] Implicit in these approaches is the assumption that the doctrine of frustration is one of 'justice' that operates to relieve parties from the terms of their agreements. By contrast, this section argues that where a party has promised to perform absolutely and unconditionally then, in respect of that obligation, the doctrine of frustration, which is ultimately a question of construction, has no role

[66] ibid [41].
[67] ibid [21].
[68] ibid [55].
[69] *Salam Air* (n 1) [47]; *Iris Helicopter* (n 1) [55].
[70] *Wilmington Trust* (n 1) [65].

to play. Absent statutory authorisation, the courts have no power to rewrite or improve the parties' agreement.

That the courts in these cases view frustration in this way is apparent from their reliance on the approach of Rix LJ in *The Sea Angel*.[71] In that case, Rix LJ (with whom Wall and Hooper LJJ agreed) made clear that in his view 'the doctrine is one of justice, as has been repeatedly affirmed on the highest authority'.[72] He said:

> If the provisions of a contract in their literal sense are to make way for the absolving effect of frustration, then that must, in my judgment, be in the interests of justice and not against those interests. Since the purpose of the doctrine is to do justice, then its application cannot be divorced from considerations of justice.[73]

According to this conception, frustration operates to relieve parties from the effects of what would otherwise be the result of enforcing their agreement as made. Thus in *Hirji Mulji v Cheon Yue SS Co*,[74] Lord Sumner said frustration 'is really a device, by which the rules as to absolute contracts are reconciled with a special exception which justice demands'. Similarly, in *National Carriers Ltd v Panalpina (Northern) Ltd*,[75] Lord Simon said that frustration operates where circumstances affecting performance of the contract have so changed that 'it would be unjust to hold [the parties] to the literal sense of its stipulations in the new circumstances'. And in *J Lauritzen AS v Wijsmuller BV (The 'Super Servant Two')*,[76] Bingham LJ said:

> The object of the doctrine was to give effect to the demands of justice, to achieve a just and reasonable result, to do what is reasonable and fair, as an expedient to escape from injustice where such would result from enforcement of a contract in its literal terms after a significant change in circumstances …

This latter statement has been said to describe 'the essence of the doctrine'.[77]

The difficulty with the 'justice' view of frustration is that it runs contrary to the 'repeated statements'[78] in the authorities that 'no Court has an absolving power'.[79] As Lord Hoffmann said in *Attorney General of Belize v Belize Telecom Ltd*, '[t]he court has no power to improve upon the instrument which it is called upon to

[71] *ACG Acquisition* (n 5) [179]; *Salam Air* (n 1) [46]; *Wilmington Trust* (n 1) [58]; *Iris Helicopter* (n 1) [21].

[72] *The Sea Angel* (n 44) 634 [112].

[73] ibid [112].

[74] *Hirji Mulji v Cheon Yue SS Co* [1926] AC 497 (PC) 510.

[75] *National Carriers Ltd v Panalpina (Northern) Ltd* [1981] AC 675 (HL) 700.

[76] *J Lauritzen AS v Wijsmuller BV (The 'Super Servant Two')* [1990] 1 Lloyd's Rep 1 (CA) 8.

[77] E McKendrick, 'Discharge by Frustration and Force Majeure Clauses' in H Beale (ed), *Chitty on Contracts*, 35th edn (London, Sweet & Maxwell, 2023) paras 27-007–27-008.

[78] English (n 3) para 6.124.

[79] *F A Tamplin Steamship Co Ltd v Anglo-Mexcian Petroleum Products Co Ltd* [1916] 2 AC 397 (HL) 404; *Joseph Constantine Steamship Line Ltd v Imperial Smelting Corp Ltd* [1942] AC 154 (HL) 185; *Denny, Mott & Dickson Ltd v James B Fraser & Co Ltd* [1944] AC 265 SC (HL) 281; *Metropolitan Water Board v Dick, Kerr & Co* [1918] AC 119 (HL) 127; *British Movietonews Ltd v London and Distict Cinemas Ltd* [1952] AC 166 (HL) 183.

construe, whether it be a contract, a statute or articles of association. It cannot introduce terms to make it fairer or more reasonable. It is concerned only to discover what the instrument means.'[80] To be fair, the courts and commentators adopting this view often seek to make clear that the court has no *general* absolving power to impose a just and reasonable solution.[81] But they nonetheless treat the doctrine of frustration as one of justice which does alter (or relieve parties from the effect of) the expressed terms of the contract.

The contrary view, which is to be preferred, is that whether a contract has been frustrated is simply a question of construction.[82] In *Davis Contractors Ltd v Farham Urban District Council*,[83] Lord Reid said:

> [F]rustration depends, at least in most cases … on the true construction of the terms which are in the contract read in light of the nature of the contract and of the relevant surrounding circumstances when the contract was made. … The question is whether the contract which they did make is, on its true construction, wide enough to apply to the new situation: if it is not, then it is at an end.[84]

In a similar vein, Lord Radcliffe spoke of frustration arising where the circumstances in which performance of a contractual obligation are called for would be 'radically different from that which was undertaken by the contract. *Non haec in foedera veni*. It was not this that I promised to do'.[85]

The best understanding of the construction theory of frustration is that it is about ascertaining whether the party who seeks to be released from their obligation has promised to perform conditionally or unconditionally. Put simply, 'to say that on the occurrence of some uncertain event the contractual obligations of the parties cease to bind – because, as a matter of construction, the contract was not intended to be binding in these circumstances – is just another way of saying that the obligations of the parties are conditional'.[86] Indeed, in *Canary Wharf v*

[80] *Attorney General of Belize v Belize Telecom Ltd* [2009] UKPC 10, [2009] 1 WLR 1988 [16].
[81] McKendrick (n 77) para 27-008; *The Sea Angel* [2007] 2 All ER (Comm) 634 [113].
[82] See English (n 3) ch 6.
[83] *Davis Contractors Ltd v Farham Urban District Council* [1956] AC 696 (HL).
[84] ibid 720–721.
[85] ibid 729. There is, admittedly, some debate about whether Lord Radcliffe was simply providing a test for frustration or a justification, or both: see E Peel, *Treitel on Contract*, 16th edn (London, Sweet & Maxwell, 2025) [19-123] and compare *National Carriers* (n 75) 688 (Lord Hailsham) with 717 (Lord Roskill). Indeed, Lord Radcliffe's dictum was cited as an appropriate 'test' and one which prevents the doctrine from 'descend[ing] into a morass of quasi-discretionary decisions' in *The Sea Angel* (n 44) [110], but clearly that case did not subscribe the construction theory as a justification for the doctrine. In *Canary Wharf v European Medicines Agency* [2019] EWHC 335 (Ch), [2019] L & TR 14 [22], [26], Marcus Smith J noted that Lord Radcliffe's dictum had found favour in the recent case law but treated it both as a test and as a theory in its own right – in particular, he treated it as a theory distinct from the construction theory. The better view, however, is that Lord Radcliffe's statement is supportive of the construction theory: see E Peel, *Treitel on Contract*, 16th edn (London, Sweet & Maxwell, 2025) [19-128], rejecting Mr Justice Marcus Smith's suggestion. To say, as Lord Radcliffe did, that '[i]t was not this I promised to do' is about the scope of the contractual obligation. It is no different to asking, as Lord Reid did, whether the contract 'is, on its true construction, wide enough to apply to the new situation'.
[86] English (n 3) para 6.97.

European Medicines Agency,[87] Marcus Smith J recognised that the construction theory was a 'more sophisticated variant' of the implied condition theory of frustration. It simply reflects the fact that rarely do parties promise to perform 'come what may' – ordinarily, promises to perform are subject to all kinds of express and implied conditions.[88]

The benefit of the 'construction theory' view of frustration is that it is consistent with the repeated judicial statements that no court has an absolving power nor an ability to improve the instrument it is called upon to construe.[89] By contrast, no good reason has been offered as to why the court should be able to intervene and rewrite the parties' bargain, which is what the 'justice' view of frustration must necessarily entail. As Professor Jonathan Morgan has observed, why does justice, at least in the context of commercial contracts, not entail parties sticking to their agreement?[90]

Sir Guenter Treitel's leading textbooks, *Frustration and Force Majeure* and *Treitel on Contract* – both now under the authorship of Professor Edwin Peel – after examining the competing theories of frustration, ask whether the 'above theoretical discussion has any practical importance'.[91] Sadly for those who spend their careers writing about the topic, those books conclude '[i]t seems to have none'.[92] But the cases examined in this part on hell or high water clauses show that it really does matter what frustration is for. In at least two of these cases, the courts, applying the approach of Rix LJ in *The Sea Angel*, treated the terms of the contract as not being determinative of the question of frustration.[93] And in the third, the question was expressly left open, it being assumed for the purpose of the case that the terms were not conclusive.[94] This is because on the 'justice' view of frustration, the effect of an argument on frustration succeeding is that the terms of the contract are not given full effect. Instead, they 'make way for the absolving effect of frustration'.[95] On this view, the terms of the contract cannot be determinative – they can only be of great weight.

But 'why should the terms of the contract *not* be "determinative"?'[96] If one had asked in these cases whether the party seeking to be relieved of their rent obligation had promised to perform conditionally or unconditionally, the answer would have been clear. While ordinarily, parties do not promise to perform 'come what may', in these cases the parties (quite literally) promised to perform 'come hell or

[87] n 85 [26(4)].
[88] For a response to the objections to the implied condition view of frustration, see: English (n 3) paras 6.85–6.117.
[89] See n 79 and n 80 above.
[90] J Morgan, 'Frustration and the Pandemic' (2021) 137 *LQR* 563, 566.
[91] Peel (n 85) para 19-130; E Peel, *Frustration and Force Majeure*, 4th edn (London, Sweet & Maxwell, 2021) para 16-015.
[92] ibid.
[93] *Salam Air* (n 1) [47]; *Iris Helicopter* (n 1) [55].
[94] *Wilmington Trust* (n 1) [65].
[95] *The Sea Angel* (n 44) [112].
[96] Morgan (n 90) 566.

high water'. Their promises were 'absolute and unconditional irrespective of any contingency whatever'.[97] In that context, the doctrine of frustration should have no role to play. If a party chooses to agree to perform come hell or high water, then they should be held to that commitment. As the Singapore Court of Appeal observed in *Lee Chee Wei v Tan Hor Peow Victor*,[98] '[p]arties to a contract can always guard against vagaries or unforeseen contingencies through express stipulation and should they voluntarily choose to accept and undertake an absolute and unconditional obligation, they forfeit the right to complain if events do not unfold as planned.'

The criticism of the approach of the courts in these hell or high water cases, however, should not be overstated. As a matter of precedent, they were bound to follow the approach of Rix LJ in *The Sea Angel*.[99] And in none of these cases did the court actually find that the contract had been frustrated. As Morgan has put it, '[f]or believers in freewheeling "justice" the operation of frustration must nevertheless come as a disappointment. … [C]ourts are reluctant to depart from what the parties have agreed.'[100] The criticism is simply that the possibility of frustration should not have been left open. If a party has promised to perform absolutely and unconditionally, then on a proper understanding of what the doctrine of frustration is for, that should preclude any argument that frustration can relieve them of their obligation to perform.

C. A Link with Common Mistake

This view of frustration may also shed light on how hell or high water clauses should operate in the context where the allegation is not that the contract has been 'frustrated' but rather that it has been entered into as the result of a 'fundamental common mistake'. This was the position in *Triple Seven Msn 27251 Ltd v Azman Air Services Ltd*.[101] In that case, the claimants had leased to the defendant two aircraft for a period of five years on hell or high water terms. It was known to both parties that 'the aircraft would be used by [the defendant] to transport passengers from West Africa to the Kingdom of Saudi Arabia for the Hajj and Umrah pilgrimages'.[102] Unbeknownst to either party though, at the time of signing, the Civil Aviation Authority of Saudi Arabia had in fact excluded the defendant from participating in the 2016 Hajj airlift.[103] A letter was sent to the defendant the day

[97] *ACG Acquisition* (n 5) [110]; *Salam Air* (n 1) [12]. See also *Wilmington Trust* (n 1) [6] in similar terms and *Iris Helicopter* (n 1) [33], substituting the word 'whatever' with 'whatsoever'.
[98] *Lee Chee Wei v Tan Hor Peow Victor* [2007] 3 SLR 537 [48].
[99] See a similar point in Morgan (n 90) 563, regarding the approach taken in *Triple Seven Msn 27251 Ltd v Azman Air Services Ltd* [2018] EWHC 1348 (Comm), [2018] 4 WLR 97, considered in the next section.
[100] Morgan (n 90) 566.
[101] *Triple Seven* (n 99).
[102] ibid [2].
[103] ibid [3].

before signing the leases but it was not received by the defendant until some hours after signing. When the defendant subsequently refused to take delivery of the aircraft and pay the first rent instalments, the claimants purported to terminate each lease pursuant to an express termination clause.

In the claimants' subsequent claim for damages for breach of the lease agreements, the defendants alleged that the agreements were void at common law for common mistake. Peter MacDonald Eggers QC, sitting as a Deputy High Court Judge, held that 'the mistaken assumption shared by the parties was not sufficiently fundamental to the lease agreements' and therefore that the doctrine of common mistake did not apply.[104] However, he went on to conclude that even if the mistaken assumption had been sufficiently fundamental, he would nevertheless still have concluded that the lease agreements were not void.[105] This conclusion was reached, in part, because of the hell or high water clause, which provided that the lessee's obligations were 'absolute and unconditional, irrespective of any contingency or circumstance whatsoever'.[106] Peter MacDonald Eggers QC said:

> This provision makes it clear that [the defendant] bears absolute and unconditional obligations under the lease agreements, and that those obligations are unaffected by 'any contingency or circumstance whatsoever'. Such a contingency must have included the failure to obtain [the civil aviation authority's] approval, which both parties recognised was a possibility.[107]

A claim that cannot be developed or defended here is that the supposed doctrine of common mistake also depends on implied conditions to be found in the parties' agreement.[108] It is differentiated from frustration only by the point in time at which the condition fails,[109] and its effect is to render the agreement 'inoperative' rather than 'void': 'the obligations of the parties are "inoperative" because, properly construed, their promises do not apply to the circumstances that have obtained.'[110]

Applying this approach to *Triple Seven*, the answer is clear. No mistake, no matter how fundamental, would have been sufficient in circumstances where the lessee had promised to perform its obligations 'come hell or high water'. The effect of the hell or high water clause is that the lessee has promised to perform absolutely and unconditionally. Unless that clause can be read to mean something else, the lessee should always be held to the agreement.

[104] ibid [89].
[105] ibid [91].
[106] ibid.
[107] ibid.
[108] But see English (n 3) ch 7.
[109] ibid paras 7.96–7.99.
[110] ibid para 7.6, citing P Aityah and F Bennion 'Mistake in the Construction of Contracts' (1961) 24 *MLR* 421, 427 and JC Smith, 'Contracts – Mistake, Frustration and Implied Terms' (1994) 110 *LQR* 400, 410.

IV. Statutory Protections against Unfair Terms

The argument in the preceding part has been that the doctrine of frustration should have no role to play where one party seeks to be relieved from the effect of a hell or high water clause. The doctrine of frustration, properly understood, is a question of construction: did the party seeking to be relieved of their obligation promise to perform conditionally or unconditionally? Where a party has promised to perform unconditionally, there is simply no role for frustration to come in and alter the parties' agreement. But just because the doctrine of frustration should have no role to play in these cases does not mean that contract law – in the broader sense, which includes statutes – has no role to play. In particular, hell or high water clauses highlight the importance of statutory protections against unfair terms, particularly for small- to medium-sized businesses who may have no choice but to agree to these clauses.

A. The Dangers of Hell or High Water Clauses

Hell or high water clauses present a number of problems.[111] In the first place, particularly in the context of equipment leasing, they are rarely, if ever, negotiated.[112] This means that in industries where their use is prevalent, a presumptive rule is created that the lessee bears the risk of a frustrating or force majeure event. In *General Electric Capital Corp v FPL Service Corp*,[113] Bennett J, sitting in the US District Court, made this point when he stated that were he free from authority, he would not enforce a hell or high water provision unless it was specifically bargained for. He said:

> As a practical matter, hell-or-highwater clauses are rarely, if ever, specifically bargained for … Because hell-or-highwater clauses are both ubiquitous and non-negotiable, presumptively enforcing these clauses creates a default rule that a commercial lessee bears the risk of an act of God. I think the default rule should be the opposite: The party best able to bear the risk of an act of God should, by default, bear that risk.[114]

The justification for the use of hell or high water clauses (and the consequent shifting of risk) in this context is, as noted earlier, that finance leases are 'functionally the equivalent of an extension of credit'.[115] Therefore just as the risk of frustrating events (ie, destruction of the equipment) would fall on a purchaser who financed

[111] A number of which arose during the pandemic: see R Simon, 'The "Hell or High Water Clause" Is Tormenting Small-Business Owners' *Wall Street Journal* (14 April 2022) www.wsj.com/business/entrepreneurship/a-lifeline-for-entrepreneurs-has-become-a-financial-albatross-for-some-11649950064.

[112] *General Electric* (n 1) fn 5.

[113] *General Electric* (n 1).

[114] ibid.

[115] *Colonial Pacific* (n 19) 807, quoting Huddleson (n 21) 660.

that acquisition through a personal loan, so too should the risk of frustrating events fall on a lessee under a finance lease.

While this may be true in respect of frustrating events, the effect of a hell or high water clause is not just that the lessee must continue to pay for the goods if, say, they are destroyed by a hurricane;[116] they must also continue to pay for the goods if they are defective or completely unsuitable for their intended purpose. And here, in addition to the hell or high water clause, the lessor 'inevitably'[117] excludes any implied or statutory warranties in respect of defects. The problem is compounded by the fact that where the goods have been supplied by a third party, the lessee (as opposed to the lessor) will not be a party to the contract with the supplier, giving rise to a privity of contract problem. The lessee therefore may be left without any remedy whatsoever for defects, while continuing to have to pay for the goods pursuant to a hell or high water clause.[118] This then raises the question: what, if any, are the statutory protections against the use of hell or high water clauses in England?

B. Statutory Protections

In considering statutory protections, it is important to distinguish between consumers and non-consumers. If a hell or high water clause is contained in a 'consumer contract', then it will be reviewable under s 62 of the Consumer Rights Act 2015 as a potentially unfair term.[119] A finance lease, in particular, may also be a consumer credit agreement, giving rise to an argument that the hell or high water clause creates an unfair relationship between the lessor and lessee under s 140A of the Consumer Credit Act 1974. But these protections are of no avail to businesses (whether individuals or companies) that have agreed to these clauses because such persons are not consumers for the purposes of either Act.

Instead, businesses must rely upon the provisions of UCTA. The provisions of that Act, however, are limited in two ways. First, s 3, which deals with liabilities arising in contract, only applies where one of the parties has contracted 'on the other's written standard terms of business'.[120] This limitation does not present a major obstacle where small- to medium-sized businesses are concerned

[116] As happened in *General Electric* (n 1) (photocopiers leased on hell or high water terms were destroyed by Hurricane Sandy).

[117] McKendrick (n 25) 157, fn 463.

[118] In the US, and in international instruments, the privity problem is dealt with by making the lessee a beneficiary of any promises made by the supplier to the lessor under the supply contract: see UCC, s 2A-209; UNIDROIT Convention on International Financial Leases, Art 10; UNIDROIT Model Law on Leasing, Art 7. But no such provision exists in England. It should also be noted that in the US, s 2A-407 of the Uniform Commercial Code, which makes the lessee's obligations under a lease contract irrevocable and independent upon their acceptance of the goods, does not apply if the lessor selects, manufactures, or supplies the goods: see UCC, s 2A-103(g) (definition of a 'finance lease').

[119] See, in particular, Sch 2, Items 2 and 18.

[120] Unfair Contract Terms Act 1977, s 3(1).

because hell or high water clauses are rarely negotiated and are usually included simply as part of the standard form in leasing transactions. Moreover, s 7, which deals with miscellaneous contracts where 'the possession or ownership of goods passes', but which are not hire-purchase agreements,[121] is not limited to standard-form contracts. The second limitation of UCTA, however, is that it principally applies to exclusion clauses.[122] And this is a significant limitation because, even on the most expansive approach to that question,[123] a hell or high water clause is not an exclusion clause. It does not seek to exclude some liability on behalf of a lessor but rather imposes (or rather expands) the obligations of the lessee.

It therefore seems that there is no direct statutory protection for small- to medium-sized businesses who may have no choice but to agree to these clauses. But there may be a way in which English statutory protections indirectly regulate the use of hell or high water clauses.

As was noted above, the use of hell or high water clauses in the finance lease context is typically justified by the fact that finance leases are equivalent to an extension of credit. However, while this argument may justify shifting the risk of frustrating events onto the lessee, it does not justify the lessee being made to continue to pay for defective goods unless they can sue somebody in respect of defects. In England, ordinarily, and irrespective of who has manufactured the goods, a lessor of goods will be subject to implied terms as to quality or fitness under s 9 of the Supply of Goods and Services Act 1982.[124] If this term is not excluded, then it seems at least plausible that the use of hell or high water clauses is acceptable (provided that one accepts the argument that finance leases are functionally equivalent to giving credit). The lessee will be able to sue the lessor for any defects but simply will not be able to withhold payment of rent while it does so.

However, as has been observed in *Chitty on Contracts*, '[f]inance leases with non-consumers inevitably exclude the terms implied by the Supply of Goods and Services Act 1982'.[125] Here is where the argument that statutory protections might indirectly regulate the use of hell or high water clauses comes in. The argument is that while hell or high water clauses might not be caught by UCTA, exclusion clauses certainly are. Section 7(1A) specifically provides in respect of contracts under which the possession or ownership of goods passes that '[l]iability in respect of the goods' correspondence with description or sample, or their quality or fitness for any particular purpose, cannot be excluded or restricted by reference to such a term except in so far as the term satisfies the requirement of reasonableness.' The

[121] Which are dealt with separately and to the same effect in s 6.
[122] eg, Unfair Contract Terms Act 1977, s 3(2).
[123] eg, *First Tower Trustees Ltd v CDS (Superstores International) Ltd* [2018] EWCA Civ 1396, [2019] 1 WLR 637.
[124] Or the Supply of Goods (Implied Terms) Act 1973, s 10 in the case of a hire-purchase.
[125] McKendrick (n 25) 157, fn 463.

submission this chapter makes is that if a lessor wishes to justify a clause excluding liability for defects, particularly where a hell or high water clause is present, then it is incumbent on them to ensure that the lessee is not left without any remedy whatsoever in respect of defects by ensuring that the lessee gets the benefits of any warranty given by the supplier.

A number of cases have considered the effect of clauses which purport to exclude a finance company's liability for express and implied warranties as to the fitness for purpose or quality of goods that have been leased to another company. The leading decision is *Purnell Secretarial Services Ltd v Lease Managements Services Ltd*.[126] In that case, Purnell Secretarial Services Ltd entered into an agreement to hire a photocopying machine for five years. Mrs Berry, who ran the company, thought that she was dealing with the supplier of the equipment, Canon (South West) Ltd, but due to the misleading way in which the form was presented, she did not realise she in fact was signing an agreement with Lease Management Services Ltd ('LMS'), a finance company. It was found to be a term of the contract that the machine was to have a specific capability, namely, the ability to produce 'paper plates'.[127] While the demonstration model that Mrs Berry had been shown was capable of producing paper plates, the model she was in fact sent was not. Mrs Berry therefore refused to make any of the monthly payments, and eventually the machine was taken away by LMS.

LMS claimed for five years' rent, less a discount for accelerated payment. Purnell sought to resist this claim on the basis that the machine did not comply with the capabilities as specified in the contract. But LMS pointed to a broadly drafted exclusion clause which, in essence, provided that LMS incurred 'no liability, and Purnell possesse[d] no rights, in respect of any condition, warranty or representation relating to the suitability or fitness of the equipment for any purpose for which it may be required'.[128] The Court of Appeal (Sir Donald Nicholls VC, with whom Hirst and Waite LJJ agreed) held that the clause failed to satisfy the requirement of reasonableness imposed by s 3(2)(a) of UCTA. Sir Donald Nicholls VC noted that the clause embraced 'virtually all liability for any shortcomings in the equipment, irrespective of seriousness and irrespective of how the warranty or condition arose' and that '[s]elf-evidently it cannot be reasonable to exclude liability for breach of a warranty or condition which has been expressly given'.[129] While not ruling out that there may be circumstances in which it could be reasonable, he added that 'where the condition excludes all liability for breach of any representation or warranty, express or implied, the burden of proving reasonableness will not be lightly discharged'.[130]

[126] *Purnell Secretarial Services Ltd v Lease Managements Services Ltd* [1999] GCCR 1841.
[127] ibid 1843.
[128] ibid 1848.
[129] ibid 1849.
[130] ibid 1851.

Importantly, the Court of Appeal also expressly rejected an argument that such clauses might be reasonable because of the finance company never having had possession of, or dealt with, the equipment.[131] Sir Donald Nicholls VC said:

> I am unable to accept, as a general proposition, that an exclusion clause which would be unreasonable in a contract for sale by a supplier will be reasonable as between a hirer and a finance company because of the latter's non-inspection of the goods and its non-participation in negotiations preceding the transaction. If there were such a general proposition, acquisition by hire from a finance company rather than by purchase from a supplier would become a trap. A customer would not expect his rights regarding defects to differ according to which of these two acquisition routes he chooses to follow.[132]

It will be recalled that the fact that the finance company (as opposed to the lessee) usually does not deal with the goods was one of the two justifications typically given for the use of hell or high water clauses.

Although *Purnell* was dealing with an express warranty, in *Sovereign Finance v Silver Crest Furniture*[133] it was applied, again in the context of a finance company, to terms implied under statute. Longmore J specifically held that the language in *Purnell* 'applies in terms to implied warranties of the kind relevant in the present case'.[134] The effect of *Purnell* then, as confirmed recently by the Court of Appeal, is that where a clause contained in a finance lease or hire-purchase agreement purports to exclude the finance company's liability for all and any defects of the goods supplied, that clause is 'prima facie unreasonable under UCTA'.[135] While it is not impossible to justify such clauses, 'the burden of proving reasonableness will not be lightly discharged'.[136]

The prima facie unreasonableness of such exclusion clauses is only exacerbated by the presence of a hell or high water clause. It is therefore submitted that if such exclusion clauses are to be justified as reasonable under UCTA then the finance company, as lessor, must ensure that the lessee is not left without any remedy whatsoever. And the most obvious way in which the finance company can do this – short of not excluding liability in the first place – is to use their bargaining power to ensure that the supplier of the goods, with whom the finance company contracts, expressly extends the benefits of any warranties to the lessee, who can then sue on their own behalf under s 1 of the Contracts (Rights of Third Parties) Act 1999. As Mr Matthew Harvey has put it:

> In view of these difficulties, and the views of the Court of Appeal expressed in [*Purnell*] … the parties ought to explore the possibility of the lessee or hirer obtaining

[131] Departing from the dictum of Dillon LJ in *R & B Customs Brokers Co Ltd v United Dominions Trust Ltd* [1988] 1 WLR 321 (CA) 331–332.

[132] *Purnell Secretarial* (n 126) 1850.

[133] *Sovereign Finance v Silver Crest Furniture* [1999] GCCR 2187. See too *Danka Rentals Ltd v Xi Software Ltd* (1998) 17 Tr LR 74.

[134] *Sovereign Finance* (n 133) 2193.

[135] *Last Bus Ltd v Dawson Group Bus and Coach Ltd* [2023] EWCA Civ 1297, [2023] 4 WLR 80 [51].

[136] *Purnell Secretarial* (n 126) 1851.

> from the supplier duplicate warranties in respect of the equipment that can be given to it on a direct basis. If the lessee or hirer has recourse to the supplier of the equipment for any faults or defects in the equipment that will help justify why an exclusion clause in the lease or hire purchase agreement is reasonable.[137]

The reason this provides an indirect method of regulating the use of hell or high water clauses is that such clauses at least have an ostensible justification – namely, that finance leases are the functional equivalent of credit – that can justify throwing the risk of frustrating events onto the lessee. But such a justification does not justify the lessee being forced to continue to pay for the goods if they are defective unless they are able to sue somebody (whether the finance company or the supplier) in respect of those defects. And in circumstances where finance companies will ordinarily be quite keen to exclude such liability, the provisions of UCTA, as interpreted by courts, seem to have the effect that if finance companies wish to do so they must ensure the lessee is not left without any remedy whatsoever. The easiest way finance companies can do this is by ensuring that the supplier confers the benefits of any warranties onto the lessee, who is the ultimate end-user of the leased item. In this way, hell or high water clauses should, in the main, only operate in the context of small- to medium-sized businesses where the lessee still has a remedy in damages against either the finance company or the supplier for any defects. In short, if the finance company does not obtain warranties from the supplier for the benefit of the lessee, then the finance company will not be able to exclude its own liability for defects under UCTA.

The proposed solution is, admittedly, not a panacea to regulate the use of hell or high water clauses. Aside from the fact that it is not directly regulating their use, UCTA also does not apply to all kinds of contracts. For example, it is unlikely that the provisions of UCTA will apply to aircraft leases because such contracts, as found by Dias J in *Spicejet*, are likely to be international supply contracts within the meaning of s 26, such that the limits on exclusions of liability do not apply.[138] But in respect of most small- to medium-sized businesses – that is, at least those not dealing in the leasing of aircraft – the arguments presented here might provide some degree of protection. In this way, contract law in the broader sense may still have some role to play when it comes to the use of hell or high water clauses in finance leases.

V. Conclusion

A party who agrees to a hell or high water clause promises to perform 'come what may' – that is, absolutely, unconditionally, and irrespective of any contingency. When faced with a frustrating or force majeure event, such a party may naturally

[137] Harvey (n 5) para N0-034.
[138] *Wilmington Trust* (n 1) [45]–[55].

wish to be relieved from the consequences of what has turned out to be an improvident bargain. But, as this chapter has argued, the doctrine of frustration is not a question of justice but a question of construction. Courts, absent statutory authorisation, do not have the power to relieve parties from the effects of the contract that they have made unless there has been some procedural defect in the concluding of the agreement.[139]

The fact that the doctrine of frustration has no role to play, however, does not mean that contract law – in its broadest sense – is powerless to help where parties have agreed to hell or high water clauses. Statutory interventions into consumer contracts directly regulate the use of such clauses. And while the statutory protections for non-consumers are considerably less extensive, this chapter has nonetheless argued that the provisions of UCTA may indirectly regulate the use of such clauses through its direct regulation of exclusion clauses.

[139] Such as in cases of misrepresentation, duress, and undue influence.

9

The Idea of Variation

CHARLES MITCHELL AND MAGDA RACZYNSKA*

I. Introduction

Parties who enter contracts can often foresee that future events may occur as a result of which one or both of them would like to change the terms of their deal. In many cases, the parties agree that neither should be able to do this. For example, it is often predictable that the market price of commodities will move up or down, and when entering a contract of sale, the parties may effectively make a bet about future market movements when they agree the contract price. In such cases, neither can complain if she loses the bet, and it would be contrary to the premise of their agreement if either were empowered to adjust the contract price up or down. In other cases, however, the parties may agree that one or both should be able to change the contract terms in response to future events, the character if not the details of which may be foreseeable (eg, new safety regulations which make it necessary to change the specifications for buildings or machinery) or unforeseeable (eg, a global pandemic which alters trading conditions).

Either way, the parties may agree to provide for the occurrence of such events by giving one party a power to vary the terms. The power-holder will then be in a strong position vis-à-vis the other party and further clauses may be inserted to protect this party from abuses of power. For example, construction contracts frequently provide that the employer has a unilateral power to change the terms but also empower the contractor to reject unreasonable changes and give the contractor rights to extensions of time and payment for extra work. For the same reason, clauses conferring unilateral powers of variation are construed restrictively, and their exercise is subject to certain limits imposed by law.

A contract may alternatively include a clause that empowers the parties to vary the terms jointly, ie, by acting together. Clauses of this kind are less common, as the exercise of bilateral variation powers may well put the parties into the same

* For drawing our attention to some of the materials discussed here we thank Eva Lomnicka and Rebecca Zaman. Declaration of interest: Charles Mitchell worked as a consultant alongside the counsel team led by David Ewart KC who represented HMRC in the *Cobalt Data* case when it went to the Supreme Court.

position as the one they would occupy if they entered a second contract under which they agreed to vary the terms of the first.[1] Given that they can do this, a clause permitting them to do it could be redundant, although clauses requiring them to do it in a particular way, if they choose to do it, are common. The best-known are no oral modification clauses requiring variations to be in writing and signed by both parties.

A question that can arise about variation by any of these routes is whether there is a difference between keeping a contract alive with varied terms and replacing a contract with a new one that has different terms. Often the answer to this will have no practical significance. In most cases, once the parties have taken either course, they know the terms which they must perform, and they do in fact perform these so that they end up in a place where they agreed they might be at the end of performance. In these circumstances it does not matter whether the parties' relationship was governed by a single continuing contract (the terms of which were varied) or two successive contracts (with different terms). The same general point can also be made about situations where one of the parties breaches after a change has been made: it usually makes no difference whether the contract by which the parties are bound at the time of breach is the one they had from the start of their relationship or another contract which they entered afterwards.

In some cases, however, there are practical reasons why the answer matters because there are rules which affect the parties only if they kept their original contract on foot, or conversely, because there are rules which affect them only if they terminated their original contract and entered a new one. In cases of this sort, parties may have a reason to argue about the correct characterisation of the changes which were made. Our goal in this chapter is to discuss cases of this kind. We consider ways in which the courts might approach the characterisation issue and the reasons why they might hold that changes to contractual terms have taken effect either as a variation or as entry into a new contract. These are questions which have not previously been examined in the literature.

II. *Cobalt Data*

Characterisation of the changes made to a contract as a variation or as entry into a new contract will not matter if application of a rule does not turn on this – and sometimes rules which may seem to turn on the characterisation question actually apply to the parties either way, so that it makes no difference whether they kept their original contract going on varied terms or ended it and started over. This

[1] One reason why parties might wish to include a bilateral variation clause is that this might enable them to avoid the common law requirement that variations must be supported by consideration. As noted in the text to n 48, however, this requirement is a weak one which parties should usually find it easy to satisfy.

was the basis on which the Supreme Court decided *R (on the application of Cobalt Data Centre 2 LLP) v HMRC*.[2] However, the judges made some obiter observations about the issue which interests us, and this was also discussed by the lower courts who decided the case. This makes it a good place for us to start.

The case concerned the Capital Allowances Act 2001 (now repealed), which entitled taxpayers to claim generous capital allowances (exceeding 100 per cent) for expenditure on certain types of building in enterprise zones, provided that the money was paid during a specified ten-year period or was paid to discharge payment obligations that accrued during the period.[3] With a view to reaping the benefits of the capital allowances regime, investors set up two firms – a developer and a contractor – and caused them to enter a contract with one another for works on a site in an enterprise zone during the ten-year period. It was not decided at the date of entry into the contract exactly what building would be constructed, and instead the contract contained a suite of options for different buildings and gave the developer the power to choose one of these options by issuing a 'change order'. The developer exercised this power, and the contractor constructed the building chosen by the developer and was paid for this work. After the ten-year period had expired, the developer then issued a second 'change order', requiring the contractor to build another building on the same site.

Whether the contract allowed the developer to issue a second 'change order' was disputed in the subsequent litigation between the developer and HMRC. HMRC argued that this was not permitted because the parties had contemplated that the developer could select only one of the options and could not afterwards select a further option and require the contractor to construct another building as well. However, the contractor made no objection of this sort at the time when the second change order was issued and did the work which the developer had requested. The developer made further payments to the contractor in respect of which it claimed further capital allowances, and HMRC denied that the statutory conditions for these had been met.

The reason why the contractor acceded to the developer's issue of the second change order was that both entities were controlled by a single set of investors whose main objective was to claim the allowances. The investors could have caused the firms to enter a new contract to construct the second building, but the developer could not then have claimed the further allowances because the new contract would have begun only after the ten-year period had ended. This was why the developer issued the second change order instead. However, this plan ultimately failed because the Supreme Court interpreted the legislation to mean that capital allowances were available only in respect of expenditure on work to which the developer had an unconditional contractual right and for which it had owed an unconditional duty to pay before the period had expired.[4] It followed that the allowances could not be

[2] *R (on the application of Cobalt Data Centre 2 LLP) v HMRC* [2024] UKSC 40, [2024] 1 WLR 5213.
[3] Capital Allowances Act 2001, ss 298–299.
[4] *Cobalt Data* (n 2) [94]–[107].

claimed even if the developer's duty to pay for the second building had arisen under the varied terms of the original contract, either because the second change order had been validly issued or because the parties had entered a second contract under which they had agreed to vary the terms of the original contract. On this interpretation of the statute, the developer was therefore unable to claim the allowances, whether its liability to pay the costs of the work arose under the (varied terms of the) original contract, or under a second contract entered when the developer requested the work and the contractor agreed to do it, or (a third possibility) because although the parties had no contract at all, the developer would have been liable to make restitution of the value of the work if it had refused to pay for this and the contractor had made a claim in unjust enrichment.

III. Variation and Party Autonomy

HMRC's arguments about this point of statutory interpretation had failed in the lower courts[5] but HMRC had successfully run alternative arguments there which had assumed that the capital allowances were available if the payments had been made under the (varied) original contract. The point of these arguments was to establish as a factual matter that the original contract had not been varied and that the parties had either created a new contract, or had ceased to have any contract at all, with the result in either case that the developer could not bring itself within the statutory capital allowances regime. In the Supreme Court, HMRC and the developer reargued these points, and the court made some obiter observations about them.

Of particular general interest is HMRC's argument that even if the parties to a contract agree that they will change the terms and, further, that this change will take effect as a variation, so that the contract subsists with varied terms, the change will nevertheless be treated in law as having brought the original contract to an end and created a new contract if the differences between the old and new terms go to the 'root' of the original contract. HMRC cited a number of authorities in support of this proposition, most prominently *Morris v Baron & Co*[6] and *British and Beningtons Ltd v North Western Cachar Tea Co Ltd.*[7]

The developer argued, to the contrary, that contracting parties are free to agree that any change to the terms of their contract will take effect as a variation, whether or not this change is a 'fundamental' one that goes to the root of the contract. In the Supreme Court, where this argument was made with particular emphasis, it was said to rest on the principle of party autonomy. The developer denied that

[5] In the Upper Tribunal (Tax and Chancery): [2019] UKUT 342 (TCC); and in the Court of Appeal: [2022] EWCA Civ 1422, [2022] STC 2041.

[6] *Morris v Baron & Co* [1918] AC 1 (HL).

[7] *British and Beningtons Ltd v North Western Cachar Tea Co Ltd* [1923] AC 48 (HL).

the cases cited by HMRC support the rule for which HMRC argued and said that these establish only that if contracting parties agree to make a change to the terms that goes to the root of the contract, then the fact they have done this is evidence from which a court may (but need not) infer that the parties have a shared intention to replace their original contract with a new one. In these circumstances a court may conclude that the original contract was replaced by a new one, or it may conclude that the original contract stayed on foot with varied terms, but in either case the question which the court decides is what effect the parties intended the changes to have.

The judgment of the Supreme Court was given by Lord Briggs and Lord Sales. They preferred the developer's interpretation of *Morris* and *Beningtons*,[8] and denied that *Morris* had established 'a rule of law to the effect that if there was a fundamental difference between the original contract and the later contract, the later contract had to be taken to "rescind" the original contract'.[9]

In other words, they denied that the parties had to be taken to have ended the original contract and replaced it with a new one in a case where the new terms were fundamentally different from the original terms. Instead, the Supreme Court interpreted *Morris* to mean that:

> the question whether the later contract set aside the original contract depended on the intention of the parties, to be gathered from all the circumstances. The fact that the agreed alterations to their contractual relationship were fundamental was certainly relevant to the ascertainment of their common intention to rescind the original contract rather than to vary it, but that fundamentality did not operate as a separate rule of law, regardless of intention.[10]

On this interpretation of *Morris*, a fundamental change to a contract may have an evidential effect, insofar as it may support an argument that the parties intended to create a new contract, but it does not have the legal effect of terminating the old contract and bringing a new contract into existence, irrespective of what the parties intended.

Lord Briggs and Lord Sales also accepted the developer's submission that contract law generally 'facilitates rather than frustrates the intentions of the parties, except where what they seek to do is contrary to public policy'[11] and that:

> the centrality and force of the principle of freedom of contract means that, purely in terms of the general common law, parties to an agreement have a wide margin of choice in deciding whether an alteration in their contractual relationship should be achieved by the mechanism of variation or replacement. This is generally a matter to be determined according to their common intention, assessed in the usual objective way, within wide parameters and subject to limits only at the margins.[12]

[8] *Cobalt Data* (n 2) [131]–[139].
[9] ibid [136].
[10] ibid.
[11] ibid [143].
[12] ibid [151].

Taking the widest possible version of this approach, as a matter of general common law, the parties' intention would *always* be determinative of whether a change to the contract terms takes effect as a variation or as the creation of a new contract. For example, if the parties to a contract to build a wooden shed agree that henceforth the contract is to build a nuclear submarine, rather than a shed, and the parties further agree that they are varying their contract and not replacing it with a new one, then as a matter of general common law the effect would *always* be that the original contract subsists on varied terms. However, while Lord Briggs and Lord Sales accepted that party intention will be determinative in most cases,[13] they did not accept that this will always be so. They held that there are limits to what the courts should go along with, because

> [at] some point it would bring the law into disrepute if the parties specified that some change in their contractual relations should take effect as a variation rather than a replacement even though that was utterly absurd, yet the law still gave effect to that specification in some way which had effects in the real world. We do not think that the general law would give effect to the intentions of the parties to the extent that it brought [the law] into disrepute and damaged its legitimacy in the eyes of the public.[14]

The judges gave two examples of cases where they seem to have thought the threshold would be crossed.[15] One was where parties enter 'a contract for a holiday in Edinburgh which is implemented and completely exhausted at the time', and the parties agree 15 years later that the contract should be varied to include new terms which provide for 'a different holiday in Paris'. The second was where the same parties 'agree to change the contract for a holiday in Edinburgh into a contract to build a nuclear submarine and agree that this will be by way of variation of the holiday contract, including if that is done fifteen years later'.[16] They also referred[17] to an example discussed in *Plevin v Paragon Personal Finance Ltd (No 2)*[18] where Lord Sumption had said that 'the description given to … transactions by the parties would not necessarily be conclusive if the alleged variation substituted a different subject matter'.[19]

Unfortunately, however, their Lordships did not explain *why* it would 'bring the law into disrepute' if parties were allowed to agree that such substantial changes should take effect as a variation, and they acknowledged that

[13] See too ibid [144]: 'In *Morris v Baron*, if the parties had expressly stated that they were varying and not replacing the original contract, it is clear from the judgments in the case that their intention would have been determinative of that issue', citing *Cumbria County Council v Dow (No 2)* [2008] CLY 1127 (Employment Appeal Tribunal) [12] where this approach was said to have been adopted.

[14] *Cobalt Data* (n 2) [147].

[15] ibid [146].

[16] *Cf Samuels Finance plc v Beechmanor Ltd (t/a Hurstwood Developments)* (1994) 67 P & CR 282 (CA) 285 (Lloyd LJ) referring to 'changes … so fundamental … that they could not properly be described as variation at all'; and see too *Triodos Bank v Dobbs* [2005] 2 CLC 95 [17] (Longmore LJ) and *Samuels Finance Group plc v Beechmanor Ltd* (1993) 67 P & CR 282, 285 (Lloyd LJ).

[17] *Cobalt Data* (n 2) [148].

[18] *Plevin v Paragon Personal Finance Ltd (No 2)* [2017] UKSC 23, [2017] 1 WLR 1249.

[19] ibid [13].

> these are vague standards which, as purely abstract statements, are not very informative about where precisely the limits lie of the ability of the parties to specify that a change to a contract is a variation rather than a replacement and by doing so to bring about some substantive legal result.[20]

In addition, the judges said that if it had affected the outcome of the dispute in *Cobalt Data*, then they would have found that the issuing of the second change order (and the contractor's compliance) had resulted in a variation of the terms of the parties' original contract rather than entry into a new contract. Their Lordships said that:

> [i]n view of the degree of respect afforded by the common law to party autonomy and the relevance of the tax context, we would incline to the view that such alterations would in such circumstances have been assessed to be by way of variation rather than replacement.[21]

This was consistent with the idea that in uncontroversial, run-of-the-mill cases the court's job is only to identify the parties' common intention and give effect to it. The judges effectively treated *Cobalt Data* as a run-of-the-mill case, found as a factual matter that both parties had wanted the developer to be able to claim the capital allowances, found that the parties had therefore wanted the change to their contract to take effect as a variation, and concluded that for this reason a variation had occurred. This assumed that *Cobalt Data* was a run-of-the-mill case and not a case 'at the margins'. However, there are reasons for thinking that the opposite was true, in particular that the second change order was issued after the contractor had fully performed its contractual obligations that had arisen following the issue of the first change order. This makes it hard to distinguish the case from their Lordships' examples of a case where it would be 'absurd' to say that a change took effect as a variation, viz 'a contract for a holiday in Edinburgh which is implemented and completely exhausted', after which the parties purport to add in new terms. How can parties which have fully performed their contractual obligations later say that they are bringing the contract back to life by adding in extra rights and duties? It is hard to make sense of this.

IV. Party Autonomy

The developer laid great stress on party autonomy as the reason why contracting parties should have unlimited freedom to choose for themselves whether or not a change to their contract counts as a 'variation'. This argument won the court's sympathy[22] but, as we have noted, the judges said that it went 'too far' and that in

[20] *Cobalt Data* (n 2) [149].
[21] ibid [156].
[22] ibid [144].

spite of it the parties will not always get their way.[23] The developer's submissions about party autonomy were pitched at a high level of abstraction, and one problem with this kind of argument is that the theory may not always cash out in a clear conclusion about the detailed content of legal doctrine. This is illustrated by *MWB Business Exchange Centres Ltd v Rock Advertising Ltd*[24] where Lord Sumption, for the majority, disagreed with Lord Briggs (and with Kitchin LJ in the Court of Appeal[25]) as to whether 'party autonomy' meant that the parties could orally agree to depart from a 'no oral modification' ('NOM') clause in their contract. Lord Sumption held that they could not and denied that this was contrary to any principle of 'party autonomy' because

> The starting point is that the effect of the rule applied by the Court of Appeal in the present case is to override the parties' intentions. They cannot validly bind themselves as to the manner in which future changes in their legal relations are to be achieved, however clearly they express their intention to do so. In the Court of Appeal, Kitchin LJ observed that the most powerful consideration in favour of this view is "party autonomy": para 34. I think that this is a fallacy. Party autonomy operates up to the point when the contract is made, but thereafter only to the extent that the contract allows. Nearly all contracts bind the parties to some course of action, and to that extent restrict their autonomy. The real offence against party autonomy is the suggestion that they cannot bind themselves as to the form of any variation, even if that is what they have agreed. There are many cases in which a particular form of agreement is prescribed by statute: contracts for the sale of land, certain regulated consumer contracts, and so on. There is no principled reason why the parties should not adopt the same principle by agreement.[26]

This decision has its supporters and critics. Supporters include Jonathan Morgan, who observes that upholding NOMs is consistent with many cases that uphold entire agreement clauses, with the result that collateral warranties cannot be enforced[27] – a point taken by Lord Sumption in *Rock*.[28] Critics include Thomas Raphael, who objects that it prioritises the parties' intentions at the formation date over their intentions at a subsequent date when there is no reason to do this.[29] In extra-judicial writing, Andrew Burrows has also identified other reasons for preferring the view that parties should be able to agree not to comply with NOMs.[30] Burrows also foretold that *Rock* might not be followed in other jurisdictions, and that prediction has been borne out by the Singapore Court of Appeal's

[23] ibid [147].

[24] *MWB Business Exchange Centres Ltd v Rock Advertising Ltd* [2018] UKSC 24, [2019] AC 119.

[25] *MWB Business Exchange Centres Ltd v Rock Advertising Ltd* [2016] EWCA Civ 553, [2017] QB 604.

[26] *Rock Advertising* (SC) (n 24) [11].

[27] J Morgan, 'Contracting for Self-Denial: On Enforcing "No Oral Modification" Clauses' (2017) 76 *CLJ* 589, 596–603.

[28] *Rock Advertising* (SC) (n 24) [14].

[29] T Raphael, 'Tying Your Own Hands: The Supreme Court's Decision in *Rock Advertising*' (2022) 138 *LQR* 299, 306–307.

[30] A Burrows, 'Anti-Oral Variation Clauses: Rock-Solid or Rocky?' in PS Davies and M Raczynska (eds), *Contents of Commercial Contracts* (Oxford, Hart Publishing, 2020) ch 3.

decision in *Lim Teng Siang v Hong Choon Hau*.[31] Nevertheless, *Rock* continues to be English law.[32]

The general relevance of this is that party autonomy is a broad theoretical concept that may lead courts and commentators in various directions when they work through the detail of what parties should and should not be able to do in particular cases. Its more immediate relevance is that one way to explain why parties should be unable to agree that fundamental changes to their contract will take effect as 'variations' might be that they have implicitly bound themselves not to do this when agreeing the original terms. These define what kind of contract the parties want to form by exercise of their autonomy, and it would compromise that choice (and the protection afforded by the law to their exercise of autonomy) if the parties could later agree that the contract should be for something fundamentally different, eg, building a submarine rather than providing a holiday in Edinburgh. Expressing this idea in the terms of Lord Sumption's analysis in *Rock*, once a contract has been formed, party autonomy operates 'only to the extent that the contract allows', and explicitly or implicitly the contract does not allow the parties to make fundamental changes, even if it does allow them to make less radical changes as they go along.

V. The Idea of Variation

There may be other reasons, too, why the Supreme Court thought that cases 'at the margins' are problematic.[33] One which the judges seem to have accepted is that 'variation' is a technical legal concept with certain content and limits as a matter of general common law. If parties attach a different meaning to the term 'variation' when purporting to 'vary' their contracts, then their actions and statements may be legally invalid essentially because they are meaningless. Another reason which seems to have played some part in the court's thinking is that allowing parties to characterise changes to their contracts either as a variation or as the creation of a new contract may be undesirable if it enables the parties to take advantage of a legal rule (or avoid its application) if this would be inconsistent with a policy the rule is meant to further.

These are separate ideas although the judges in *Cobalt Data* elide them in parts of their judgment.[34] It does seem, though, that they thought the idea of 'variation'

[31] *Lim Teng Siang v Hong Choon Hau* [2021] SGCA 43, [2021] 2 SLR 153; noted T Liau, 'No-oral-variation Clauses and Our Powers to Vary Contracts' [2022] *Singapore Journal of Legal Studies* 225.

[32] See also Vienna Convention on Contracts for the International Sale of Goods ('CISG') (1980), art 29(2) (not ratified by UK); US Uniform Commercial Code, Art 2 – Sales (2002), Part 2 Modification, Rescission and Waiver, s 2-209(2); UNIDROIT Principles of International Commercial Contracts (2016), Art 2.1.18.

[33] *Cobalt Data* (n 2) [146]–[147].

[34] ibid [146]–[147].

has conceptual content and limits, hard though these are to define, and if that is correct, then the fact that contracting parties agree they have effected a 'variation' cannot ever be conclusive in itself. For in every case it must still be asked whether the parties' understanding aligns with the courts' understanding of what they have done, albeit that the answer will often be an uncontroversial 'yes'. The reason is that sometimes, in cases at the margins, the courts may still decide to give the answer 'no' after they have interpreted the parties' statements and characterised their effect in law, this being the two-stage process which Lewison LJ took to be required when deciding the *Cobalt Data* case in the Court of Appeal.[35]

In the rest of this chapter, we will consider three aspects of the view, to which we subscribe, that variation is a technical legal concept. In section VI we will suggest that powers to vary contracts are distinct from powers to form contracts. In section VII we will discuss why it is justified for legal systems to insist that 'variation' is a term of art defined by law in the same way that, eg, 'lease' and 'licence' are terms denoting certain sets of legal relations that are deemed by law to exist in certain situations regardless of whether the parties agree they have created one or the other.[36] In section VIII we will observe that the application of some legal rules turns on the question of whether a 'variation' has occurred, that in such cases it is relevant but not necessarily determinative whether changes have taken place which align with a general legal definition of the concept, as the policy underpinning the rules may require the court to adopt a narrower or wider definition when deciding the case.[37]

VI. Powers to Vary Contracts and Powers to Form Contracts

The idea of variation is that a state of affairs exists which undergoes a change with the result that an altered state of affairs comes into being. A variation of a contract occurs when there is a set of contractual rights and duties which is replaced by an altered set of rights and duties between the parties.[38] This is achieved by the

[35] [2022] EWCA Civ 1422, [2022] STC 2041 [106]–[111]. General discussion: G McMeel, *McMeel on the Construction of Contracts: Interpretation, Implication and Rectification*, 3rd edn (Oxford, OUP, 2017) paras 1.30–1.32 and ch 3; R Catterwell, *A Unified Approach to Contract Interpretation* (Oxford, Hart Publishing, 2020) 231–238; Sir K Lewison, *The Interpretation of Contracts*, 8th edn (London, Sweet & Maxwell, 2023) paras 4.16ff.

[36] *Street v Mountford* [1985] AC 809; *AG Securities v Vaughan* [1990] AC 417; *Bruton v London & Quadrant Housing Trust* [2000] 1 AC 406, 413; *Mexfield Housing Co-operative Ltd v Berrisford* [2011] UKSC 52, [2012] AC 955 [17] and [63].

[37] *Cf* S Elliott (ed), *Snell's Equity*, 25th edn (London, Sweet & Maxwell, 2024) para 21-016, citing *Gartside v IRC* [1968] AC 553, 617–618 to illustrate an analogous observation about the liabilities of beneficiaries to tax as parties with an 'interest' in the trust property: 'The terms of tax legislation, rather than any abstract conception of ownership, may determine whether a beneficiary is to be treated as having a sufficient interest in the trust to be liable to tax.'

[38] *Brikom Investments Ltd v Carr* [1979] 1 QB 467 (CA) is sometimes said to be a possible exception to the idea that there must be a pre-existing contract for there to be variation, but this cannot be right: S Wilken and K Ghaly, *The Law of Waiver, Variation, and Estoppel* (Oxford, OUP, 2012) [2.12]–[2.13].

exercise of variation powers held by one or more parties, and not, for example, by a court order or an administrative decision.

When powers of variation are validly exercised, the effect is therefore to create a new set of rights and duties, and of course a similar effect is produced when parties exercise powers to form contracts for the first time. Historically, the resemblance led some courts to regard the power to vary a contract as a type of power to form a contract and to hold that for this reason fresh consideration is needed for the variation of a contract to be binding.[39] A well-known example of this view in American jurisprudence is Cardozo J's dictum in *Beatty v Guggenheim Exploration Co* that:

> Those who make a contract, may unmake it. The clause which forbids a change may be changed like any other. The prohibition of oral waiver, may itself be waived … What is excluded by one act, is restored by another. You may put it out by the door, it is back through the window. Whenever two men contract, no limitation self-imposed can destroy their power to contract again.[40]

On this view, it seems, powers to form and powers to vary contracts are linked to the principle of party autonomy in the same way. If parties are free to enter a contract and decide its content, the reasoning goes, then they must also be free not only to change their agreement but also to decide whether this change takes effect as a variation or formation of a new contract. The better view, however, is that powers to vary contracts are not a sub-set of powers to form contracts. They are different powers, and this difference is reflected in various dissimilarities between the two.[41]

First, a power to vary can be derived from a contractual term, but terms requiring parties to enter a new contract ('agreements to agree') are invalid.[42] Second, powers to vary can be unilateral, and the power-holder can vary the terms without the agreement of other contracting parties,[43] although the effect is to alter their position (and the power-holder's position, in many cases). In contrast, powers to form a contract are always bilateral. This is best explained with reference to the structure of powers. Following Hohfeld,[44] a power is the ability to change legal relations. In contract formation, each party has the power to affect the legal position of the other by agreeing to terms, but in order to bring the contract into existence, the parties' respective powers must be collectively

[39] eg, *Bret v JS* (1599) Cro Eliz 756; 78 ER 987; *Pinnel's Case* (1602) 5 Coke Rep 117a, 77 ER 237, in which alteration of an obligation was seen as an assumption of a new obligation by the obligor, thus conferring a fresh benefit on the obligee. See, too, *Goss v Lord Nugent* (1883) 5 B & Ad 58, 64–65; 110 ER 713, 716: 'By the general rules of the common law … it is competent to the parties at any time before breach of it, by a new contract … to … vary or qualify the terms of … the former agreements.'

[40] *Beatty v Guggenheim Exploration Co* 225 NY 380, 388 (1919); endorsed in *Lim* (n 31) [44].

[41] As argued by, eg, Liau (n 31) 231.

[42] *Hillas & Co Ltd v Arcos Ltd* (1932) 43 Ll L Rep 359 (HL) 368, 370 (Lord Wright).

[43] But note *Felthouse v Brindley* (1862) 11 CBNS 869, 142 ER 1037 (a specific provision to vary is needed for a party to be able to vary a contract unilaterally).

[44] W Hohfeld, 'Some Fundamental Legal Conceptions as Applied in Judicial Reasoning' (1913) 23 *Yale Law Journal* 16, 49–51.

or 'jointly'[45] exercised,[46] because an agreement by definition entails a doing by *both* parties.[47]

Third, the requirement of consideration in relation to variation, while present, is less burdensome than in the case of contract formation: receipt of a practical benefit appears to be enough to support variation.[48] It is difficult to justify the difference in the consideration requirement unless variation differs from formation of contract.

Fourth, the idea that powers to form and vary contracts are distinct aligns with Lord Sumption's view in *Rock*, cited above,[49] that once a contract has been entered, party autonomy operates 'only to the extent that the contract allows'. This means that powers to form contracts, when they are exercised, have the potential to constrain the exercise of powers to vary.

All of this gives us reason to think that variation has its own criteria for application and plays a distinct role in legal systems. This is consistent with the view, which we favour, that variation is a technical concept with content and boundaries set by law. Variation is not whatever parties agree it is, subject to some limit demanded by the concern that affirming ridiculous statements will bring the courts into disrepute. Rather, in every case, variation is a legal concept. The idea of variation is that it is a change to the terms of the contract, and negatively, it is not a change that is so radical that it would be absurd to say the same contract exists. If what parties intend is to effect a variation, their changes must accord with the law's idea of what 'variation' means. In most cases, what parties intend as a variation to an existing contract will fall easily inside the legal concept, but in some cases it will not. Where the changes are fundamental, the effect will be to create a new contract, which may – but need not – terminate and replace the parties' previous agreement.

VII. Justifying the Legal Conception of Variation

Is it justified for the law to insist on a general legal conception of 'variation' and to prevent parties from invoking a different conception of their own in circumstances where this suits them better? A possible justification is that even if parties agree how they wish to characterise changes they have made to a contract, they may be labouring under a misapprehension as to what, if anything, they have achieved. If the parties' ideas about this are confused and even meaningless, then it is not in their interests to treat them as though they were meaningful.

[45] *Lim* (n 31) [42]–[46], [51], [55], [58].

[46] Technically, by making an offer, the offeror undertakes a conditional liability to be bound (conditional on the acceptance of the offer) and exercises a power to affect the position of the offeree (the offeree is placed in a position they were not in before, since – by accepting the offer – a new legal relationship is formed between the parties). The offeree – by accepting the offer – exercises a power affecting the position of the offeror, not least by triggering the condition (and thus, the liability) of the offeror.

[47] R Stevens, 'Binding our Future Selves' in PS Davies and M Raczynska (eds), *Contents of Commercial Contracts. Terms Affecting Freedoms* (Oxford, Hart Publishing, 2020) 18.

[48] *Williams v Roffey Bros & Nicholls (Contractors) Ltd* [1991] 1 QB 1.

[49] See text to n 26.

The same rationale underlies the rule that contracts to do the impossible are void, whether they are impossible due to facts about the real world, such as, eg, contracts for the sale of non-existent goods,[50] or conceptually impossible, such as, eg, contracts which contain mutually contradictory terms or contracts purportedly entered by parties which do not exist. An example of the latter is contracts that are purportedly entered by companies prior to their incorporation. English law provides that contractual rights and duties can only be held and owed by legal persons, which are deemed to possess capacity to hold rights and owe duties. Human beings may have such capacity, but only if they are alive; likewise, companies, but only after they have been incorporated – before then they do not 'exist' and cannot enter contracts. Hence, English law does not permit company promoters to enter contracts in the name of a non-existent company which will be incorporated later and then cause the company to ratify the contract after incorporation. Legislation has therefore been passed to cover this situation, as noted in *Rolle Family & Co Ltd v Rolle*, '[i]t is … because of the conceptual impossibility of assuming an obligation conditional upon the obligee coming into existence, that pre-incorporation contracts are commonly dealt with by specific statutory provision.'[51]

The point of the general rule invalidating contracts to do the impossible is that supporting 'party autonomy' means supporting parties' freedom to make choices about their life, but this is only a policy to support parties' freedom to make choices which are meaningful. The law does not support the freedom to make meaningless choices. Further, the goal of supporting the freedom to make meaningful choices would be frustrated by upholding contracts which are conceptually meaningless or confused because doing this would undermine parties' ability to recognise that they are confused, have acted in a self-defeating way, and would be better off if they started again and thought things through more clearly.

A similar rationale underlies the rule that contractual terms must be certain. As Lord Wright said in *G Scammell & Nephew Ltd v HC and JG Ouston*, the courts generally strive to give effect to parties' intentions, but:

> the test of intention is to be found in the words used [and if] these words, considered however broadly and untechnically and with due regard to all the just implications, fail to evince any definite meaning on which the court can safely act, the court has no choice but to say that there is no contract.[52]

[50] This is a small extension of Sale of Goods Act 1979, s 6: see M Bridge, *The Sale of Goods*, 4th edn (Oxford, OUP, 2019) [4.77], and see [4.70]–[4.72]. Note that the contract will not be void if the seller has given a warranty that the goods are in existence: *McRae v Commonwealth Disposals Commission* (1950) 84 CLR 377 (High Court of Australia).

[51] *Rolle Family & Co Ltd v Rolle* [2017] UKPC 35, [2018] AC 205 [10].

[52] *G Scammell & Nephew Ltd v HC and JG Ouston* [1941] AC 251 (HL) 268. See too Toulson LJ's comments in *Durham Tees Valley Airport Ltd v BMI Baby Ltd* [2010] EWCA Civ 485, [2011] 1 Lloyd's Rep 68 [88]: 'Where parties intend to create a contractual obligation, the court will try to give it legal effect. [But it will] hold that the contract, or some part of it, is void for uncertainty if it is legally or practically impossible to give to the agreement (or that part of it) any sensible content.'

VIII. Variation in Context

What we have discussed so far is the idea of variation that is laid down as a matter of general common law. In many cases, the question of whether a change to contractual terms takes effect as a 'variation' can be decided by reference to this idea without generating answers that subvert the purpose of legal rules which are at issue between the parties. However, cases can arise where reference to the general common law idea of variation may have this effect. In such cases the context may demand that the court ascribes a different meaning to the term 'variation' when this is used, for example, in a piece of legislation.

Consider *Alesayi v Bank Audi SAL*.[53] Sheikh Alesayi wanted to transfer money from certain bank accounts to an account in Geneva, but his bank refused the transfer. Alesayi brought a claim as a consumer against the bank under ss 15B and 15E of the Civil Jurisdiction and Judgments Act 1982. The bank denied that the 'consumer jurisdiction' was engaged on the basis that Alesayi had not contracted as a consumer within the meaning of the 1982 Act because he had not been domiciled in England at the time of contract formation. Resolution of this issue turned in part on the question of when the banking contract was concluded. Alesayi had first entered a banking contract with Saradar Bank in 1994, but Saradar later became a subsidiary of Bank Audi SAL (in 2004), and in November 2016 Alesayi signed various contractual documents, including new terms and conditions. Alesayi argued that for the purposes of the 1982 Act, the contract had been concluded in November 2016, but Bank Audi argued that the 2016 changes had taken effect as variations of the 1994 contract. Constable J found that the 2016 changes had been fundamental and that, at least for the purposes of section 15E, a new contract had therefore been formed in 2016, even if this 'did not amount to formal novation in law'.[54] Noticeably, the judge did not hold that the changes had been so fundamental as to mean that the original contract had been replaced by a new one as a matter of general law: he confined himself to saying only that this had occurred for the purposes of the 1982 Act.

The idea that the meaning of 'variation' for the purpose of particular legal rules can differ from its general common law meaning makes it possible to reconcile *Alesayi* with another Lebanese banking case, *Khalifeh v Blom Bank SAL*.[55] There Foxton J found new contract terms to have taken effect only as variations of the parties' original contract, which did not amount to entry into a new contract for the purposes of Article 6 of Rome I.[56] Under Article 6, a contract concluded by a consumer is governed by the law of the country where the consumer has his

[53] *Alesayi v Bank Audi SAL* [2025] EWHC 1033 (KB).

[54] *Alesayi* (n 53).

[55] *Khalifeh v Blom Bank SAL* [2021] EWHC 3399 (QB).

[56] Regulation (EC) No 593/2008 of the European Parliament and of the Council of 17 June 2008 on the law applicable to contractual obligations ('Rome I').

habitual residence at the time when the contract is formed.[57] Khalifeh argued, among other things, that a new contract had been formed when the parties' original contract had been amended in 2019, when he had been resident in England. Foxton J emphatically rejected this argument.[58] One of the reasons he gave was that characterising the changes made to parties' contracts as variations would be more conducive to the purpose of Rome I because this would mean that there was less fluctuation in the potential applicability of different laws than would be the case if changes were characterised as entry into a new contract.[59]

A second example concerns the Consumer Credit Act 1974, section 82. The section governs bilateral and unilateral variations of agreements regulated under the Act. For unilateral variation, such as a change in the interest rate under a regulated credit agreement, there is a disclosure duty that must be fulfilled before the variation can take effect.[60] But of more interest for current purposes are bilateral variations. If parties agree, for example, that additional equipment is to be let under an existing hire-purchase agreement, this constitutes an agreement that 'varies or supplements' an earlier agreement, termed a 'modifying agreement' under section 82 of the 1974 Act.[61] The effect of such an agreement is stipulated by section 82(2):[62] the modifying agreement is treated for the purposes of the statute as 'revoking the earlier agreement' and giving rise to a new agreement, which subsumes the terms of the earlier agreement.[63] This appears to be a protective measure aimed at ensuring that both the customer and the lender have clarity about their contractual rights and duties. The result of characterising changes to the contracts as entry into new contracts is that lending firms must issue consumers with the full suite of fresh pre-contract and contractual information documents.[64]

[57] Rome I, Art 19(3).

[58] *Khalifeh* (n 55) [73].

[59] Rome I, recital (6): 'to improve the predictability of the outcome of litigation [and] certainty as to the law applicable'.

[60] Consumer Credit Act 1974, s 78A.

[61] See *Chitty on Contracts*, 35th edn (London, Sweet & Maxwell, 2023) para [40-148].

[62] Section 82(2) does not apply if the earlier agreement or the modifying agreement is an exempt agreement under the Financial Services and Markets Act 2000 (Regulated Activities) Order 2001/544, arts 60C and 60D. See further *Chitty on Contracts* (n 61) paras [40-148]–[40-149].

[63] Consumer Credit Act 1974, s 82(2). *Cf Chitty on Contracts* (n 61) para [40-145], where it is said that 'in view of s 82(2), it seems probable that an agreement which "varies or supplements an earlier agreement" will not be construed as a termination and substitution unless such is manifestly the intention of the parties'. On the view advanced in this chapter, the question of whether an agreement has been varied or whether it has been terminated and replaced with a new agreement depends on whether the changes to the contract fall within the meaning of variation, whether variation under the general common law or variation in a given context; it is not, therefore, solely a matter of parties' intention. In addition, it seems that s 82(2) of the 1974 Act provides for a replacement agreement (and termination of the old one) irrespective of whether parties intended to give effect to this when they agreed to change their agreement.

[64] HM Treasury, *Consumer Credit Act Reform – Phase 1. Consultation* (May 2025) 25–26, noting that the 'provision currently results in a lot of unnecessary complexity which makes it difficult for firms and consumers to agree changes to their credit agreement', and a repeal is recommended.

A third example comes from the law of guarantees. This concerns a complex situation involving three parties, and so it calls for a few words of explanation. In the law of guarantees, there is a rule that protects the guarantor from the creditor and principal debtor agreeing a modification to the contractual obligations for which the guarantor is liable without first obtaining the guarantor's consent. The creditor might, for example, agree to give the debtor more time to pay. Unless the guarantor consents to such a modification, the guarantor is released from liability for the principal debtor's obligation, as determined by the well-known case of *Holme v Brunskill*.[65] Although the law has been described as being unduly favourable to guarantors,[66] it is thought that the reason the guarantors are protected is because they obtain no benefit for undertaking a heavy burden, namely a liability for another person's debt.[67] This rule applies whether the modification takes place by way of a variation or a new contract, and so if that were all there was to say about the rule, then it would be of little interest in the present context. However, relevant issues arise in cases where parties try to contract out of the rule.

Given the risk faced by the creditor of losing a guarantor, it is common for the guarantor to consent to variation of the contract in advance, typically in the guarantee.[68] In practice such clauses are drafted broadly (eg, the 'guarantor's liability is not affected by any variation of or amendment which might operate to vary the liability under to the underlying contract'). The question that typically arises in practice is whether the modification of the contract that the creditor and the debtor effected falls within the scope of the consent clause in the guarantee. The answer rests in the construction of the guarantee.[69] It often comes down to identifying whether the change to the contractual duties and liabilities is a variation (and within the clause) or amounts to a new liability arising under a new contract. It is clear that the courts have attempted to identify some limits to variation. Some seem to be conceptual, as mentioned earlier ('if the change were so fundamental that it could not be described as a variation'). But courts are clearly, albeit not uniformly, concerned about the burden placed on the guarantor.

In *Triodos Bank v Dobbs*,[70] for example, Dobbs guaranteed to a bank the obligation of a company under two loan agreements. The company borrowed £900,000 under those agreements, partly to refinance existing borrowings and partly to complete a stage of a particular project. The guarantee provided that the guarantee extended to variations and amendments of the existing facility. The loan agreements were replaced in 1998 by another two loan agreements and a further one in 1999, all of which, in effect, increased the facility to £2,600,000.

[65] *Holme v Brunskill* (1878) LR 3 QBD 495 (CA) and see, too, *Ankar v National Westminster Finance (Australia)* [1987] HCA 15, (1987) 162 CLR 549, 559.

[66] See, eg, *GPP Big Field LLP v Solar EPC Solutions SL* [2018] EWHC 2866 (Comm) [147].

[67] *Triodos Bank v Dobbs* (n 16) [34] (Chadwick LJ). See also R Calnan, R Oliver, M Raczynska, *Calnan on Taking Security*, 5th edn (London, LexisNexis, 2024) para [12.6].

[68] eg, *Perry v National Provincial Bank of England* [1910] 1 Ch 464 (CA).

[69] *Samuels Finance* (n 16).

[70] *Triodos Bank* (n 16).

The purpose of the increased loan was to finance a second stage of the project. The Court of Appeal held that the guarantee did not extend to the new facilities. Longmore LJ and Chadwick LJ each gave his own reasons for this conclusion, and Neuberger LJ agreed. Longmore LJ suggested that a new obligation arises where variation is fundamental (a conceptual limit), and also said the 1998 and 1999 agreements were not variations 'within the purview of the 1996 agreements'.[71] Chadwick LJ's reasons leant towards the policy of protecting the guarantor, as he emphasised that it is the guarantor who must be able to decide what she is liable for. If the modified liability is to be more onerous than the liability initially assumed, there must accordingly be 'clear words in the guarantee which show that he did agree to be bound to a more onerous obligation in the future imposed without further reference to him'.[72] In other words, the guarantor must spell out that she *really* consents to be liable for more. Chadwick LJ then mixed the policy-driven analysis with a conceptual one when he found that while the guarantee permitted the guarantor's liability to become more onerous through variation of the obligations under the 1996 loan agreement, it did not permit the guarantor's liability to become more onerous by covering new obligations of the company. And the liability as guarantor for the obligations under the 1998 agreement would have been substantially more onerous than the liability for obligations under the 1996 agreement.

The reference to variations not being 'within the purview' of the guarantee has become problematic. In *CIMC Raffles Offshore (Singapore) Ltd v Schahin Holding SA*, Sir Bernard Rix drew attention to the various possible meanings of the doctrine. One is that the doctrine is about 'pure construction, albeit of particular application to contracts of guarantee', while the other is that it is 'a doctrine of law, reflecting the equitable concerns of *Holme v Brunskill*, however much it may be influenced by matters of interpretation'.[73] Rix LJ then identified two sets of situations to which the doctrine might apply. However, of more interest here is what the discussion of those situations reveals, namely that there are two very different approaches to determining whether the guarantor's liability extends to variation. The first approach makes it a matter of the parties' intentions at the time of the guarantee whether the alterations are covered by the guarantee. The second approach seems to involve identifying whether the burden generated by the alterations of the underlying contract (its 'onerousness') is contemplated in the original guarantee, specifically whether it is one to which the guarantor consented (as stressed by Chadwick LJ in the *Triodos* case[74]).

Although courts generally prefer to couch the issue of variations in the guarantee context in the language of common intention (essentially the first approach), in actual fact they are concerned about the burden that variations might

[71] ibid [19].
[72] ibid [34].
[73] *CIMC Raffles Offshore (Singapore) Ltd v Schahin Holding SA* [2013] EWCA Civ 644, [2013] 2 All ER (Comm) 760 [51].
[74] See text to n 72.

generate, which is a policy concern. A clearer example is *Downing LLP v Sanguine Hospitality Ltd.*[75] Sanguine guaranteed payment of 'the Liabilities', and this in turn was broadly defined to mean 'all monies and liabilities which from time to time … are due and owing or incurred from the Borrower [LCSC] to the Security Trustee [Downing] and the Lenders.' The judge looked at the 'factual matrix as it stood when the Guarantee was entered into'[76] and found that the 'commercial situation had changed materially'.[77] The material change involved 'different overall sums [that] were owed to a different group of [lenders], and in respect of different liabilities, and with (it seems) modified security arrangements'.[78] The judge did not explicitly refer to the increase of (or a change in) the burden that would be faced by the guarantor, but it is difficult to avoid the impression that the reason why the material changes mattered was that they significantly changed the liability faced by the guarantor, and the general policy is that guarantors are not liable for obligations unless they have very clearly agreed to this.

The courts' reluctance to identify and uphold policy considerations that appear to underpin guarantees is perhaps unsurprising. First, the protection of guarantors is already thought to be unduly generous. It is unsurprising that courts are reluctant to appeal to a shaky policy. Second, the protections available to guarantors are not available to indemnifiers, even though parties who give indemnities undertake a similarly burdensome liability. This difference of treatment may be difficult to justify. Nevertheless, the policy of protecting guarantors remains detectable, and it is plausible that it imposes a limit on variations of contracts between the principal debtor and the creditor when the question arises whether the guarantor is liable notwithstanding the variation.

The policy limits at issue in cases of the kind we are discussing are easier to identify when the rule the parties have in their sights is generated by a statute which itself spells out the policies underpinning the rule. An example is a variation of a public contract governed by legislation. In *Edenred (UK Group) Ltd v HM Treasury*,[79] a government department and a company (Atos) entered a contract for the provision of services that the government wished to outsource (relating to retail savings and investment products). The government later decided to use the department to deliver its tax-free childcare scheme, which was designed to replace the existing scheme of employer-supported childcare. The department then proposed to modify its existing contract with Atos to include these services. Other service providers (such as a trade association for providers of childcare vouchers) claimed that the modification of the existing contract would be substantial under the European procurement regime (under the Parliament and Council Directive 2014/24/EU, implemented by the Public Contracts Regulations 2015, regulation 72). In determining whether the

[75] *Downing LLP v Sanguine Hospitality Ltd* [2020] EWHC 3011 (Ch).
[76] ibid [86].
[77] ibid [90].
[78] ibid [91].
[79] *Edenred (UK Group) Ltd v HM Treasury* [2015] UKSC 45, [2016] 1 All ER 763.

modification was substantial, the Supreme Court considered the purpose of the EU procurement law (which it stated was to develop effective competition in the field of public contracts). It held that there was no substantial modification (as defined in the 2015 Regulations) because the modification would not extend beyond the level of services initially provided for.

The foregoing cases suggest that the question of whether a change to a contract is so fundamental that it becomes a new contract is one that may well require consideration of policy issues relating to rules the application of which turns on this question. The courts are usually well aware of this but the way in which such issues are addressed in judgments varies. Sometimes the courts consider the policy that a rule is meant to further in the course of deciding whether there has been a variation (eg, the variation of public contracts considered in *Edenred*). At other times, the policy discussion takes place when the courts consider whether a rule engaged by the contract is applicable to the facts, and then it may be less obvious that the policy is also relevant when the variation point is discussed. In guarantee cases, the policy furthered by guarantee contracts is rarely spoken about. More often courts take context into account when deciding whether the parties' intention was to vary or replace an existing contract. This is unsurprising, as contracts are read in context.[80] But it seems that in deciding whether a contract is varied, the context taken into account also captures the policies furthered by the legal concepts that the contract created. This is perhaps less surprising than it might seem at first glance. A concept (such as a guarantee) conveys a particular meaning to a reasonable person. Once a contract engaging the concept is created, the concept exists to the extent allowed by the contract and the law. The reasons, including policy reasons, why a concept is given effect to remain valid and relevant when the courts consider whether a contract has been varied.

IX. Envoi

In his *Life of Theseus* Plutarch tells us that:

> The ship on which Theseus sailed with the youths and returned in safety, the thirty-oared galley, was preserved by the Athenians down to the time of Demetrius Phalereus. They took away the old timbers from time to time, and put new and sound ones in their places, so that the vessel became a standing illustration for the philosophers in the mooted question of growth, some declaring that it remained the same, others that it was not the same vessel.[81]

[80] See, eg, *Investors Compensation Scheme v West Bromwich Building Society* [1998] 1 WLR 896 (HL) 912 (Lord Hoffmann); *Chartbrook Ltd v Persimmon Homes Ltd* [2009] UKHL 38, [2009] AC 1101 [14] (Lord Hoffmann), endorsed in *Arnold v Britton* [2015] UKSC 36, [2015] AC 1619 [15] (Lord Neuberger).

[81] B Perrin (trans), Plutarch, *Lives, Volume I: Theseus and Romulus. Lycurgus and Numa. Solon and Publicola* (Loeb, 1914) 48–49.

Modern philosophers, like their ancient counterparts, enjoy discussing the 'Ship of Theseus' paradox; commercial lawyers may recoil from the task of examining a problem framed in such an abstract way and apparently offering so little in practical cash-out. *Cobalt Data* shows us, though, that contract law, like every other part of our law, is built upon foundational concepts and that although these are not often examined by lawyers and judges, there are times when the task of examining them is unavoidable. Our objective in this chapter has been to explain why we think variation is a foundational concept of this kind, to discuss why defining it is not, and should not be, something that can simply be left to the parties, and to consider some of the ramifications of this, both theoretical and practical. When changes are made to a contract, does it remain the same contract? We hope that our thoughts about this question will promote further reflection and discussion.

10

Specific Performance Clauses

SOLÈNE ROWAN*

I. Introduction

It is common for sophisticated contracting parties to seek to allocate the risks of breach of their agreements by expressly stipulating the remedies that will follow. The aim is to provide a level of protection that they judge appropriate for those risks. This will often go beyond or address perceived uncertainties in the default remedial regime for breach of contract.

The subject of this chapter is one such provision, the specific performance clause. This form of agreed remedy has been brought into greater focus by the COVID-19 pandemic and front-page headlines about high-profile corporate takeover deals, such as Elon Musk's initially on-off acquisition of Twitter.[1] Typically, the clause will provide that specific performance – which in England is not available as of right – can be obtained at the election of the injured party in the event of a breach or certain types of breach. This can be supplemented by, or the parties might instead include, an express acknowledgement that the requirements for specific performance, such as irreparable loss and damages being inadequate, will be met where there is a breach.[2]

The utility of specific performance clauses to parties desirous of managing contractual risks has the potential to be significant. As a remedy, specific performance generally protects contractual expectations to a greater degree than other remedies. It does so by compelling the defaulting party to fulfil their promise and perform their contractual obligations. However, it is at the discretion of the court and in practice is rarely awarded, to the point of being exceptional. The specific

* My thanks go to Sushma Ananda, Gregg Rowan, and the organisers and participants of the 'Contract Law and the Unexpected' UCL conference for their comments on an earlier draft. I would also like to thank Caroline Rae for her helpful insights on M&A transactions in England.

[1] See also *Cineplex v Cineworld*, 2021 ONSC 8016 (Canada) and *Travelport Ltd & Ors v WEX Inc*, [2020] EWHC 2670 (Comm) (England).

[2] For examples of boilerplate specific performance clauses, see R Christou, *Boilerplate: Practical Clauses*, 5th edn (London, Sweet & Maxwell, 2019) para [12-168]; T Arnold, A Dixon, H Tanne, M Whalen Sherrill and M Gulati, 'Lipstick on a Pig': Specific Performance Clauses in Action' [2021] *Wisconsin Law Review* 359.

performance clause is an attempt to overcome these challenges by the creation of a contractual entitlement to the remedy. It is likely to be particularly attractive to contracting parties who wish to obtain the actual performance of their counterparty and not simply an award of damages. They may perceive that damages would not satisfactorily compensate a breach. By including the clause, they seek to strengthen the protection of their contractual expectations beyond the default entitlement.

Despite their potential utility, there is barely any mention of specific performance clauses in the English case law. Nor is there any clear authority as to whether they are enforceable. Indeed, when they have been obliquely considered, the approach of the courts appears to have been one of circumspection. There is a discernible reluctance to allow contracting parties to fetter or oust the equitable discretion of the court as to whether to grant specific performance. At most they are regarded as lending evidential support to a contention that damages are inadequate.

This chapter examines the circumspection historically shown by the English courts to specific performance clauses and whether this continues to be warranted. These are topics that the author first explored 15 years ago in an article in the *Law Quarterly Review*.[3] Under the auspices of the 'Contract Law and the Unexpected' theme of this book, it is timely to revisit them. This is due in particular to the greater receptiveness recently shown by the Supreme Court to a different type of agreed remedy, the damages clause, in *Cavendish Square Holding BV v Talal El Makdessi*.[4] The chapter reflects on the current state of the law on specific performance clauses and how it might now evolve in the light of that decision.

Its thesis is that the caution of English courts towards specific performance clauses should be reconsidered, and that they have a valuable role to play in commercial transactions. It is natural and legitimate for sophisticated contracting parties to wish to ensure that the remedies available for breach meet their interests and needs, particularly where they perceive that the default remedial regime does not adequately do so. On close examination, the objections that have been or might be made are capable of being surmounted.

For the courts to uphold specific performance clauses would promote contractual freedom and give primacy to the common intention of the parties, as well as transactional certainty. It would also be consistent with the approach in *Makdessi* to damages clauses that impose greater liability on the defaulting party than would standard damages for breach of contract. The Supreme Court redefined the test for ascertaining whether such a clause is penal and put an end to the binary search for a genuine pre-estimate of loss in favour of a more nuanced and evaluative enquiry into whether the clause is justifiable and proportionate.

[3] S Rowan, 'For the Recognition of Remedial Terms Agreed *Inter Partes*' (2010) 126 *LQR* 448.

[4] *Cavendish Square Holding BV v Talal El Makdessi* [2015] UKSC 67, [2016] AC 172 (SC), with its conjoined appeal *ParkingEye Ltd v Beavis*. For ease of reference, the conjoined appeals will be referred to in this chapter simply as *Makdessi*.

Now the courts have greater flexibility to assess the enforceability of damages clauses by reference to notions of legitimate interest, unconscionability, exorbitance and extravagance.

The chapter begins by examining the limited availability of specific performance as a remedy under the default regime for breach of contract in England. It then identifies certain deficiencies in the regime, which it is argued could be mitigated were specific performance clauses to be enforceable. A brief comparative analysis shows that these provisions have become increasingly prevalent in high-value and complex agreements elsewhere in the world. The chapter turns next to the scepticism of the English courts, explaining and seeking to address the concerns that have been raised in the cases. Drawing parallels with damages clauses and the new approach in *Makdessi*, it concludes by arguing that there are no insurmountable objections to specific performance clauses, provided that there are safeguards to weed out abusive and unacceptable terms. English contract law could readily adapt to such a change.

II. The Limited Availability of Specific Performance

Specific performance and injunctive relief seek to ensure that the injured party receives their bargained-for performance. To this extent, in the arsenal of remedies available under English law for breach of contract, they are the most powerful.[5] However, they are also discretionary. They are therefore not available as of right. In fact, the practical reality is that they are relatively exceptional. This is particularly true of specific performance. Since Lord Hoffmann's seminal speech in the defining case of *Co-operative Insurance Society Ltd v Argyll Stores (Holdings) Ltd*,[6] the remedy has largely been marginalised. Only where compensatory damages are inadequate can it be claimed.[7] It is also unavailable where granting the remedy would cause undue hardship to the defaulting party[8] or require continuous supervision by the court to ensure compliance.[9]

In most situations, English law regards damages as an adequate remedy. This is why specific performance is exceptional. The injured party is generally thought to be satisfactorily and effectively protected by monetary compensation. Where, for example, the injured party is able to acquire a suitable replacement from a third party,

[5] J O'Sullivan, 'Loss and Gain at Greater Depth: the Implications of the *Ruxley* Decision' in F Rose (ed), *Failure of Contracts – Contractual, Restitutionary and Proprietary Consequences* (Oxford, Hart Publishing, 1997) 1 at 18; D Harris, 'Incentives to Perform, or Break Contracts [1992] *Current Legal Problems* 29 at 30.

[6] *Co-operative Insurance Society Ltd v Argyll Stores (Holdings) Ltd* [1998] AC 1 (HL). Although the focus of this chapter is on specific performance, the arguments made also apply to mandatory injunctions, the availability of which is subject to the same principles.

[7] ibid at [11] (Lord Hoffmann).

[8] *Co-operative v Argyll* (n 6) at [15], [18] (Lord Hoffmann).

[9] ibid at [12] (Lord Hoffmann).

their expectations are deemed to be fulfilled.[10] There is deemed to be an equivalence between the promised performance and substitute performance, to which the injured party is treated as being indifferent. This is in keeping with the mitigation principle, which will reduce a compensatory award where the injured party fails to take reasonable steps to minimise the loss flowing from the breach. Typically, mitigation will involve buying a replacement elsewhere. The difference between the contract price and the price of that replacement, together with additional damages for any recoverable consequential losses, are regarded as being adequate compensation.

The English courts have been faithful to this approach, even in extreme circumstances. This is illustrated by *Société des Industries Métallurgiques SA v Bronx Engineering Co Ltd*.[11] In breach of contract, the defaulting party failed to supply a large machine weighing over 220 tonnes and valued at more than £270,000. It would take between 9 and 12 months for a replacement to be sourced by the injured party, which would suffer substantial consequential losses in the meantime. Nevertheless, the Court of Appeal found that damages were an adequate remedy and refused specific performance. These losses, which would also be difficult to quantify accurately, were held not to suffice for a finding that damages were inadequate.

The supremacy of damages is additionally said to place fewer demands on scarce judicial resources and to draw a once-and-for-all line under disputes, which might otherwise be prolonged by specific performance. In *Co-operative v Argyll*,[12] the House of Lords refused to order specific performance of a covenant in a 35-year lease which required the defendant-tenant, a supermarket which was the anchor unit in the claimant-landlord's shopping centre, to remain 'open for retail business'. Whilst recognising the seriousness of the consequences of breach, and also the difficulty in accurately quantifying the loss suffered by the landlord, the court held that only damages should be awarded. It was unwilling to countenance the risk of first instance courts having to police whether specific performance orders have been breached. A once-and-for-all inquiry as to damages would put much less strain on judicial resources.[13]

III. Specific Performance as an Agreed Remedy

The premise that performance and damages fulfil the expectations of contracting parties in equal measure is questionable. In reality, these outcomes can be starkly different. It is therefore scarcely believable that the parties will always be neutral or

[10] A frequently cited example, and one of the few instances where specific performance is routinely awarded, is contracts for the sale of land. Each plot of land is regarded as being unique and irreplaceable. Damages for the breach of such contracts will therefore seldom be adequate.

[11] *Société des Industries Métallurgiques SA v Bronx Engineering Co Ltd* [1975] 1 Lloyd's Rep 465 (CA).

[12] n 6.

[13] ibid at [12] (Lord Hoffmann). According to P MacMahon, 'Conflict and Contract Law' (2018) 38 *OJLS* 270 at 284, the commitment to compensatory damages over specific performance contributes to 'conflict minimisation'.

indifferent between them. Some or even many may prefer to obtain the promised performance rather than damages.

A middle way that would recognise this possibility would be to allow the parties to provide in their agreements for specific performance. Such clauses would enable any perceived inadequacies in the default remedial regime to be circumvented. It is presumably for these reasons that they have attracted interest and become more prevalent in the US.

A. Specific Performance Clauses

Situations abound in which the parties may regard specific performance as preferable to damages.[14] It may be that potential substitutes are not close enough to the original, in short supply, or time-consuming or slow to obtain.[15] In contrast, performance may be less disruptive and inconvenient to the injured party. It may be said that serious disruption and inconvenience are compensable by damages, but *Bronx Engineering* and *Cooperative v Argyll* illustrate in practice that the extent of the loss actually suffered may be difficult to assess.[16] There is also a risk that the injured party will be under-compensated due to the operation of the principles of remoteness and loss mitigation.

In some cases, only performance in a particular manner or personally by the defaulting party will fulfil the expectations of the injured party. This might be because the promised performance is perceived to have intrinsic value. It might also be that the interest of the injured party is not commercial in nature.[17] Compensation will not always be capable of fulfilling subjective value;[18] only specific performance can do so. The very fact that the injured party requests specific performance implies that they prefer performance over damages.[19]

Specific performance being granted where the parties have so agreed could readily be assimilated into English law. It would, after all, give effect to their common intention and the fundamental principle of freedom to contract. These are both articles of faith in England. The result would be to enhance the protection

[14] G Jones and W Goodhart, *Specific Performance*, 2nd edn (London, Butterworths, 1996) 4; D Friedmann, 'Economic Aspects of Damages and Specific Performance Compared' in R Cunnington and D Saidov (eds), *Contract Damages: Domestic and International Perspectives* (Oxford, Hart Publishing, 2008) 66–71.

[15] Jones and Goodhart (n 14) 147.

[16] See also *CN Marine Inc v Stena Line A/B and Regie voor Maritiem Transport (The 'Stena Nautica') (N° 2)* [1982] 2 Lloyd's Rep 336 (CA) citing the observation of the trial judge that 'in many cases there are items of inconvenience which may not be capable of quantification or which the law regards as too remote to sound in damages but such matters do not, without more, justify the granting of an order for specific performance' at 342 (Buckley LJ).

[17] *Ruxley Electronics and Construction Ltd v Forsyth* [1996] AC 344 (HL) 353 (Lord Bridge); TS Ulen, 'The Efficiency of Specific Performance: Toward a Unified Theory of Contract Remedies' [1984] *Michigan Law Review* 341, 350–56.

[18] D Harris, A Ogus and J Phillips, 'Contract Remedies and the Consumer Surplus' (1979) 95 *LQR* 581.

[19] A Schwartz 'The Case for Specific Performance' (1979) 89 *Yale Law Journal* 271, 277.

of their interests, but only where they jointly desire it. It would encourage and empower them to consider and negotiate, at the time of the formation of the contract, how breach should be dealt with. There would also be an ancillary benefit of encouraging the parties to perform and deterring breach of the contract.[20]

For example, the parties in *Bronx Engineering* would have known when they entered the contract that a failure by the manufacturer to supply the machine would inevitably lead to the buyer suffering pecuniary loss, delay, and considerable inconvenience. In *Co-operative v Argyll*, the business plan of the landlord relied heavily on the tenant abiding by its covenant to remain 'open for retail business'. Even at the time of the inception of the lease, it was known that without the presence of that particular tenant, which operated a Safeway supermarket described by Lord Hoffmann as 'by far the largest shop and the greatest attraction'[21] at the shopping centre, fewer retail customers would come. In turn, it would be less viable for the occupiers of smaller retail units and ultimately for the landlord.[22] In both cases, these consequences may well have been avoided by enforceable specific performance clauses. Given the choice, both injured parties may even have been prepared to pay a premium for the inclusion in the agreement of such a clause, and for the comfort of not being confined to a damages award that could result in under-compensation.

B. Comparative Perspectives

It is unclear to what extent specific performance clauses are used in practice in England. In the case law and literature, they have received scant attention. This is in contrast with the US, where they have generated real interest[23] and are enforced in some situations. For sale of goods contracts, section 2-719 of the Uniform Commercial Code allows the parties in non-consumer contracts to shape their remedies to their particular needs.[24] This is subject to a requirement of reasonableness. Only 'reasonable agreements limiting or modifying remedies are to be given effect'. In addition, 'any clause purporting to modify or limit the remedial

[20] Harris (n 5) 38.

[21] *Co-operative v Argyll* (n 6) at [9].

[22] In the Court of Appeal, this fact was heavily relied on in the judgments of Leggatt and Roch LJJ: *Co-operative v Argyll* (n 6).

[23] Articles on the subject include A Kronman, 'Specific Performance' [1978] *University of Chicago Law Review* 351; I Macneil, 'Power of Contract and Agreed Remedies [1962] *Cornell Law Quarterly* 495; P Rubin, 'Unenforceable Contracts: Penalty Clauses and Specific Performance' (1981) 10 *Journal of Legal Studies* 237; D Frisch, 'Remedies as Properties: A Different Perspective on Specific Performance Clauses' [1993–94] *William & Mary Law Review* 1691. In Australia, see R Carroll, 'Agreements to Specifically Perform Contractual Obligations' (2012) 29 *Journal of Contract Law* 155.

[24] Section 2-719 states that 'the agreement may provide for remedies in addition to or in substitution for those provided in this Article and may limit or alter the measure of damages recoverable under this Article, as by limiting the buyer's remedies to return of the goods and repayment of the price or to repair and replacement of non-conforming goods or parts.'

provisions of this Article in an unconscionable manner is subject to deletion'.[25] There are at least two cases in which specific performance clauses have been given effect pursuant to section 2-719 of the Uniform Commercial Code.[26]

Specific performance clauses have been shown to be widely used in commercial practice in the US, although the extent to which they are enforced is less apparent.[27] There is empirical evidence that, over the last 15 years, they have become the market standard in Mergers and Acquisitions (M&A) transactions where one or both parties is a public entity. In a review of data collected from 1,000 M&A agreements over a ten-year period (2010–19), it was found that specific performance clauses were included in 85 per cent (in 2010) to 95 per cent (in 2019) of them.[28] This was true whether the M&A transaction was aimed at generating financial or strategic value and whether the parties were both public entities or one was public and the other a private enterprise. A similar study was undertaken in 2002, and at that time only 50 per cent of M&A transactions were found to contain such clauses.[29]

This strikingly high rate has been attributed to the perceived inability of the courts to award adequate compensation for losses resulting from failed mergers.[30] The parties are incentivised to close their deal. In turn, this helps to assuage seller-side fears of being 'left at the altar' and perceived as 'damaged goods'.[31] As an alternative to closing the deal, there is also an incentive for the parties to negotiate an out-of-court monetary settlement that more accurately compensates the injured party for its losses than might be the case, if that party had to pursue a damages claim.[32]

A high-profile illustration of a specific performance clause in an M&A context can be seen in Elon Musk's turbulent acquisition of Twitter in 2022.[33] Mr Musk initially sought to terminate the so-called merger agreement by which he would acquire Twitter. He did so on the ground, amongst others, that Twitter had breached its information-sharing and cooperation covenants in relation to 'spam/fake accounts'. In the view of Twitter, his change of heart was in fact due to movements in the market which made the fixed-price deal less attractive to him. To force the deal through, it invoked the specific performance clause in the agreement.[34] It is difficult to measure the extent to which this clause was a factor in

[25] See the Official Comments to s 2-719, UCC.

[26] *Martin v Sheffer* (contract for the sale of a printer valued at US$17,000) and *Frank Leroux Inc v Burns* (contract for the sale of the assets of a pharmaceutical business).

[27] See Arnold, Dixon, Tanne et al (n 2) and for cases not enforcing them: *301 East 60th Street LLC v Competitive Solutions LLC*, 217 A.D.3d 79 (NY App 2023); *26 Capital Acquisition Corp v Tiger Resort Asia Ltd*, 309 A3d 434 (Del 2023); *In re Cellular Tel P'ship Litig*, 2021 WL 4438046 (Del Ch 28 Sept 2021).

[28] Arnold, Dixon, Tanne et al (n 2) 359, 363 and 375.

[29] T Eisenberg and GP Miller, *Damages Versus Specific Performance: Lessons from Commercial Contracts* (2015) 12 *Journal of Empirical Legal Studies* 29.

[30] Eisenberg and Miller (n 29) 68–69; Arnold, Dixon, Tanne et al (n 2) 389.

[31] Arnold, Dixon, Tanne et al (n 2) 380.

[32] ibid 380–81.

[33] See section 9.9 of the takeover agreement: www.sec.gov/Archives/edgar/data/1418091/000119312522120474/d310843ddefa14.htm.

[34] www.corpgov.law.harvard.edu/2022/07/14/twitter-vs-musk-the-complaint/.

Mr Musk's eventual decision to complete, but it was widely seen by commentators in the US as giving Twitter a significant advantage.[35]

Another context in which specific performance clauses have made the front pages in the US is the leases of sports stadiums from municipalities to professional sports franchises. In one case, the group that owned the Cleveland Browns, an American football team, sought to relocate from Cleveland to Baltimore. To prevent the relocation, the City of Cleveland, which owned the stadium in which the Browns played, invoked a specific performance clause in the stadium lease. In another case, the owner of the Sonics, a basketball team, wished to escape from a fixed-term lease in order to move the team from Seattle to Oklahoma City. Again, the lease contained a specific performance clause, which the City of Seattle relied on in order to keep its prize tenant.

Both cases were compromised prior to final determination,[36] but they illustrate the utility of specific performance clauses in this context. If there were no such clauses and the entitlement of the municipalities to specific performance was left entirely to the discretion of the court, the risk of an adverse decision would increase. The effect would be to deprive the municipalities not only of their tenants but also of the civic pride, prestige, and capacity to attract new businesses and inhabitants that flow from a major sports franchise being in residence. These benefits would be very difficult to measure in monetary terms, and similarly difficult to compensate adequately in damages.

The US is not the only jurisdiction in which contracting parties can provide for specific performance. Such clauses are also enforced in some civilian jurisdictions, for example, France. This is so even where the remedy is not available under the default regime.[37] In sale of goods contracts, clauses that specify that the purchaser can require defective or otherwise non-conforming goods to be repaired or replaced are not infrequently upheld.[38] The parties may also agree to the opposite outcome and exclude specific performance. Clauses that provide that damages should be the remedial consequence of breach, to the exclusion of other remedies, have also been upheld.[39]

[35] See, eg, R Anderson, 'Limited Specific Performance in the Musk-Twitter Case and Beyond (2022) (available at www.papers.ssrn.com/sol3/papers.cfm?abstract_id=4222557); M Bobelian, Twitter Has a Far Stronger Case as It Heads into Trial Against Elon Musk, *FORBES* (27 July 2022), www.forbes.com/sites/michaelbobelian/2022/07/27/twitter-has-a-far-stronger-case-as-it-heads-into-trial-against-elon-musk/.

[36] K Leone, 'No Team, No Peace: Franchise Free Agency in the National Football League' [1997] *Columbia Law Review* 473. The owners of the Browns and the NFL negotiated a deal that allowed the team eventually to move to Baltimore, whilst guaranteeing the City of Cleveland an expansion franchise that kept the 'Browns' name.

[37] Civ (3) 27 March 2008, RDC 2008 n03.734 noted by D Mazeaud; CA Paris, 26 Oct 2006, RDC 2007.795, noted by F Collart Dutilleul.

[38] Y-M Laithier 'La prétendue primauté de l'exécution en nature' RDC 2005.161, 168; C Grimaldi, 'Les clauses tournées vers le maintien du contrat: exécution par remplacement, exécution forcée, réduction de prix', RDC 2024.111; R Libchaber, 'Le juge du contrat peut-il être tenu à l'écart d'une clause ?' RDC 2024.10.

[39] Com 20 Jan 1981, Bull civ IV no 41; Civ (1) 21 March 1995, n°93-12.177; Com 1 Feb 1994, n°92-12.621; Civ (1) 11 Jan 1967, Bull civ no 15 and Com 7 Mar 1984, JCP 1985.II.20407. Also Civ (3) 3 Nov 2011, no 10-26203 CA Rennes, 9 Dec 2010, no 08/03916.

IV. The Response of the English Courts to Specific Performance Clauses

Firm conclusions cannot easily be drawn as to the use, validity and enforcement of specific performance clauses in England, given that they have been so neglected in the case law and literature. When they have been litigated, the courts have shown an aversion to permitting the parties to fetter or oust the equitable discretion to grant specific performance. There must therefore be real doubt about whether, as things currently stand, a court in England would enforce such a clause. It will be argued that this is regrettable and the objections that have weighed on the English courts do not withstand close scrutiny.

A. Reluctance to Enforce Specific Performance Clauses

The circumspection of English courts towards specific performance clauses is illustrated by *Quadrant Visual Communications Ltd v Hutchison Telephone (UK) Ltd*.[40] In that case, the Court of Appeal refused to award specific performance on the ground that the claimant did not come to equity with 'clean hands'. It rejected the submission that a clause providing that the consideration should be paid in cash 'free from any equity cross-claim set-off or other deduction whatsoever' could preclude the operation of the 'clean hands' bar. On the question of whether the discretion of the court could be excluded by agreement, Stocker LJ said:

> Once the court is asked for the equitable remedy of specific performance, its discretion cannot be fettered. Once the assistance of the court is involved by one of the parties in a discretionary matter, that party is bound by the general discretion of the court to grant or refuse the remedy sought. If … [the] submission that the court is bound by the terms of the contract and therefore has no discretion to exercise is correct, the function of the court would be reduced to that of a rubber stamp. In my opinion, this could not be and is not the situation.[41]

This reasoning is hardly surprising on the facts. The claimant had deliberately breached the agreement and behaved dishonestly. There would have been an understandable aversion to upholding a clause purporting to confer remedies on

[40] *Quadrant Visual Communications Ltd v Hutchison Telephone (UK) Ltd* [1993] BCLC 442 (CA); See also S Shiffrin, 'Remedial Clauses: The Over-Privatization of Private Law' (2016) 67 *Hastings Law Journal* 407. See also *Awbury Technical Solutions LLC v Karson Management (Bermuda) Ltd* [2019] EWHC 233 (Comm) [2019] Bus LR 559 at [44]–[59] and [68]; *TP Global Operations Ltd (t/a 1Global) v Insightful Technology Ltd* [2024] EWHC 3106 (Comm) at [19]–[20]. Note, however, that an agreement to exclude the remedy being granted is valid: *Mills v Sportsdirect.com Retail Ltd* [2010] EWHC 1072 (Ch) at [88] (Lewison J); see also the dicta of Leggatt LJ in *Co-operative v Argyll* (n 22) at [294]. In the context of arbitration, see *Vertex Data Science Ltd v Powergen Retail Ltd* [2006] EWHC 1340 (Comm) at [28].

[41] *Quadrant v Hutchison* (n 40) 451 (Stocker LJ); see also at 452 (Butler-Sloss LJ).

a party that had behaved reprehensibly. One can only speculate as to whether the outcome would have been different had the claimant not been so tainted.

The circumspection can also be divined from *Warner Bros Pictures Inc v Nelson*.[42] An actress had agreed to work exclusively for a film producer. There was a clause in the contract stating that her services were 'of a special, unique, extraordinary and intellectual character', 'the loss of which [could not] be reasonably or adequately compensated in damages'. It also acknowledged that breach may 'cost [the film producer] great and irreparable injury and damage' such that they should be entitled to injunctive relief to restrain breach. When the actress sought to work for a third party in breach of her undertaking, Branson J granted an injunction without relying on the clause. By the following remarks, he indicated that, although relevant, injunction clauses should not be determinative:

> Of course, parties cannot contract themselves out of the law; but it assists, at all events, on the question of evidence as to the applicability of an injunction in the present case, to find the parties formally recognizing that in cases of this kind injunction is a more appropriate remedy than damages.[43]

It would be wrong to contend that the courts in these cases really grappled with whether clauses that provide for specific relief should be enforceable. The cases do, however, offer instructive guidance and suggest that these clauses will be approached with at least a degree of scepticism. Until there is judicial authority to the contrary, it would therefore be unsafe to regard specific relief clauses as being anything other than evidential in nature, probative to the question of whether damages are adequate. Whilst the wishes of the parties may be taken into account, the courts reserve the final word to themselves. It follows that specific performance and injunction clauses should currently be regarded as of correspondingly limited utility.

B. Rejecting the Objections to Specific Performance Clauses

The attribution of no more than evidential value to specific performance clauses is, it is submitted, unfortunate. It is at odds with the fulfilment of the parties' contractual expectations. There is also an incongruity with the deference to freedom of contract and the promotion of transactional certainty that prevail with relatively few exceptions in the context of primary contractual obligations.[44] Specific performance clauses are a logical incident of the principle of freedom of contract. The enforcement of an agreement insofar as it relates to the promised

[42] *Warner Bros Pictures Inc v Nelson* [1937] 1 KB 209.
[43] ibid 220–221.
[44] For a recent decision in which the importance of freedom of contract and commercial certainty was stressed by the Supreme Court, see *RTI Ltd v MUR Shipping BV* [2024] UKSC 18; [2024] 2 WLR 1350; P MacMahon, 'The Costs of Contractual Certainty: *RTI* v *MUR Shipping*' (2024) 88 *MLR* 404.

substantive performance but not the consequences of breach is difficult to rationalise.[45] As Lord Diplock said in *Photo Production Ltd v Securicor Transport Ltd*,[46] a 'contract … is just as much the source of secondary obligations as it is of primary obligations … and like primary obligations that are implied by law, secondary obligations too can be modified by agreement between the parties'.[47]

A consequence of the limited effect of specific performance clauses is that the parties can side-step the allocation of risk that they have agreed. The injured party may have specifically negotiated and paid a premium for the additional protection conferred by the clause.[48] This is undermined if the clause is disallowed. The defaulting party can pocket the premium without bearing any of the corresponding risk. In return, the injured party receives nothing other than an argument of questionable value that the court should take account of the clause when exercising its discretion.

The contrariness of these outcomes and the broader discordance with the fundamental principles of freedom of contract and contractual certainty necessitate an examination of why the courts are apparently unwilling to enforce specific performance clauses. The starting point for this exercise is the reasoning in *Quadrant Visual* and *Warner Bros* that their purpose and effect are to usurp the decision-making role of the court. It also requires consideration of the reasons for the narrow availability of specific performance in English law. These include the concern that the remedy would require an unacceptable degree of judicial supervision or cause undue hardship to the defaulting party, particularly since non-compliance would constitute contempt of court. It will be argued that these objections are largely overemphasised, and they lose their force or can be managed where the parties have agreed to specific performance as a remedy.

i. *The Usurpation of the Role of the Court Objection*

Probably the main ground of objection to specific performance clauses is that they are antithetical to established principles that determine when the remedy should be awarded. To uphold such a clause would be to permit the contracting parties to circumvent the clear preference in English law for compensatory damage over mandatory orders. The role of the court would be correspondingly diminished, confined to implementing their agreed remedy, rather than applying the equitable rules developed and finessed in the cases over many years.

[45] On the usefulness of the distinction between primary and secondary obligations, see D Foxton, 'How Useful is Lord Diplock's Distinction between Primary and Secondary Obligations in Contract?' (2019) 135 *LQR* 249. A Georgiou, 'Making Contract-breakers Pay' (2025) 141 *LQR* 104, for whom the principles that justify judicial recognition of primary obligations do not, necessarily, justify secondary obligations.

[46] *Photo Production Ltd v Securicor Transport Ltd* [1980] AC 827 (HL).

[47] ibid 849.

[48] Harris (n 5) 39; R Sharpe, 'Specific Relief for Contract Breach' in B Reiter and J Swan (eds), *Studies in Contract Law* (London, Butterworths, 1980) 123, 135.

It is submitted that this reasoning is unpersuasive. So developed and finessed are the equitable rules that the discretion of the court to award specific remedies is, in many cases, more theoretical than real.[49] In practice there is rarely any real discretion.[50] More often than not, damages are an adequate remedy and are ordered as a matter of course. Only in borderline cases is the court called upon to exercise discretion, but otherwise there is no real discretion to oust. This objection to specific relief clauses therefore falls away.

There is ample precedent in a remedial context for contracting parties being permitted to exclude the decision-making role of the court. These include force majeure clauses, termination clauses and exclusion clauses. Taking the force majeure clause as an example, its very purpose is to enable the parties to avoid the strictures of the doctrine of frustration. It does so by defining as force majeure events that would not, at common law, suffice to frustrate their agreement.[51] In doing so, they side-step the application of the default rule.

Termination clauses serve a similar purpose. The injured party is able to bring the contract to an end where there has been an event of default that engages the clause. It does not matter whether the breach constitutes a repudiation or even that it is trifling in nature. It is true that on occasions the courts have interpreted termination clauses narrowly, but even this can generally be prevented by the parties using clear and unequivocal wording.[52]

Exclusion and limitation clauses enable the parties to depart from the conventional approach to determining recoverable damages to compensate for loss, subject to statutory and regulatory safeguards.[53] If contracting parties are at liberty to narrow the remedial consequences of breach, there is a strong argument for saying that their enlargement to uphold the contractual expectations of the injured party through specific performance clauses should also be allowed.[54]

ii. Onerous Performance and the Undue Hardship Exception

A further objection to specific performance clauses is that, even if they are not unfair at the time they are agreed, they have the potential to become so when they are enforced. It may be, for example, that mandatory performance initially appeared manageable, but by the time the clause is invoked, circumstances have

[49] *Co-operative v Argyll* (n 6) at [9] (Lord Hoffmann).

[50] For an excellent article questioning the orthodoxy that specific performance orders are truly 'discretionary', see T Liau and A Georgiou, 'Are Equitable Remedies Discretionary' (2025) 18 *Journal of Equity* 246.

[51] E McKendrick, 'Force Majeure Clauses: The Gap between Doctrine and Practice' in Burrows and Peel (eds), *Contract Terms* (Oxford, OUP, 2007) 233.

[52] *Rice v Great Yarmouth BC* [2003] TCLR 1, criticised by S Whittaker, 'Termination Clauses' in A Burrows and E Peel (eds), *Contract Terms* (Oxford, OUP, 2007) 253.

[53] Unfair Contract Terms Act 1977, s 3. Where the Act does not apply, the only means by which the courts may be able to police the reasonableness of contractual clauses is interpretation.

[54] M Chen-Wishart, 'Controlling the Power to Agree Damages' in Birks (ed), *Wrongs and Remedies in the Twenty-First Century* (Oxford, OUP, 1996) 280.

changed and performance has become onerous. The undue hardship bar to specific performance is underpinned by similar considerations.[55]

However, this objection is arguably too accommodating to the defaulting party. After all, to enforce the specific performance clause is to do no more than hold them to their promise. It is the very remedy to which they expressly agreed and reflects the agreement of the parties as to how to balance their competing interests and allocate the risk of breach. Having by their own volition agreed to the clause, they should not be able to resile from it, simply because they underestimated its implications.

For the courts to disregard a specific performance clause on this basis would conflict with the steadfast refusal in English law to offer relief against bad bargains. According to this principle, the court should not concern itself with whether an agreement is harsh or one-sided.[56] In the words of Diplock LJ in *Robophone Facilities Ltd v Blank*[57] in the context of penalty clauses, 'the court has no general jurisdiction to re-form terms of a contract because it thinks them unduly onerous on one of the parties. … *Pacta sunt servanda* is still a useful principle of English law which in my view applies'.[58]

If anything, it would be entirely conventional for the courts *not* to disturb the contractual allocation of risk just because it has turned out to have harsh consequences. This is precisely the approach to termination clauses. The injured party is able to exercise their right to terminate unfettered. It makes no difference that the defaulting party will suffer serious detriment[59] or could easily cure the breach, or even that the loss is trivial.[60]

A case could potentially be made for limiting the scope for enforcement of a specific performance clause where there would be extreme undue hardship to the defaulting party. However, if there were to be such an exception, it should not cover mere miscalculation of risk. It would therefore not extend to cases such as *Co-operative v Argyll*.[61] In the next section of this chapter, a possible solution to accommodate these extreme cases is suggested.

iii. The Constant Supervision Objection

An objection to specific performance that must logically extend to clauses providing for the remedy is that their enforcement would require an unacceptable

[55] S Waddams, 'The Choice of Remedy for Breach of Contract' in J Beatson and D Friedmann (eds), *Good Faith and Fault in Contract Law* (Oxford, OUP, 1997) 471, 482.

[56] *Gaumont-British Picture Corp v Alexander* [1936] 2 All ER 1686 (KB).

[57] *Robophone Facilities Ltd v Blank* [1966] 1 WLR 1428 (CA).

[58] ibid at 1446, 1449.

[59] eg, *Union Eagle Ltd v Golden Achievement Ltd* [1997] AC 514 (PC).

[60] E Peel, *Treitel on the Law of Contract*, 16th edn (London, Sweet & Maxwell, 2025) para [18-072]. On occasions, the courts have taken a narrow approach to the interpretation of widely drafted termination clauses: see *Rice v Great Yarmouth BC* [2003] TCLR 1 (CA).

[61] Note the absence of undue hardship finding in the Irish decision *Wanze Properties (Ireland) Ltd v Five Star Supermarket and Tesco (Ireland) Ltd* Unreported (High Court, 24 October 1997) (an Irish case) and *Highland Universal Properties Ltd v Safeway Properties Ltd* 2000 SLT 414 (a Scottish case), which were both factually close to *Co-operative v Argyll* (n 6).

degree of judicial supervision.[62] This has, however, been the subject of judicial[63] and academic doubt.[64] In most cases the perceived difficulties relating to court supervision are more apparent than real. Intentional transgression of court orders should be relatively rare. It seems likely that a binding and enforceable specific performance clause would encourage voluntary performance. This could even lead to an overall reduction in court involvement, thereby saving time and cost.[65] If a solution to this objection is necessary, Treitel has proposed the appointment of a neutral individual or body to supervise and give directions regarding performance.[66] It would be open to the parties to make provision alongside their specific performance clause for the appointment of such a person, how they should discharge their function, and how the cost should be borne.

iv. The Contempt of Court Objection

The scope for proceedings for contempt of court for breach of a specific performance order and the attendant threat of imprisonment loom large over the remedy. For the parties to agree that the remedy should be available for breach might therefore be seen as equating to an appropriation of this draconian machinery for enforcement as a means of compelling compliance with their private contractual obligations.

It is undoubtedly true that exposure to contempt proceedings can be intimidating and onerous. However, to focus on the ultimate sanction for non-compliance with a specific performance order risks imputing to the parties an intention that they do not have. In many cases, a fairer characterisation will be that they are simply concerned to be able to insist on performance. It would be an exaggeration to suggest that this equates to invoking the strong arm of the courts, at least in a manner that

[62] Waddams (n 55) 482.

[63] *CH Giles & Co Ltd v Morris* [1972] 1 WLR 307 Ch D at 318 (Megarry VC); *Tito v Waddell (No.2)* [1977] Ch 106 at 321–323 (Megarry VC); *Rainbow Estates Ltd v Tokenhold Ltd* [1999] Ch 64 at 73 (Lawrence Collins QC).

[64] A Burrows, 'Specific Performance at the Crossroads' (1984) 4 *LS* 102, 110; F Lawson, *Remedies of English Law*, 2nd edn (London, Butterworths, 1980) 224; G Treitel, 'Specific Performance in the Sale of Goods' [1966] *Journal of Business Law* 211, 228.

[65] Kronman (n 23) 351, 373; contra MacMahon (n 13) 288 for whom the continuing ability of the courts to invalidate penalties and their reluctance to enforce specific performance clauses minimise conflict between the parties and put an end to a conflict-ridden contractual relationship.

[66] Peel (n 60) para [21-045] (in the context of specific performance generally). Dr Tim Liau has suggested to me a solution that is similar but of more general application. This is that, even if the courts were readily to enforce specific performance clauses, thus rendering specific performance more widely available, this would not necessarily equate to the courts giving up their freedom to fashion the contents of the specific performance order. It would always be open to a court to formulate the order as it considers appropriate in the circumstances of the case, for example, by making the order conditional or subject to other terms. In this way, issues about constant supervision and even oppression and abuse could potentially be dealt with at the time of trial, taking into account any change in circumstances that has occurred since the contract was made (on conditional orders, see A Burrows, *Remedies for Torts, Breach of Contract, and Equitable Wrongs*, 4th edn (Oxford, OUP, 2019); see also Liau and Georgiou (n 50) 247, 264–65).

is abusive. The injured party seeking to enforce a specific performance clause can hardly be held responsible to the point of being deprived of an effective remedy because English law chooses to sanction a failure to comply with an order for performance as a contempt of court. In reality, rare will be the occasions when they go so far as to bring contempt proceedings, not least because the seriousness of the sanction should persuade most to comply. Where resort is made to such proceedings, imprisonment is not the sole available sanction. The court can order monetary penalties. Indeed, that is the only possible sanction where the contemnor is a corporation, which by its nature cannot be the subject of a custodial sentence.

v. The Personal Freedom Objection

A further possible objection that is also made against specific performance generally is that the remedy risks encroaching on the freedom of choice of the defaulting party. Over many years, a concern to protect individual liberty has been discernible in the reasoning of English courts in a range of contexts. It has undoubtedly contributed to the limited availability of specific performance as a remedy. This is borne from a fear that to compel performance might constitute an unreasonable encroachment on personal freedom. The same logic could be said to apply, albeit perhaps to a lesser extent, even where the parties have agreed that the remedy should be available.

There is a degree of force in this objection, but it should not be overstated. A specific performance clause will only ever require the injured party to honour their promise and fulfil the obligation that they voluntarily accepted and agreed that they could be compelled to perform. Considerations of personal freedom will also be less convincing where the defaulting party is a corporation or can fulfil the obligation from a range of available resources.

Where this objection does have greater force is in respect of obligations that are personal in nature.[67] An obvious example is the employment contract. There would be real difficulty in compelling an employee to work against their will. However, this should not result in specific performance clauses being disallowed entirely. A more tailored solution would be to make an exception for contracts that have a strong personal element.

V. The Possible Supervisory Jurisdiction of the Court

Even if one accepts some or all of these objections, it does not follow that specific performance clauses never have a role to play and should be disallowed on a blanket basis. Such a solution would be unnecessarily far-reaching. Its effect would

[67] P Saprai, 'The Principle against Self-Enslavement in Contract Law' (2009) *Journal of Contract Law* 26 at 34–43.

be to prevent contracting parties from agreeing to specific performance, even where the objections do not apply. A more measured and rational approach would be for the remedy to be generally available, but subject to any objections that outweigh the countervailing considerations of freedom of contract and contractual certainty. This would give primacy to the will of the parties. It would also be consistent with the increasingly liberal and light-touch approach of the courts in the related context of agreed damages clauses.

A. Consistency with the Greater Liberality Toward Damages Clauses

The courts have shown greater openness in recent years to upholding damages clauses that go beyond the level of damages that would ordinarily be available at common law. In the conjoined appeals of *Cavendish Square Holding BV v Talal El Makdessi* and *ParkingEye Ltd v Beavis*,[68] the Supreme Court rewrote the law on penalties and jettisoned the familiar requirement that a damages clause[69] must represent a genuine pre-estimate of loss in order to be enforceable. The inquiry has shifted to whether the damages clause is justifiable and not unconscionable. It will now be enforceable if it creates a secondary obligation which seeks to protect a legitimate interest of the injured party in the performance of the contract and imposes a detriment that is not extravagant, exorbitant or unconscionable in comparison with the interest protected.[70]

This brought an end to the long-established rule that invalidated any damages clause that conferred an entitlement to compensation above the default level, regardless of whether or not it was objectionable.[71] Loss has ceased to be the only measure against which these clauses are assessed. Even if the clause goes beyond compensation, it can still be valid. The parties therefore have greater latitude to adapt the level of recoverable damages to fulfil their contractual expectations.

[68] n 4. See A Summers, 'Unresolved Issues in the Law on Penalty' [2017] *Lloyd's Maritime and Commercial Law Quarterly* 95; F Dawson, 'Determining Penalties as a Matter of Construction' [2016] *Lloyd's Maritime and Commercial Law Quarterly* 207; J Morgan, 'The Penalty Clause Doctrine: Unlovable but Untouchable' [2016] *CLJ* 11; C Conte, 'The Penalty Rule Revisited' (2016) 132 *LQR* 382; J Fisher, 'Rearticulating the Rule Against Penalty Clauses' [2016] *Lloyd's Maritime and Commercial Law Quarterly* 169; W Day, 'Disproportionate Penalties in Commercial Contracts' in PS Davies and M Raczynska (eds), *The Contents of Commercial Contracts Terms Affecting Freedoms* (Oxford, Hart Publishing, 2020); E Peel, 'Penalties' in W Day and S Worthington (eds), *Challenging Private Law: Lord Sumption on the Supreme Court* (Oxford, Hart Publishing, 2020) 95; R Halson, 'Liquidated Damages and Penalties – a Review of the *Cavendish* Decision by the Singapore Court of Appeal' [2021] *LQR* 375.

[69] Or any other type of clause that falls within the scope of the penalty rule.

[70] *Makdessi* (n 4) at [32] (Lords Neuberger and Sumption); [152] (Lord Mance); [255] (Lord Hodge).

[71] Note that there had already been growing recognition that the blanket invalidation of all such damages clauses simply in order to guard against unfairness that might occasionally arise was a crude and inexact solution and the courts had shown an increasing willingness to allow large but not oppressive clauses: *Philips Hong Kong Ltd v The AG of Hong Kong* (1993) 61 BLR 41 (PC); *Murray v Leisureplay plc* [2005] EWCA Civ 963 (CA).

There are three important aspects of the reasoning in *Makdessi* that lend support to specific performance clauses being similarly enforceable. The first is the recognition by the Supreme Court that where the damages that would ordinarily be available fail to uphold the wider, non-compensatory, contractual objectives of the parties, they can themselves achieve greater protection by supplementing the remedy.[72] Importantly, it is the parties that identify this need and develop a solution to meet it.[73] This reflects a more permissive approach to the contractual objectives of the parties. It also allows them greater freedom to tailor the level of protection to meet their particular circumstances.

The second aspect is the clear recognition in the reasoning of the Supreme Court of the importance of freedom of contract and commercial certainty in secondary obligations. Lord Hodge put it this way: 'there is beyond doubt real benefit in parties being able to agree the consequences of a breach of contract'.[74] Lord Neuberger and Lord Sumption criticised the penalty rule as 'an interference with freedom of contract … [which] undermines the certainty which parties are entitled to expect of the law'.[75] Promoting freedom of contract and certainty was said to be especially relevant where the parties are commercial entities negotiating at arm's length. They should be taken to understand the interests at play and the implications of their agreement. The 'strong initial presumption must be that the parties themselves are the best judges of what is legitimate in a provision dealing with the consequences of breach'.[76] There should only be limited interference with their chosen solution.[77] It is not for the court to impose its own views over theirs as to which interests are deserving of protection.[78]

The third aspect is the recognition that deterring breach and incentivising performance can be legitimate contractual objectives. To seek to deter is justifiable where 'there is a legitimate interest in influencing the conduct of the contracting party which is not satisfied by the mere right to recover damages for breach'.[79] There may be good reasons for the parties to place heightened value on obtaining the very performance that was promised, and therefore to fashion secondary obligations that deter breach or incentivise performance. The acceptance of deterrence as a legitimate aim for damages clauses has been described as a 'most

[72] *Makdessi* (n 4) at [28]–[32] and [99] (Lords Neuberger and Sumption); [152] (Lord Mance); [255] (Lord Hodge).

[73] Specific performance was cited by Lords Neuberger and Sumption (at [29]–[30]) in their rationalisation of the new test on penalties as a context in which the courts require, before granting relief, that the injured party has a legitimate interest in performance that goes beyond compensation. However, this requirement is not formally part of the test for specific performance. As explained earlier, the most important hurdle to obtaining the remedy is that damages are inadequate. Additionally, and importantly, in the context of damages clauses, it is the parties themselves, and not the courts, that identify and, by agreeing the clause, stipulate that obtaining the promised performance has heightened value that warrants more robust protection.

[74] ibid [259] (Lord Hodge).

[75] ibid [33] (Lords Neuberger and Sumption).

[76] ibid [35] (Lords Neuberger and Sumption).

[77] ibid [33]-[35] (Lords Neuberger and Sumption).

[78] Summers (n 68) 95.

[79] *Makdessi* (n 4) [99].

fundamental change in the law'.[80] It has been said to amount to 'something which had never before been done in the common law of contract', and to authorise 'the prevention of breach as a final remedy' irrespective of the adequacy of damage.[81]

Promoting freedom of contract and transactional certainty, empowering the parties to provide for the consequences of breach, recognising that they are best placed to do so, and acknowledging that they may wish to deter breach in order to secure performance, are all factors that also point towards upholding specific performance clauses. They justify their enforcement, in the same way that they underpin the enforceability of damages clauses. If the penalties doctrine can be 'modernised by a new broom which erects legitimate business purpose as the basis for upholding penalties, why should a similar revolutionary change'[82] not occur with respect to specific performance clauses? There is nothing inherently wrong with them, as has already been shown. The real question is what safeguards ought to be put in place to prevent them from being a source of oppression.

B. Safeguards to Prevent Oppression and the Supervisory Jurisdiction of the Courts

To hold a defaulting party to perform obligations to which he has voluntarily agreed is not inherently unfair or unreasonable, although it may in fact be so in some cases, particularly where there is an inequality of bargaining power between the parties. For example, the specific performance clause may have been incorporated into the agreement as a result of the stronger party's oppressive conduct or insistence on its standard terms.

A possible solution would be a general requirement of reasonableness. In the US, for example, specific performance clauses are enforceable in the context of sale of goods contracts under the Uniform Commercial Code, subject to such a requirement.[83] Another would be to shield groups that are known to be vulnerable to exploitation against unfairness. An obvious example is consumers, although the reality is that, in consumer contracts, the obligation on the consumer is usually to pay money, and specific performance clauses therefore seem unlikely to have much of a role in this context.

If the need for protection were nevertheless to arise, there is already sweeping legislation to protect consumers in England. The Consumer Rights Act 2015 is the main enactment. It is expansive in scope, applying to all types of contract terms with the exception of core terms that are transparent and prominent.[84] In most

[80] Day (n 68) 227.

[81] D Campbell and R Halson, 'By Their Fruits Shall Ye Know Them' (2020) 79 *CLJ* 405, 407.

[82] To use Lord Briggs' words in the context of relief against forfeiture: Lord Briggs, 'Equity in Business' (2019) 135 *LQR* 570, 579.

[83] See s 2-719 of the UCC, which allows parties to such contracts to shape their remedies and the Official Comments to s 2-719 for the reasonableness requirement.

[84] Consumer Rights Act 2015, s 64(1).

and arguably even all cases, specific performance clauses will fall outside the scope of this exclusion. They should therefore be capable of challenge on the grounds of unfairness. In each case, the question would be whether the clause, 'contrary to the requirement of good faith', causes 'a significant imbalance in the parties' rights and obligations to the detriment of the consumer'.[85] Clauses that are ambiguous or favour the stronger party over the consumer would be particularly at risk. These safeguards should serve to mitigate the harsher effects of specific performance clauses in consumer contracts.[86]

In a non-consumer context, there is materially less need for protection.[87] However, as the Supreme Court observed in *Makdessi*, there are 'significant imbalances in negotiating power in the commercial world. Small businesses often contract with large commercial entities and have little say as to the terms of their contracts'.[88] They share 'many of the characteristics of consumers which are thought to make [them] worthy of legal protection' but do not benefit from the same statutory protections.[89] It was thought that they were sufficiently at risk of oppression to warrant judicial intervention.

For this group, a possible way to guard against abusive specific performance clauses would be to adopt similar protections to those that apply to damages clauses. This is closely analogous since both are agreed remedies founded on similar principles. In *Makdessi*, the Supreme Court sought to protect the defaulting party from extortionate demands and severe hardship by requiring that the clause must serve a 'legitimate interest in performance' and impose a detriment that is not extravagant, exorbitant or unconscionable in comparison with the interest protected.[90]

The threshold requirement of a 'legitimate interest in performance' means that there must be some acceptable basis or rational justification for the entitlement to overcompensation upon breach and/or deterrence.[91] In the absence of a good reason, the clause cannot be enforced to recover more than the amount

[85] Consumer Rights Act 2015, s 62.

[86] Whether it is unfair will depend on the particular circumstances of the case. In *Makdessi* (n 4), the majority of the Supreme Court decided that, on the facts, the £85 parking charge was not unfair under the Unfair Terms in Consumer Contracts Regulations 1999: see [102]–[113] (Lords Neuberger and Sumption); [200]–[213] (Lord Mance) and [295]–[309] (Lord Toulson dissenting). For a criticism, see J Spooner, 'Contract Law When the Poor Pay More' [2024] *OJLS* 257.

[87] The Law Commission report *Unfair Terms in Contracts* considered extending the protection against unfair terms to all businesses that trade on non-negotiated standard terms, regardless of their size. It concluded that such a change had the potential to cause uncertainty and might also be deployed abusively as a delaying tactic: Law Commission, *Unfair Terms in Contracts* (2005), Law Com. No.292.

[88] *Makdessi* (n 4) at [262] (Lord Hodge).

[89] ibid at [38] (Lords Neuberger and Sumption).

[90] S Rowan, 'Abuse of Rights in English Contract Law: Hidden in Plain Sight?' (2021) 84 *MLR* 1066.

[91] ibid; see also S Rowan, 'The "Legitimate Interest in Performance" in the Law on Penalties' (2019) 78 *CLJ* 148; Day (n 68); R Halson, 'The Critical Reception of *Cavendish Square Holdings v Makdessi*' in E Peel and R Probert (eds), *Shaping the Law of Obligations- Essays in Honour of Professor Ewan McKendrick KC* (Oxford, OUP, 2024); and Georgiou (n 45) who argues that the jurisdiction of the court to grant relief against penalties is actually an application of the *White & Carter* 'legitimate interest' bar that applies to other debt claims.

of the loss suffered. Requiring that the detriment be measured against the interest that is being protected effectively precludes extreme or disproportionate levels of overcompensation.[92] The agreed sum cannot be substantially greater than is necessary to protect that interest. This should serve to prevent excessive levels of recovery that bear no relation to the interest.[93]

It is apparent from the case law since *Makdessi* that there is now a high threshold for a finding that a damages clause is penal and should not be enforced.[94] Rarely have the courts reached such a conclusion, especially in cases involving sophisticated commercial parties and where the object of the clause is shown to protect a commercial interest.[95] Court intervention is confined to egregious cases at the far end of the spectrum.[96]

If a similarly permissive approach were extended to specific performance clauses, it would be necessary in each case for the court to consider whether the clause serves an interest of the beneficiary in obtaining what they were promised and whether to compel performance would be an unconscionable or disproportionate response to breach. No longer would specific performance be supplemental to damages, only available where that remedy is inadequate. The role of the court would also change. Its equitable discretion to grant specific performance would be replaced by or 'elided' with a lighter, and merely supervisory, review,[97] effectively confined to ascertaining whether the clause is abusive.

A new set of factors would be relevant to whether specific performance should be awarded under a specific performance clause.[98] These would be wider than those presently applicable, and the adequacy of damages would not be decisive.[99]

[92] *Makdessi* (n 4) at [152] (Lord Mance); [255] (Lord Hodge); [293] (Lord Toulson).

[93] ibid at [32] (Lords Neuberger and Sumption); [249] and [255] (Lord Hodge); [266] (Lord Hodge).

[94] The high threshold is apparent from *Makdessi* itself: ibid at [32]–[33] (Lords Neuberger and Sumption): the detriment must be 'out of all proportion to any legitimate interest of the innocent party'; [152] (Lord Mance); at [249] and [255] per Lord Hodge. For post-*Makdessi* cases, see, eg, *Gray v Braid Group (Holdings) Ltd* [2016] CSIH 68 (Court of Session Scotland); *Signia Wealth Ltd v Vector Trustees Ltd* [2018] EWHC 1040 (Ch); *BHL v Leumi ABL Ltd* [2017] EWHC 1871 (QB); *Holyoake v Candy* [2017] EWHC 3397 (Ch); *Eco World – Ballymore Embassy Gardens Co Ltd v Dobler UK* [2021] EWHC 2207 (TCC); *Luxury Italian KBB Co Ltd v Boutros* [2021] EW Misc 5 (CC); *Permanent v Makin* [2021] EWHC 467 (Ch); *Houssein & Ors v London Credit Limited & Ors* [2024] EWCA Civ 721.

[95] ibid and also *ZCCM Investments Holdings Plc v Konkola Copper Mines Plc* [2017] EWHC 3288 (Comm); *Cargill International trading Pte Ltd v Uttam Galva Steels Ltd* [2019] EWHC 476 (Comm); *Houssein & Ors v London Credit Limited & Ors* [2024] EWCA Civ 721; *Lombard North Central Plc v European Skyjets Ltd (in liquidation)* [2020] EWHC 679 (QB); see M Abdussalam and C Rickett, 'A Restatement of the Legitimate Interest Criterion in the Law of Remedial Contractual Terms' [2023] *Lloyd's Maritime and Commercial Law Quarterly* 41.

[96] eg, *Ahuja Investments Ltd v Victorygame Ltd* [2021] EWHC 2729 (Ch); *Slowikowska v Rogers* [2021] EWHC 192 (Ch); *Blu-Sky Solutions v Be Caring Ltd* [2021] EWHC 2619 (Comm).

[97] J Grower, 'The Overlap of Equity and Contract' (2021) 137 *LQR* 573.

[98] In the context of damages clauses, see Rowan (n 92) for an analysis of the factors that may be relevant in determining whether a legitimate interest exists.

[99] This approach has parallels with the expansionist approach that saw a broader range of factors taken into account to determine whether specific relief was granted and greater judicial recognition that damages might not be adequate, which was the trend prior to *Co-operative v Argyll* (n 6), and which had found favour in certain academic quarters, being described as a 'sensible and pragmatic approach … to be welcomed' by Jones and Goodhart (n 14) 5.

It would involve examining the full range of considerations that might justify the clause in question,[100] such as the context and nature of the contract, the (commercial) objectives of the parties (including securing performance and deterring breach), the importance of the obligation, the extent of the possible loss suffered by the injured party as a result of breach, the delay and inconvenience caused by the breach, the 'consumer surplus',[101] the difficulty of assessing damages, and the attributes of the parties.

Where a specific performance clause relates to an essential obligation of the contract and the breach could have serious consequences, it would be more likely to be acceptable. The same is also true where the clause protects non-monetary expectations. It will be particularly unusual for the courts to intervene in cases involving substantial commercial concerns that negotiated their agreement at arm's length and benefitted from legal advice. By contrast, there may be a greater propensity to intervene in contracts that involve a personal relationship or where a specific performance order would risk encroaching on the personal freedom of a party or otherwise significantly overburden them in a way that is more than just financial. The weaker the party's bargaining position, the more intensive the review would be and the more likely the court would be to interfere.[102]

For the court to be confined to a limited supervisory role would also align with trends in other contexts in which its role is to review whether a contractual term, or the exercise of a right under a term, is abusive. As an illustration of the former, restraint of trade clauses are enforceable only when reasonable, having regard to the interests of the parties and not contrary to the public interest.[103] An example relating to the exercise of a right can be found in cases concerning the exercise of a unilateral discretionary power conferred under a contract. When scrutinising the exercise of such a power, the courts will imply a term that the discretion should be exercised honestly, in good faith and not for an improper purpose, capriciously, perversely, arbitrarily or irrationally.[104] Rather than substitute itself as the decision-maker, the court reviews the manner and process by which the decision was made and is concerned only with decisions that are egregious.[105]

VI. Conclusion

It is legitimate for contracting parties who consider that the default remedial regime for breach of contract does not achieve a satisfactory outcome to craft secondary obligations to suit their interests and needs. If specific performance

[100] Similar to those in the context of penalties: see Rowan (n 92) and the cases referenced above.
[101] Harris, Ogus and Phillips (n 18).
[102] On the intensity of the review in the context of damages clauses, see Rowan (n 91).
[103] Beale, *Chitty on Contracts* 35th edn (London, Sweet & Maxwell, 2023) paras [19-203] ff.
[104] *Braganza v BP Shipping Ltd* at [2015] UKSC 17 (SC); *Paragon Finance plc v Nash* [2002] 1 WLR (CA); *Socimer International Bank Ltd v Standard Bank London Ltd* [2008] Bus LR 1304 (CA).
[105] See Rowan (n 91).

clauses were enforceable, it would enable the parties to agree that the innocent party should be able to insist upon receiving the actual performance of the defaulting party. The prevalence of these clauses in the M&A context in the US shows that they can be useful to supplement and overcome perceived inadequacies in conventional remedies.

English courts have thus far been averse to allowing the parties to agree to specific performance and thereby to fetter or oust the equitable discretion of the court to grant specific performance. It has, however, been shown that there is nothing inherently wrong with specific performance clauses. Many of the objections to specific performance as a remedy lose their force when it has been consensually agreed by the parties. In that case, the focus should instead be on appropriate safeguards that would prevent them from being a source of oppression.

This chapter has sought to draw parallels with the more permissive approach enunciated by the Supreme Court to damages clauses in *Makdessi*. Similar safeguards to those that now invalidate abusive and objectionable damages clauses could be introduced to prevent abuse in the context of specific performance clauses. Where the parties have agreed such a clause, the role of the court would be to decide whether their chosen remedy serves an interest in securing performance and that compelling performance is not unconscionable or disproportionate. This would uphold an agreement freely and willingly made by the parties while enabling intervention in cases of unacceptable oppression.

INDEX

www.ingramcontent.com/pod-product-compliance
Ingram Content Group UK Ltd.
Pitfield, Milton Keynes, MK11 3LW, UK
UKHW020909180926
475645UK00003B/45